Traffic Investigation
and Control
Second Edition

BRUCE A. HAND
Golden West College

ARCHIBLE W. SHERMAN, JR.
Bakersfield College

MICHAEL E. CAVANAGH
University of San Francisco

Charles E. Merrill Publishing Company
A Bell & Howell Company
Columbus   Toronto   London   Sydney

Published by Charles E. Merrill Publishing Co.
A Bell & Howell Company
Columbus, Ohio 43216

This book was set in Optima
Production Editor: Jo Ellen Gohr
Cover Design Coordination: Will Chenoweth
Cover photograph by H. Armstrong Roberts

Library of Congress Catalog Card Number: 79–92133

International Standard Book Number: 0–675–08112–2

89   91 90 89

Printed in the United States of America

To our wives, Lee, Norma and Marie,
as well as our children
whose patience was unending.

Preface

Each year law enforcement agencies are faced with an ever-increasing death and injury rate due to traffic crashes. By the late 1970s, deaths on our highways reached totals of over 50,000 per year. The U.S. Department of Transportation reported that for every 100 million vehicle-miles traveled, there were 3.27 deaths directly related to motor vehicle operation.

Furthermore, over 11 million persons are disabled. Motor vehicle collisions significantly lead *all other causes of death* for individuals from ages one to forty-five. Property damage caused by motor vehicle collisions is approximately six billion dollars each year.* So the traffic officer, both in his role as enforcer and as investigator, is dealing in a very direct way with the preservation of human life and property.

Searching for material for a traffic control class quickly revealed an abundance of reference material. However, the material was highly technical and submerged in technical and legal jargon. Most of the volumes we encountered dealt with specific subjects and involved sophisticated theoretical models and algebraic equations and therefore did not lend themselves to a general class of traffic control designed to address broad areas of traffic supervision, traffic engineering, enforcement, records systems, and accident investigation.

What was lacking was a single text that covered subjects relative to traffic control and investigation in comprehensive and understandable terms. A small number of publications were available; however, they were too simplistic and/or lacking in content.

After identifying the need for a single source of reference for traffic control and investigation, we felt that such a publication should have

---

*Statistics from *Accident Facts*, 1978 (Chicago, Ill.: The National Safety Council) and the National Highway Traffic Safety Administration, U.S. Department of Transportation.

v

national application because of the universality of the traffic problem. Thus, our efforts were directed toward sorting and assimilating a vast amount of secondary data and combining it with many years of knowledge gained through field traffic experience. It is our hope that this book will fill the gap and provide a single comprehensive and understandable text which has national application.

To simplify the language of this text, we have consistently used the pronouns *he, him,* and *his*. It is hoped that no reader will be offended by this compromise.

Acknowledgments

The authors wish to acknowledge the following for their generous assistance in the preparation of this text: The California Highway Patrol; Los Angeles Police Department; Ohio Highway Patrol; Michigan State Police; Florida Highway Patrol; Tiburon (California) Police Department; Wisconsin State Patrol; Traffic Institute, Northwestern University, Evanston, Illinois; and the School of Public Administration, University of Southern California.

Individually we would like to thank the following persons for their assistance in providing materials, suggestions, and review of the chapters, and most of all their support and encouragement in the publication of this material: Chief John Bailey (Tiburon Police Department); and Thomas W. Rice, Kenneth Freyer, and Warren E. Clark, Ph.D. (presently Sergeant, California Highway Patrol, and Instructor at Golden West College).

Contents

10 • SPECIAL ACCIDENT INVESTIGATION PROBLEMS   207

11 • DETERMINATION OF SPEED FROM SKID MARKS   231

BIBLIOGRAPHY   249

INDEX   253

chapter 1

The Traffic Problem

The success of any traffic investigation and control program is dependent upon the control of the rate and severity of traffic accidents. Critical to control of traffic accidents is the determination of their causes and remedies, which minimize their recurrence. Thus, traffic accident investigation evolves as the primary source of data for analysis of highway safety.

HISTORICAL DEVELOPMENTS

Traffic accident investigation is nothing new. From the time a human first shouldered a burden and collided on a narrow trail with another human, traffic accidents have occurred. The taming of wild animals and their subsequent training as beasts of burden brought an increasing number of traffic accidents. The development of the wheel and the corresponding development of transportation vehicles over the ages contributed to the growth of the traffic problem.

Progress and improvement in thoroughfares paralleled advances in transportation first with trails, then roads. In ancient times, a road network consisting of hard surface pavements was developed by the Romans to spread their civilization. These roads were so well constructed that some of them still remain visible today.

The Romans were responsible for the development of the term *highway*. During their military exploits in England, the Romans built cities on high ground above the low moors and marshes. Since they developed roads to connect their cities, they built raised roads to span the low lands. These "high ways" soon became known as highways.

Traffic accidents occurred on these roads then, even as they do now. Those investigated by the Romans led to certain control measures. Weight limits were imposed to prevent breakdown of vehicles and destruction of pavements. Restrictive laws were passed to regulate the movement of persons and property. Encroachments upon right-of-way by roadside businesses were discouraged and restricted. Roads were designed with a minimum of grades and curves to facilitate travel. In fact, it was here that the concept of the three "E's" — engineering, education, and enforcement — was discovered. Today this is still the basis for traffic investigation and control.

The methods of supervising traffic adopted during the Roman Empire were so advanced that they supplied many future generations with sufficient control for their own safety. Because there were no appreciable improvements in the means of travel, there were no real necessities to improve or alter the early practices. It was not until the twentieth century that the need arose for any major change, for it was during this period that transportation took a tremendous upswing with the advent of the automobile. This upswing was accompanied by a colossal upsurge of traffic problems, which resulted in the need for new regulations and adjustments.

RAPID GROWTH

In September, 1899, H.H. Bliss stepped off a trolley car and was run over by a horseless carriage. It was the first time on record that a citizen had been killed in an automobile accident.[1] Since then the death on the highways has reached a proportion unequaled by war and other man-made calamities. Approximately two million persons have died in automobile accidents since the automobile's invention. Using 1900 as the base year for automobiles, in about seventy-eight years the annual average death rate has been approximately 27,000 persons. For young people under 25 years of age, the number one killer in the United States is traffic accidents. Statistics show that more than 20,000 young adults are killed in traffic crashes each year. There were 46,400 traffic deaths in 1975; 46,700 in 1976; 49,200 in 1977; and 50,145 in 1978 in this country alone! These figures were exceeded only in 1973, when the nation's fatalities reached an all-time high of 54,052.[2]

Improved roads, better signs, seat belts, shoulder harnesses, padded dashboards, collapsible steering columns, and improved tires and brakes

---

1. Walter Pudinski, "Fatal Accident Studies," *Journal of Traffic Safety Education* 17, no. 3 (March 1971): 17.

2. Howard C. Shook, "Editorial," *Police Chief* (September 1978): 8, and U.S. Department of Transportation (Washington D.C., March 1979).

have made driving a safer activity in the last decade. The reduction of the maximum speed limit to 55 miles per hour has proven to be an effective piece of legislation. As a result, the death rate has decreased significantly over the past several years. Although we will never eliminate traffic fatalities, we can try to control their escalation. The use of scare tactics may bring attention to the problem, but it is the driver who needs to take positive steps by being careful and observing traffic laws. Possibly, this is where the emphasis should be—reminding drivers directly and bluntly of this obligation behind the wheel.[3]

FINDING AN ANSWER

There is no simplistic answer to the traffic problem. However, we are now at a point where the traffic problem has to be attacked systematically. Since, as individuals, we do not have the legal power, labor, or resources to immediately and unilaterally eliminate the traffic problem, we must develop priority programs for corrective action collectively.[4] We must define specific problem areas, determine realistic levels of expectation, and identify those areas that can be improved upon with available resources. This can be accomplished through detailed nationwide cooperative study and analysis of traffic accidents and their causes and a systems approach to highway safety. It is through research that efforts are better directed because it supplies the necessary information for enforcement, engineering, and education programs.[5]

Roads and vehicles, like other inanimate objects, can be reshaped and made over, but not so easily the driver. He must be governed by the rules of driving conduct in order to minimize highway chaos. Driver conduct must be guided and controlled for the welfare of all highway users. Through the years effort progressed along various lines of training, education, and by traffic laws and ordinances designed to promote orderly passage of vehicles over the streets and highways and the relief of traffic congestion.[6]

Once attention was focused on these methods of control, the authorities and others concerned with traffic safety found themselves confronted by a variety of legal questions. By or through what agency or agencies of government could valid restrictions on use of the highways be promoted? To what extent and for what purposes could use of the streets and highways be limited or restricted? In other words, first attempts to

---

3. Richard Bauman, "The Absurd Statistic," *The California Highway Patrolman* 39, no. 4 (June 1975): 29.
4. Pudinski, "Fatal Accident Studies."
5. Ibid., p. 41.
6. Donald R. Drew, *Traffic Flow Theory and Control* (New York: McGraw-Hill, 1968), p. 28.

control the mass of people through restrictive regulations affecting the driving of their own vehicles posed some highly complex and interesting questions for the courts as well as for the legislative and executive branches of government. In the area of traffic every person was concerned, either as a driver or a pedestrian, and means of control and enforcement had to be devised for a volume of offenses quite unknown before. The making of the early traffic laws followed an erratic and unrealistic course. Archaic laws and regulations, some of which aggravated the situation rather than helped it, had to be eliminated. New concepts of driver control had to be devised. New theories and practices of enforcing laws and regulations had to be contrived and developed. What had to be done was not terminal but a continuous process, because conditions change swiftly, requiring new adaptations of old principles and the development of new ones.[7]

Control of the driver posed questions not only for law-making bodies and enforcement officials, but it also called for supplementary activity on the part of educators and traffic engineers. It is our conclusion that the human element is a crucial factor in the effective control of traffic. Intelligent, efficient enforcement of well-devised regulations, with certainty and consistency, can and will offer the hope and promise of solutions to the traffic problem.

Progress toward an ultimate solution is threefold. Continuous traffic supervision effort has to be directed toward the utilization of: (1) modern enforcement methods and techniques, together with improvement in the education and training of drivers; (2) modern traffic engineering concepts which provide for the reduction of driver decision-making situations and the compatability of the highway system with driver behavior and vehicle kinematic and dynamic characteristics; and (3) realistic laws designed to prevent collision and congestion, enforced by police officers specially trained for traffic work. These laws must be administered and adjudicated by courts functioning according to modern standards for the administration of justice in traffic cases. Concentrated effort in these areas can be effective in reducing the toll of deaths, injuries, and property damage resulting from the operation of motor vehicles upon streets and highways.[8]

SCOPE OF THIS TEXT

Some provocative issues of traffic investigation and control have been touched upon in this introductory chapter. The purpose of this text is to look at some of these issues and at the same time explore some of the variables that have an impact on highway safety. Also, some basic concepts of traffic

----

7.   Ibid.
8.   Ibid., p. 29.

investigation and control as developed through engineering, enforcement, and education efforts, which attempt to integrate people, vehicles, and highways within a relatively safe traffic environment, will be explored.

The specific areas we will cover are (1) traffic supervision and the monumental task of identifying overall problem areas and directing resources strategically to effectively remedy the situation; (2) how the traffic officer's testimony in court brings together the need for sound investigative techniques and good communication skills; (3) psychology of enforcement tactics as these relate to the psychological factors and interactions that determine whether a traffic stop is a positive, neutral, or negative learning experience; (4) traffic directing, which emphasizes the practical aspect of uniform signals and gestures and flare patterns; (5) traffic laws and their legitimate purpose of establishing standards of procedure to be followed by drivers in vehicle operation so as to promote the safe and orderly flow of traffic; (6) traffic accident investigation and its importance in collecting and assimilating relevant information for complete analysis of traffic accident causes; and (7) special accident investigation problems which focus on critical issues in terms of method and evidence required for the establishment of traffic violations. The last chapter gives in-depth exposure to the techniques of determining speed from skid marks.

We have attempted to expose the reader to the vast subject of traffic investigation and control. It is our hope that this text will provide the reader with an insight into the variables that have an impact on the traffic environment in terms of highway safety. Furthermore, it is hoped that unanswered questions will provide an impetus for future research.

chapter **2**

Traffic Engineering

The amount of traffic in existence in American cities at the turn of the century was amazing. As one might expect, this was not motorized traffic but animal traffic. Initially, automobiles were a rare sight and their existence was known to most people by word of mouth only. Within a few years horses, which were used extensively for transportation, began to disappear from the highways, giving way to horsepower in the form of motorized vehicles. By 1927, the transition from horses to automobiles was well underway. By the 1950s, the automobile had become recognized as an indispensable means of conveyance and transportation. Automobiles along with other types of motorized vehicles had taken full control of the highway transportation scene.

The impact of motor vehicles upon the social, economic, and political structures of modern society has been enormous. As a result, changes in social customs, business and industrial methods, and American habits and lifestyles have been dramatic. The phenomenal growth of motor vehicle use came before many were ready for it. The demand for additional streets and highways far outstripped efforts to increase highway capacity (supply). Existing highways were incapable of accommodating the increased number and use of motor vehicles. To improve the situation, vast sums of money were spent not only for the development and construction of highway systems, but also for maintenance of highways and facilities for the operation of motor vehicles, which have perpetual needs.

It was not long before the interaction of three elements (highways, people, and vehicles) of the highway transportation system created a high-risk highway environment in which traffic congestions and conflicts were prevalent factors. Deficiencies inherent in each contributed to devastating traffic tolls. Traffic engineers approached this problem by straightening and grading roads, eliminating sharp turns, and establishing improved routes such as sophisticated freeways and turnpike systems. With better roads came motor vehicles equipped with bigger engines capable of greater speeds. The traffic toll did not decline. The accident patterns merely changed in type and at the same time increased in number. The pattern of cars turning over on rutty roads and sharp turns or colliding at obscure unmarked intersections changed to colliding at high speeds with other vehicles, pedestrians, and fixed objects.

The increasing number of accidents brought a trend toward safer cars. Car tops were manufactured with more structural support. Such cars could turn over and not crush their occupants, as was the case in so many cars previously manufactured without this feature. In addition, padded dashes, collapsible steering wheels, anti-lock brakes, energy absorption bumpers, and safety harnesses were designed to improve car safety. As manufacturers improved cars and as these cars were driven to the extent of their speed potential, accident tolls continued upward.

Higher speeds inevitably brought a corresponding increase in traffic fatalities. Obviously, better roads and better cars did not supply the ultimate answer to the traffic problem. Authorities began to realize that whatever engineering improvements and innovations might be made or adopted, it was not the mechanical inadequacies of the motor vehicles nor the defective, outmoded highways alone that were causing the trouble. Even though these factors are an integral part of the problem, the influential effect of the driver is considerable.

Yet, the general public believes that the main reason for devastating traffic accident tolls is the deficiency of the highway systems. Traditionally, better roads through traffic engineering were viewed as being the transportation system panacea.

Through the centuries, and into the early period of the automobile, the engineering approach to highways was almost exclusively structural. The emphasis was placed on the composition of the highway and how well it supported weight rather than its geometrical features. With the advent of more sophisticated automobiles, the functional requirements of the new type of traffic gradually became recognized. Emphasis began to shift from the static aspect of road design to the dynamic factors which are so important to efficient movement. The engineering shift was toward geometric design, and during the transition a concern for aesthetic highway design developed. How well highway structures harmonized with their environment became important.

Geometric design deals with roadway elements such as cross section, gradient, curvature, sight distance, and clearances as well as with combinations of these elements. There are many traffic factors which influence geometric design. Prime consideration is given to the abilities and limitations of the driver, vehicle, and road, either individually or collectively. Traffic composition, volume, speed, and stopping and turning abilities of vehicles are also important, especially when the demand for highway use is great and the ability of various highways to accommodate existing traffic is limited. Stated in a different way, the geometry of the highway system must be in harmony with traffic performance and traffic demand in order to achieve traffic operation which is safe, efficient, and economical. Accomplishing this is the goal of traffic engineering.

Traffic engineering is a relatively modern procedure for coping with the three elements of street and highway traffic: (1) the road user, (2) the vehicle and its load, and (3) the road itself. This process attempts to improve the driving efficiency of road users by reducing the number of decisions required of drivers. By improving the design and operation of roads, the traffic engineer curtails the accident potential inherent in any street or highway by avoiding the need for the driver to make a decision. Through channelization, adequate signs and pavement markings, and other devices for traffic control, the engineer removes the attendant conflict and confusion when one or more drivers are required to make a decision. The traffic engineer deals in reportable accidents (injuries and fatalities). When these accidents add up to meaningful totals, they constitute a warrant for some form of traffic engineering action.

Highway traffic engineering is popularly thought of as the installation and administration of controls essential to maintaining the movement of vehicles over highway systems. Actually traffic engineering is much more. It is the combination of art and science directed toward determining traffic demand and highway capacity and determining the relationship between traffic variables, plus the application of this knowledge to planning, designing, and operating highway systems to achieve the safe and efficient movement of persons and goods. The essential elements of this definition are measurement of traffic demand and highway capacity; studying and determining the relationship between traffic variables; and application of knowledge to planning, designing, and operating highway systems.

MEASUREMENT OF DEMAND AND HIGHWAY CAPACITY

Measurement of demand and highway capacity involves measuring the traffic flow (volume). The value of measuring the flow of traffic is the determination of whether the demand is as large as the capacity during any significant length of time during a day. Volume is the number of vehicles passing a given point during a specified period of time. Volume studies are one of the processes used for traffic flow evaluation.

Volume studies are made to obtain factual data concerning the movement of vehicles and/or persons at selected points on highway systems. Volume data are expressed in relation to time, such as Average Daily Traffic (ADT). The type of data collected in a specific volume study depends upon how the information will be applied.

Average Daily Traffic in vehicles per day is used for measuring the present demand for service on a street or highway by evaluating the present traffic flow with respect to the street system, developing the major or arterial street system, and locating areas where new facilities or improvement to existing facilities is necessary. Although ADT volume is important in determining the classification of a highway or street and designing the structural element, the direct use of it in geometric design is not practical because it does not indicate the cyclical traffic patterns.

Hourly traffic in vehicles per hour is used for determining length and magnitude of peak periods and evaluating traffic controls. Volume studies of this type are usually among the criteria for the installation of signs, signals, and markings; designation of through streets, one-way streets, unbalanced flow, and traffic routing; and prohibition of parking, stopping, and turning. Geometric design or redesign of streets and intersections is influenced by hourly traffic volume studies.

Dividing hourly volume by the average speed of traffic will determine the density of traffic. Density is the number of vehicles per mile on the traveled way at a given instance. Density may be a better measure of street service than volume since it continues to increase as congestion increases. Conversely, volume reaches a maximum under moderate congestion and then decreases with greater congestion. Density is at its maximum and volume is zero when complete blockage occurs.

Traffic studies conducted by the California Department of Transportation indicate that the greatest number of vehicles passing a given point travel at 35 mph. It was found that more traffic was expedited between the speed range of 30 to 35 mph than any other speed ranges. For example, on a two-lane highway with traffic using both lanes, lane capacity was most efficient (1500 vehicles per hour passing a given point) when the speed of traffic was 35 mph. On the freeway, undesirable congestion developed when traffic volume increased to the point where operating speeds were reduced below 35 mph. Speeds under 25 mph inevitably produced stopping, starting, and very jerky operation.

This phenomenon is partially attributed to the reaction of drivers in the traffic stream. The longitudinal position of vehicles in the traffic stream is the single factor which gives a driver either a sense of safety with some freedom of movement or a sense of hazard and congestion with no freedom of maneuver. At speeds greater than 35 mph, the spacing or *headway* between vehicles increases and the corresponding lag reduces the number of vehicles passing a given point. At lesser speeds, the slower pace coupled with congestion delays act to reduce the number of vehicles being measured.

Basically, congestion is the direct result of an imbalance between the supply and demand of a highway system. Congestion will occur whenever the demand exceeds capacity. In traffic engineering terms, capacity is the supply. The demand (volume) is generated by those motorists seeking to use the system. Demand can be estimated by origin and destination surveys if the times of the desired trip are obtained.

Capacity and Level of Service Criteria

The ability of a highway system to accommodate traffic is a major factor of highway capacity and level of service. Capacity is the maximum number of vehicles that can pass a point on a lane or roadway during a given period of time under prevailing roadway and traffic conditions. It is a particular rate of flow — the maximum rate. Level of service, as applied to the traffic operation on a particular roadway, refers to the quality of the driving conditions afforded the driver by a particular highway system. Variables include speed of vehicles, spacing between vehicles, and the relative interference between vehicles as well as the number of vehicles that can pass a point on a roadway in a specified period of time.

Prevailing Conditions. Roadway capacity depends primarily upon (1) composition of traffic, (2) alignment of the roadway, (3) number and width of lanes, and (4) speeds of vehicles using the roadway. The prevailing conditions are divided into two groups: (1) prevailing roadway conditions and (2) prevailing traffic conditions.[1]

Prevailing roadway conditions. These conditions are determined by the physical characteristics of the roadway and do not change unless some construction or reconstruction work is performed. Poor planning and design of a highway may result in a roadway whose prevailing conditions make it difficult to move traffic without accidents when the roadway is operated well within the limits of planned capacity.[2]

Prevailing traffic conditions. Conditions of traffic are determined upon the vehicles and pedestrians using the roadway. These conditions may change during various seasons of the year, periods of the day, and, in some locations, from hour to hour. Prevailing traffic conditions are also affected

1. J. Stannard Baker and William R. Stebbins, Jr., *Dictionary of Highway Traffic* (Evanston, Ill.: Traffic Institute, Northwestern University, 1964).

2. Paul B. Weston, *The Police Traffic Control Function*, 2d ed. (Springfield, Ill.: Charles C Thomas, 1964).

by holidays, parades, sporting events, construction, and other traffic generators or hindrances. Possibly the worst prevailing traffic conditions exist just before and immediately following major holidays.[3]

Capacity. There are three levels of roadway capacity: (1) basic capacity, (2) possible capacity, and (3) design capacity.

Basic capacity. This is the maximum number of vehicles that can pass on a given lane or roadway during one hour under the most nearly ideal roadway and traffic conditions. Actually, this is a theoretical measure, as it is most difficult to secure ideal conditions when roadways are subject to maximum use.[4]

Possible capacity. This is a measure of the maximum number of vehicles that can pass a given point on a lane or roadway during one hour under the prevailing roadway and traffic conditions. This is a positive measure or quantity. It cites a traffic volume that cannot be exceeded without changing one or more of the prevailing conditions.[5]

Design capacity. This is the number of vehicles that can pass over a given section of a roadway in one direction during one hour under specified traffic conditions and operating at a "level of service." A design capacity is a volume generally selected for design purposes which will provide a desirable level of service. This definition replaces the concept of "practical capacity." The "practical capacity" concept dealt with the maximum number of vehicles that could pass a given point per hour without traffic density being so great as to unduly restrict the driver's freedom of maneuver under prevailing roadway and traffic conditions, and the maximum number of vehicles that could enter and clear an intersection without waiting for more than one complete signal cycle.[6]

These terms for roadway capacity levels have been found to be more applicable for rural conditions where higher speed is desirable. The desire, in urban conditions, for a more dependable and higher quality of service has brought about a change in the application of "capacity" in the design and operation of streets and highways. This new application has been termed the "level of service" concept.

Level of Service. Level of service is a qualitative measure of the effects of a number of factors, including speed and travel time, traffic interruption, freedom of maneuver, safety, driving comfort and convenience, and ve-

---

3. National Committee On Uniform Traffic Laws and Ordinances, *Uniform Vehicle Code and Model Traffic Ordinances* (Washington, D.C., 1972).

4. Committee on Highway Capacity of the Highway Research Board, *Highway Capacity Manual* (Washington, D.C.: U.S. Bureau of Public Roads, Government Printing Office, 1960).

5. Ibid.

6. Ibid.

hicular operational costs. Each of these factors is somewhat related to all the others. The volume of traffic using a facility affects all the factors; and, in general, the greater the volume, the more adverse are the effects. As the ratio of the volume of traffic on a highway and the ability of the highway to accommodate traffic approaches unity, congestion increases.[7]

Both capacity and level of service are functions of the physical features of the highway system and the interaction of vehicles in the traffic stream. The distinction between them is that a given lane or roadway may provide a wide range of levels of service but only one possible capacity. The various levels for any specific roadway are a function of the volume and composition of traffic. A given lane or roadway designed for a given level of service at a specified volume will operate at many different levels of service as the flow varies during different periods of time. In other words, fluctuations in demand do not cause fluctuations in capacity but do effect changes in the quality of operation afforded the driver. In a very general way, then, highway planning, design, and operational problems become a question of whether a certain roadway capacity can handle the projected or measured demand at an acceptable level of service.

There are various factors which inhibit the ability of a highway system to accommodate traffic. The most important factors that may reduce highway capacity are:

1. Lanes less than twelve feet wide have a lower capacity.

2. Retaining walls, bridge abutments, parked cars, and the like all reduce the effective width of a traffic lane, cause lane-straddling and result in lower capacity.

3. Inadequate shoulders also reduce the effective width of a traffic lane by causing vehicles to shy away from the edge of the pavement and travel toward the center of the roadway. Greatest reduction in capacity is when the width of the shoulders of a road will not permit the parking of a disabled vehicle outside of the traffic lane.

4. Commercial vehicles occupy a greater road space and influence other traffic more than other passenger cars. They are slow moving, especially on grades, and are slower to close gaps.

5. When drivers are restricted in their freedom of movement by restricted sight distances, the capacity of the road will be lowered.

6. Controlled intersections impair highway capacity by depriving the traffic stream of a portion of the time during which it would otherwise be on the move.

---

7. Ibid.

STUDYING AND DETERMINING THE RELATIONSHIP BETWEEN TRAFFIC VARIABLES

In studying and determining relationships between traffic variables, we must evaluate certain characteristics of traffic dynamics. Traffic dynamics involve drivers' actual experiences while operating vehicles on the highway system. A collection of vehicles on a particular segment of the system forms a stream of traffic. The quality of service and the potential for conflict depend upon the number of vehicles in the traffic stream and the ability of the highway system to handle the volume. When the number of vehicles approaches capacity levels, the quality of service diminishes and the potential for conflicts increases. That is, increased congestion factors adversely affect available space and opportunities to maneuver in terms of entering, exiting, and crossing the highway system.

Information derived from studies of traffic flow and patterns is important to traffic engineering planning. Such information may include (1) the presence or absence of acceptable gaps in the traffic stream, which either decreases or increases the potential for conflicts; (2) speed zones, which provide a better level of service by influencing consistent operating speeds and thus reduce conflicts attributed to widely differentiated operating speeds; and (3) traffic control device warrants, which provide justification for the installation of traffic control devices to expedite traffic flow and to improve safety. Factors of gap acceptance, conflict patterns, control devices, and speed zoning are discussed later in greater detail.

Vehicular movement in one or more lines in the same direction on the street or highway usually represents the traffic stream.[8] The operators of motor vehicles, while a part of the traffic stream, act in such a manner that it is difficult to predict their reactions. Each operator is a separate and distinct unit, limited in his relationship to other units on the street or highway.[9]

The longitudinal and lateral positions of vehicles in the traffic stream are factors that can give a driver a sense of safety with some freedom to maneuver or a sense of hazard and congestion with no freedom to maneuver. As the traffic congestion increases, each driver is affected more and more by his fellow motorists, with the high-speed driver feeling this restriction more than the driver operating at lower speeds. This sensitivity of drivers affects their ability to maneuver and to react to gaps and conflicts.

Gap Acceptance

One of the most important aspects of traffic operation is the interaction of vehicles within a stream of traffic or the interaction of two separate traffic

---

8. Baker and Stebbins, *Dictionary of Highway Traffic*, p. 23.
9. Weston, *The Police Traffic Control Function*.

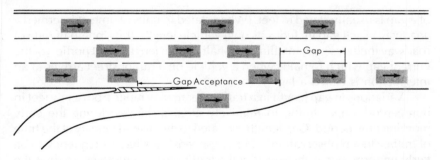

FIGURE 2-1

Gap Acceptance

streams. This interaction takes place when a driver changes lanes, merges into a traffic stream, or crosses a traffic stream. Inherent in the traffic interaction associated with these basic maneuvers is the concept of gap acceptance.

Gap acceptance is best illustrated in the analysis of freeway ramp connections (fig. 2-1). The driver uses the acceleration lane to gain speed in order to flow into the traffic stream. In doing so, he takes advantage of an acceptable gap.

The two-way stop intersection, another location in which gap acceptance provides the basis of operation, is essentially just a special case of ramp-freeway connection in which there is no acceleration lane (fig. 2-2).

Unoccupied road spaces ahead of each vehicle determine the distribution of vehicles in any traffic stream. The road spaces are commonly referred to as gaps. A gap is the elapsed time between the arrival of successive vehicles on a roadway at a specified reference point (see fig. 2-1). Gaps are measured from head to head of successive vehicles. The size

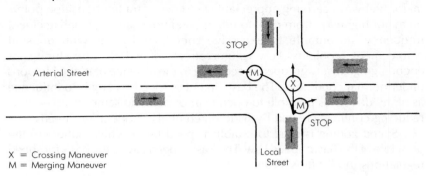

X = Crossing Maneuver
M = Merging Maneuver

FIGURE 2-2

Gap Acceptance: Two-way Stop

of a gap is usually stated in feet. (When stated in units of time, it is termed a *headway*.) Each gap includes its own vehicle length; thus, one-half mile of roadway includes gaps totalling one-half mile in length. That portion of the current gap which remains when a vehicle on a minor street arrives at an intersection is called a lag.

Variations in gap length in a traffic stream may range from a few feet in bumper-to-bumper traffic to relatively great distances during the early morning time period. Gap length is related to the overall density at the time of traffic stream observation. At lower speeds gaps have a tendency to be fairly uniform, but as the speed of the traffic stream increases, so does the variation in gap length.

Gaps of adequate lengths provide a driver with an opportunity to either accept them or reject them. A gap is accepted when the driver crosses or enters the traffic flow between two vehicles on the roadway. Gap acceptance is based on the probability that a gap is acceptable to a vehicle waiting to enter or cross the traffic stream (both acceptable to the driver and present in the traffic stream).

It is possible to determine gap acceptance for a specified intersection and hence the number of vehicles that can be handled on a minor street without the need of a signal to interrupt the flow of the traffic on a main street. Justification for traffic signal control can be established for the intersection of a main street and a minor street by using the relationship between the availability of gaps in the traffic stream on a main street and the lag and/or gap acceptance by the drivers on a minor street.

Speed Zoning

Speed zoning is a traffic engineering tool used to derive the best traffic service for a given set of conditions. Generally, speed zoning is applied to major highways carrying appreciable volumes of traffic; transition points on major highways from rural to urban conditions; areas of high accident frequency attributable to excessive speed; and areas with unusual enforcement problems. Low-volume streets offer little opportunity for encouraging closely grouped speeds due to the absence of traffic platoons under normal conditions. The basic intent of speed zoning is to influence as many drivers as possible to operate at or near the same speed — thus reducing conflicts created by wide differentials in operating speeds.

Speed zoning is used to establish speed limits which adhere to the principle of the Basic Speed Law. The Basic Speed Law is the basis for speed regulations in all fifty states:

> No person shall drive a vehicle upon a highway at a speed greater than is reasonable or prudent having due regard for weather, visibility, the traffic

on, and the surface and width of, the highway, and in no event at a speed which endangers the safety of persons or property.[10]

Inherent in the Basic Speed Law is the driver's recognition of driving conditions, which vary widely from time to time and place to place. No set of fixed driving rules can adequately serve all conditions. The Basic Speed Law is founded on the belief that most motorists are able to modify their driving behavior properly, as long as they are aware of the conditions around them.

Many times, unfortunately, drivers are unaware of all the conditions around them. Because of this, engineering and traffic surveys are needed to establish certain speed zones. An engineering and traffic survey is a survey of highway and traffic conditions which includes but is not limited to (1) prevailing speeds as determined by traffic engineering measurements; (2) accident records; and (3) highway, traffic, and roadside conditions not readily apparent to the driver.

The data collection phase of speed surveys is extremely important and requires considerable care due to the many variables involved and the source of possible bias in sampling (sample size should consist of at least 100 select observations). Some common errors that tend to introduce bias, and the procedure for eliminating these errors, are:

1. Selecting the first vehicle in a platoon of traffic. When traffic is constantly platooned, vehicles from varying positions in the platoon should be selected. In platoons which are densely packed, the traffic may be too heavy to permit a good survey and should be avoided.

2. Selecting too large a proportion of trucks. The same proportion of trucks in the sample as exist in the traffic stream should be obtained.

3. Selecting too large a proportion of higher speed vehicles. Ignoring measurement of normal speed vehicles to measure high-speed vehicles will result in the survey being biased toward the upper speed ranges. Normal speed vehicles should be considered.

Important to speed surveys are inventories of road conditions and accident records. Information about existing speed zones, prevailing speeds, location of accidents, roadway alignment, traffic volumes, and other general roadside physical characteristics should be obtained. Visibility restrictions should be recorded and deficiencies corrected to assure compatibility with the prevailing speed.

---

10. State of California, *Vehicle Code* (Sacramento: Department of Motor Vehicles, 1978).

When a concentration of reported accidents or an accident rate significantly higher than normal for the type of roadway under study is discovered, a detailed accident analysis should be made, including a collision diagram for the route or intersection as necessary. Adequate consideration may then be given to other corrective measures, the degree of enforcement needed, and the general applicability of any posted speed limit at all.

Analysis of Speed Survey Data

Two characteristics developed from prevailing speed data are of primary importance in the selection of a reasonable speed limit: the critical (85th percentile) speed and the pace. The critical speed is the speed at or below which 85 percent of the traffic is moving. The critical speed can be determined directly from a field speed data sheet specifically designed for speed surveys by counting from the top speed the number of vehicles equaling 15 percent of the total number of vehicles observed. Experience has shown that the 85th percentile speed is the one characteristic of high speeds that most nearly conforms to a safe and reasonable limit.

The 85th percentile speed is usually within 2 miles per hour of the upper limit of the pace speed. The pace is the 10 mph range of speeds containing the largest number of observations. A normal speed distribution will contain approximately 70 percent of the sample within the pace with 15 percent above and 15 percent below. These are plotted on a speed zone survey sheet (see figures 2-3, 2-4, and 2-5), vehicle speed data sheet, and a cumulative speed curve graph.

As a final aid to establishing realistic speed zones, the following practical considerations should be kept in mind:

1. Intermediate speed limits are applicable to through routes having positive intersection controls, good signing, striping, and markings to accommodate appreciable volumes of traffic from beyond the immediate neighborhood.

2. Unusually short zones of less than one-half mile in length should be avoided whenever possible.

3. Speed zone changes should be coordinated with visible changes in roadway conditions or roadside development.

4. Successive 5 mph speed zone changes should be avoided by properly selecting longer speed zones in 10 mph increments.

5. Speed zoning should be coordinated with adjacent jurisdictions to assure compatibility.

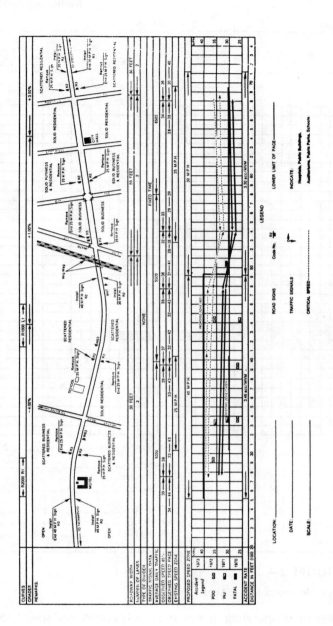

FIGURE 2-3

Speed Zone Survey Sheet

19

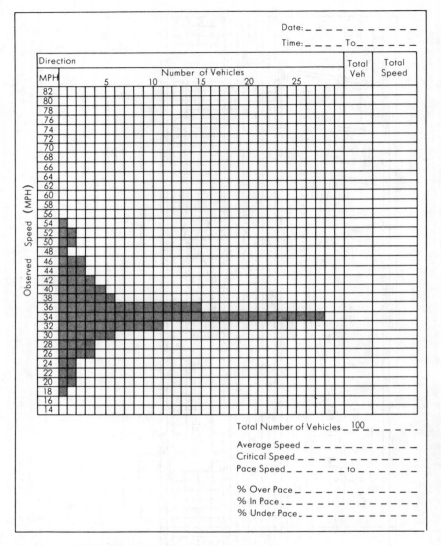

FIGURE 2-4

Vehicle Speed Data Sheet

An after-study of operating speeds in a newly established speed zone should be made to verify appropriateness, relative effectiveness, and general acceptance by the motoring public.

Local Street. The function of local streets is to provide access from a collecting street to abutting land and properties. The characteristics of local

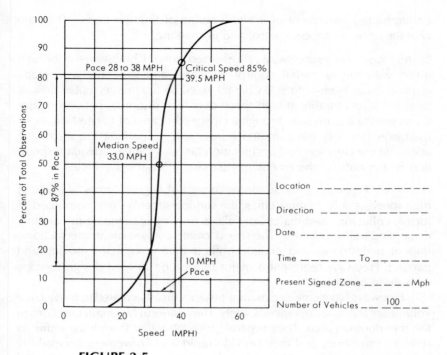

FIGURE 2-5

Cumulative Speed Curve

streets are (1) low speeds, (2) low volume, (3) access to abutting lands, (4) space for turning moves to give access to local establishments, and (5) curb parking.

Collector Street. A collector street serves the internal traffic movement within an area of the city, such as a subdivision, and connects with the major arterial system. A collector street does not handle long through trips and is not continuous for any great length.[11] While speeds are as low as on local streets, a collector street handles a greater volume of traffic and provides only limited curb parking.

Major Arterial Highway. This street serves those major movements of traffic within or through the metropolitan area not served by expressways. Major arterials interconnect the principal traffic generators within the city and the important rural routes.[12] While streets in this category may serve abutting property, the primary purpose of these roadways is to provide

---

11. Baker and Stebbins, *Dictionary of Highway Traffic.*
12. Ibid.

uninterrupted movement of a high volume of through traffic. They are characterized by access control and no parking.

Expressway.   An expressway is a divided arterial highway for through traffic with full or partial control of access and generally with grade separations at intersections.[13] Characterized by the uninterrupted flow of large volumes of traffic at high speed over long distances between major traffic generating areas or through a city or other area of congestion, these roadways not only have limited access and no parking but also have adequate deceleration and acceleration lanes as well as adequate shoulders or turnouts for the emergency parking of disabled vehicles.

Freeway.   Freeways provide for movement of large volumes of traffic at high speeds safely. In most cities, the surface-street system, composed of locals, collectors, and major arterials, is proving inadequate in handling expanding traffic volumes. The streets create congestion at intersections, imperil pedestrians, and create conflicts among vehicles moving and parking. Freeways represent a major innovation in road design to cope with these conditions.

Freeways have emerged as facilities specifically created to move large volumes of traffic at high speeds safely. They perform two main functions in the metropolitan area. They separate through traffic from local traffic to relieve congestion, and they provide rapid and convenient accessiblity between different parts of the area and between one metropolitan area and another.

A freeway is a divided arterial highway for through traffic. This preference to through traffic is achieved by providing specially designed ramps that allow traffic to enter or leave at designated points and by prohibiting crossings at grade through the use of over- and underpasses. The biggest departure of the freeway from the surface street design is in its controlled access feature.

Conflict Patterns

Lane Changing.   An operator who moves from one lane to another because of diminishing gap length has made a forced lane change. Any other change of lanes is termed an optional lane change. These terms give a general indication of the actions of the driver. When a driver is faced with a rapidly closing gap between his vehicle and the car ahead, he finds the longitudinal position of his vehicle unsatisfactory. He may accept gaps in adjacent lanes as short as 125 feet at speeds from 30 to 40 mph. Drivers making optional lane changes look for longer gaps before they move from their lane of operation (fig. 2-6).

---

13.   Ibid.

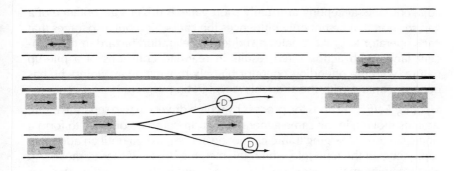

D = Diverging
      Maneuver

FIGURE 2-6

Lane Change Gap Acceptance

The maneuver of overtaking and passing the car ahead when approaching zero headway also requires lane changing. The first movement places the overtaking vehicle in the adjacent traffic stream and the second movement returns the passing vehicle to its original lane of travel.

In either case a definite conflict occurs. This conflict in lane changing usually results from lack of opportunity to move into the adjacent lane. When the change is made in lanes of a traffic stream moving in the same direction, the conflict is mainly with the rear vehicle in the adjacent lane. When the lane change is made as a part of an overtaking and passing maneuver there is a greater potential conflict in the oncoming vehicle. A lesser conflict exists at all times in lane changing between the overtaken vehicle and the overtaking or lane-changing vehicle.

Possibly the greatest enemy of effective lane distribution and the most effective creators of conflict are lane-straddling drivers. These individuals test the patience of fellow drivers in the traffic stream and offer an excellent opportunity for police remedial action. Normally lane-straddlers will make up about 20 percent of the volume on a highway. While a certain amount of this percentage will be operators efficiently shifting from lane to lane for legitimate reasons, the great majority are true lane-straddlers.

The careless driver straddling two lanes of a one-way traffic stream is an offender literally screaming for police attention, as he often causes two lanes of traffic to line up behind his vehicle. Next in importance in relation to the traffic stream, but possibly most important in minor accident causation, is the driver who timidly waits in his lane of travel until an over-size gap appears in the adjacent lane of travel. Vehicles that line up behind this driver create increased conflict because their impatient drivers dart into the adjacent lane, accepting unusually short gaps. A driver's acceptance of a gap so short that he not only influences the car behind but also forces that car's operator to brake creates a sudden deceleration hazard in the adjacent lane. Such action often results in rear-end collisions of a pile-up nature, with the offending operator blithely moving away, unless he has been in contact with the suddenly decelerating vehicle.[14]

Merging Traffic.   This is the process by which drivers in two separate traffic streams moving in the same general direction combine or unite to form a single stream.[15] Merging traffic cannot be accomplished until an adequate gap occurs in the lane into which the merging driver wishes to move. An ideal merging maneuver should be carried out without retarding the rear vehicle concerned. While most delays occur to the merging vehicles, there is also delay to vehicles in the lanes of traffic into which the merging takes place.

When the merging vehicle is stationary (as occurs when entering the traffic stream after a required full stop) or moving slowly, average drivers require larger gaps for merging; but when the merging vehicle's speed approaches that of the rear vehicle, relatively short gaps are accepted for merging by most drivers. Acceleration and deceleration lanes on modern highways provide space for merging vehicles to adjust speeds for the purpose of entering or leaving a fast-moving traffic stream.

All merging maneuvering has a definite conflict area. This area begins at a safe distance back of the collision area and extends to a point beyond where the merging vehicle has gained approximately normal speed. The collision area extends from the point of entry of the merging vehicle to the far end of the area of conflict.

Diverging Traffic.   The diverging vehicle develops an area of conflict in the lane from which it departs, and when this maneuver is made from the wrong lane of a multilane roadway the inherent hazard of leaving a highway is increased and the conflict area extends from the point of initial movement to the point where the diverging vehicle clears the path of the rear vehicle.

Even when made from the correct lane, this diverging maneuver creates some conflict unless traffic volume is very low because the diverging vehicle must slow up in order to make a turn. This creates the possibility of a rear-end collision as long as the turning vehicle remains in its original lane of travel.

The Crossing Maneuver.   No greater conflict exists in the time-space relationship of vehicles to each other than in this maneuver. The conflict area extends some distance from the intersection or crossing. The speeds of

---

14.   Weston, *The Police Traffic Control Function.*
15.   Ibid.

the vehicles concerned, the type of vehicle crossing contemplated (right-angle, oblique, and opposed left-turn), and the volume of vehicles in each flow determine relative degrees of interference to crossing traffic. Safety at the intersection may require some form of traffic control. Control lessens the capacity of the entering traffic streams but reduces conflict in the interests of safety.

Intersections are heavy conflict areas in which collisions may occur; for this reason they are of particular interest to persons engaged in accident reduction. The normal right-angle intersection of two-way streams of traffic develops thirty-two conflict points, of which half are of the collision potential crossing type (see fig. 2-7). The number of potential conflicts per hour is dependent upon vehicle volume in each flow of traffic. When the entering stream carries 200 vehicles per hour, approximately 1200 potential conflicts are created in each hour.

Traffic engineering techniques are available to minimize traffic conflicts. For example, the construction of left-turn lanes controlled by traffic signals can reduce conflicts at intersections and improve pedestrian safety by providing turning priority for drivers and favored crosswalks at each intersection entrance for pedestrians.

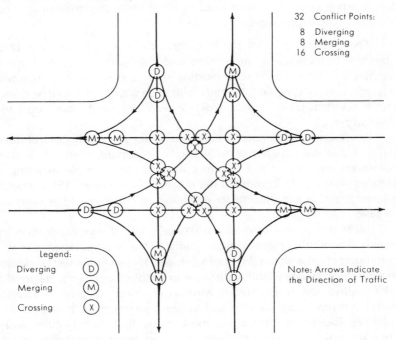

FIGURE 2-7

Conflict Points at an Intersection

Control Devices

Maximum efficiency and safety in the use of roads can be obtained only with the employment of the appropriate traffic control devices. Traffic control devices are all pavement markings, traffic signals, signs, and markers placed on, above, or adjacent to a roadway by authority of officials having the responsibility to regulate, warn, or guide traffic.

Traffic control devices are basically safety devices. Their function is to guide the motorist to his destination, warn of potential hazards, point the right of way, channel traffic, and otherwise regulate conduct in the traffic stream.

There are three types of traffic control:

1. Regulatory controls have the authority of law and impose precise requirements upon the road user.

2. Warning controls inform road users of potentially hazardous road conditions or unusual traffic conditions not readily apparent to them and thus impose responsibility upon the individual driver to employ caution as he proceeds through the danger area.

3. Guiding controls inform road users of route designation and other pertinent information.

These three types of traffic control devices point out the overall objective in their use — movement with safety. The individual driver is regulated in accordance with existing rules and regulations, warned of hazards, and is expected to comply with such warnings so that he does not create accident-prone situations while searching for the best route to his destination.

There are six elementary requirements for any traffic control device: (1) it should be capable of fulfilling an important need; (2) it should command attention; (3) it should convey a clear, simple meaning at a glance; (4) it should command the respect of road users; (5) it should be located to give adequate time for response; and (6) it should be sanctioned by law.

All traffic control devices are basically visual communication techniques. The traffic engineer uses signing as the principal means of visual communication with the driver of a vehicle. This signing must be designed to provide adequate visibility distance to enable the driver to respond and take positive action. To avoid hazardous situations, careful consideration must be given to sign design and to sign placement with respect to the roadway. Design of the signing must assure that such features as size, contrast, colors, shades, composition, and lighting or reflectorization where needed are combined to draw attention to the device; that shape, size, colors, and simplicity of message combine to produce a clear meaning; that legibility and size combine with placement to permit adequate time for response; and that uniformity, reasonableness, size, and legibility elicit compliance.

In order for the driving public to continue to respect these control devices, it is important that they be promptly removed from the public highway when no longer required or if for any reason they tend to encourage disrespect for control devices in general.

TRAFFIC ENGINEERING APPLICATION

By correcting engineering deficiencies which contribute to accidents, accidents can be reduced. The key is the remedial treatment of locations where the roadway environment is contributing to an accident hazard. The engineer must relate the physical and environmental characteristics of each location to the accident pattern. He must have firsthand knowledge of the signal head locations, street width, sight restrictions, lane marking (or lack thereof), grades, crown, and particularly any physical characteristics that make this location different from similar locations in the community. He should also be aware of traffic volumes and turning movements, parking restrictions, signal timing, composition of traffic, lining up tendencies, and other environmental characteristics which may have an effect on accident hazards.

The most effective way of gathering this information is to analyze accident records while observing traffic operations at the study location. The role of enforcement officers in such analysis cannot be overemphasized. Frequently, local police officers who have attended accidents at a given location can provide insights about the factors which may have caused accidents. Although each location will present unique hazards, a partial list of factors follows which will enable recognition of some common techniques for reducing hazards.

Primary Collision Factors	Corrective Measures
Left-turning vehicles struck by opposing cars (not at an intersection).	This pattern is usually found in areas where there is a lack of driveway control. Clusters of these accidents usually are found at drive-in restaurants, bowling alleys, or other traffic generators of this type. Such accidents can be reduced by installation of curb and gutter to prohibit high-speed, low-angle turning movements.

Primary Collision Factors	*Corrective Measures*
Right-turn accidents.	If a heavy volume of right turns is found in association with a high number of right-turning accidents, provision of right-turn lanes and channelization can frequently reduce this hazard.
Rear-end collisions involving left-turning vehicles (at an intersection).	These accidents can be reduced by provision of left-turn storage lanes. Such lanes can frequently be created by removing parking at an intersection or by widening the shoulder where sufficient width cannot otherwise be found to create such turning refuges.
Left-turning vehicles struck by on-coming cars (signalized intersections).	If sufficient left-turning volumes are found, this type of accident can be reduced with a separate signal phase to protect left-turning vehicles.
Right-angle collisions (nonsignalized intersections).	Right-angle collisions are usually associated with substandard sight distance or lack of acceptable gaps in through street traffic. There are three common solutions to these problems: 1. If a signal warrant is met, installation of a semi-actuated traffic signal will reduce this type of collision. 2. Removal of obstructions which restrict the view of oncoming traffic. This treatment will permit the driver to choose a safe crossing gap. 3. Channelization may be used to reduce the conflict area of the intersection, thereby increasing the number of acceptable gaps available to crossing vehicles.

Primary Collision Factors	*Corrective Measures*
Rear-end collisions.	A pattern of rear-end collisions, usually on a downgrade, at locations approaching stop signs or traffic signals can often be attributed to a low coefficient of friction. A rough-textured seal coat can be used to reduce this hazard.
Right-angle and rear-end collisions (signalized intersections).	A combined pattern of this type usually can be attributed to poor signal timing or poor signal head visibility. Utilization of dual, far side signal indications can reduce this hazard. If approach speeds are relatively high or if long lines of traffic can be expected, use of 12-inch signal lenses can also effect an improvement.

Evaluating Corrective Measures

Each improvement that is implemented as the result of the traffic accident analysis program should be documented. A "before and after" study should be conducted to test the effectiveness of various corrective measures in reducing the frequency of specific types of collisions. Locations that do not respond as expected should be studied to determine why accidents continue to occur and what additional measures can be taken to bring about the desired accident reduction. In addition, any accident types that increase in frequency as the result of an improvement should be noted. This follow-up procedure provides the traffic engineer with information concerning the effects of various corrective measures on specific types of accidents. This information helps to promote installation of proper traffic control devices and to discourage measures that have been proven ineffective.

The most important engineering facts to be gained from accident data are physical location and type of collision, both of which can be important indicators of deficiencies of the roadway system. Traffic engineers use accident reports to study physical locations that have been identified as hazardous to see if a pattern of accidents exists. If such a pattern exists, it is compared with the physical elements at that location to see if some element is causing the pattern.

Engineers actually need very little information from each accident report. But they do need accurate and complete reporting on the direction of travel, time of day, day of week, unusual pavement conditions, noninvolved vehicles, and driver intent.

Identifying Hazardous Locations

Traffic accident data must be filed by location for use by engineers. Accident reports should be filed by intersection; other location identities, such as the street number where the collision occurred; or highway mile post markers.

Certain intersections and highway segments are more prone to accidents than others. The traffic records system should identify these locations and provide information that indicates whether or not plans to reduce accidents are working. A detailed summary of all accidents within a specified time period at a given location can provide clues as to the underlying traffic flow problem.

Selecting Locations for Study

One method is to select for analysis all intersections having ten or more accidents in a twelve-month period. If the number of intersections selected by this method is less than fifteen or more than forty, some other number of accidents per location should be used as a guide.

An alternative method assigns a rating number to each accident, and the weighted result is used instead of total accidents. Each fatal accident is given a factor such as 12, each personal injury accident rates 3, and each property damage 1. This method recognizes accident severity as a prime factor in selecting intersections to be studied.

A combination method is also possible. An intersection would qualify for study if, for example, it showed (a) ten or more total accidents or (b) a weighted factor, based on severity, of twenty or more. In this way, a location with twelve property damage accidents and one personal injury accident would qualify for study under (a), while another with one fatal, two personal injuries, and three property damage accidents (total: 21 points) would qualify under (b). Either method separately, or the combination of both, may be used as desired.

It is not uncommon to find intersections in medium-sized cities with thirty to forty accidents per year. Such experience indicates needed improvement, and the accident reports will reveal some of the probable changes required. The accident problem is relative, as evidenced by the feeling in many cities that five accidents per year at any location is cause for official alarm. There is no acceptable number of accidents, unless it be zero. It is a matter of local decision as to what constitutes a tolerable number of traffic accidents per year and what measures must be employed to reduce the total rate.

Collision Diagrams. Preparation of these diagrams requires complete accident reports for the locations under study, covering all accidents occurring within the last one to five years. The collision diagram shows graphically the nature of all accidents occurring at the location by means of symbols (see fig. 2-8).

The collision diagram need not be drawn to scale but should indicate by arrows the direction of movement of each vehicle or pedestrian involved. The exact point of impact need not be to scale either, although a key number may be added to each collision arrow to provide a cross-reference to the original accident report.

The date and hour of the accident should be written alongside each arrow. Unusual weather or pavement conditions or driver action should also be indicated if it has an important bearing on the accident. If visibility is an important factor in the accident study, night accidents may be circled to provide a comparison between night and day collisions. This same idea may be applied to any single causative factor deserving special recognition.

The collision diagram is particularly useful in revealing accidents falling into one or more of the following classifications, which are clues to needed remedies:

1. Right-angle collisions between vehicles entering on intersecting streets.

2. Left-turn collisions involving vehicles approaching one another.

3. Rear-end collisions.

4. Pedestrian versus vehicle collisions.

5. Collisions between vehicles traveling in the same direction involving turning, lane changing, or sideswiping.

6. Head-on collisions.

7. Vehicles running off the roadway at curves or constrictions in the roadway.

8. Collisions with fixed objects near the roadside or within the intersection.

9. Collisions with parked vehicles.

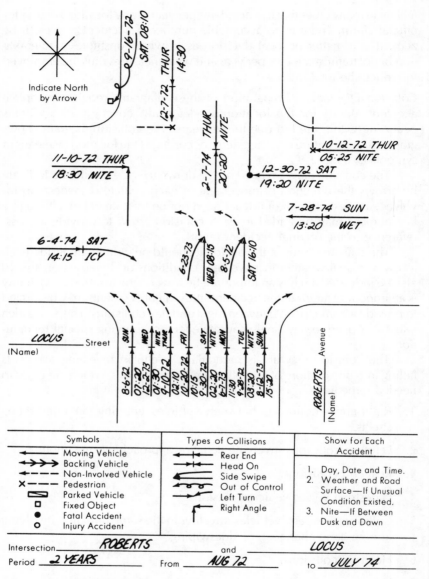

Indicate North
by Arrow

FIGURE 2-8

Collision Diagram

The collision diagram may also reveal certain months, days, or hours when most accidents tend to occur, as well as the effect of weather conditions.

Condition Diagrams. Often it is desirable to supplement the collision diagram with a drawing that portrays the existing physical features at, and adjacent to, an intersection or high-accident-frequency location (see fig. 2-9). This will not always be necessary, however, since physical features of the roadside or intersection may have little bearing on the accident experience. In cases where view obstructions, location, or other factors are suspected, a sketch of physical features should be prepared. Also, it may be possible to add such items to the collision diagram, thus making a combination sketch rather than two separate drawings.

As an alternative to the condition diagram, many engineers agree that photographs of the location taken during times when most accidents occur are more useful than condition sketches. Furthermore, it is widely agreed that personal visits to each high-accident location are far more revealing and valuable in the final analysis of accident causes.

Summarization. A summary should be made for the total number of each type of accident such as left-turn, sideswipe, rear-end, and so on; for the

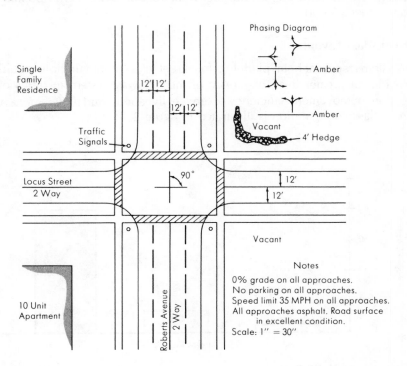

FIGURE 2-9

Condition Diagram

number of fatal, personal injury, and property damage accidents; and for the number of collisions on each approach to the intersection or other location. The numbers of accidents occurring at various seasons of the year and during various periods of the day are also summarized, together with the number of collisions occurring under different weather conditions, such as wet, snow, fog, and dry. Once the summary has been prepared, all outstanding facts should be identified to aid in future references.

THE HIGHWAY TRANSPORTATION SYSTEM

Often omitted in highway transportation system development is a systems approach. Planning and designing highway systems develops from land use, new developments, and the attendant need for *travel corridors*. A systems approach to highway system planning would take into consideration acceptable street class mileage distribution to maximize efficiency and minimize conflicts. The mileage distribution depicted in figure 2-10 is considered normal for cities outside of metropolitan areas with populations under 75,000.

Street Class Layout

A systems approach in planning for street class configuration would provide for greater level of service of the highway system in terms of freedom of movement, efficiency of service, liveability, and traffic safety. A street class configuration is illustrated in figure 2-11.

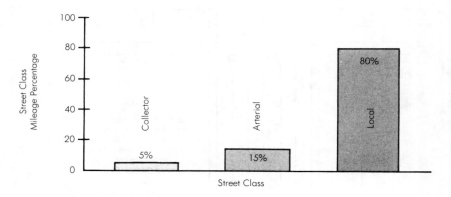

FIGURE 2-10

Street Class Mileage Distribution

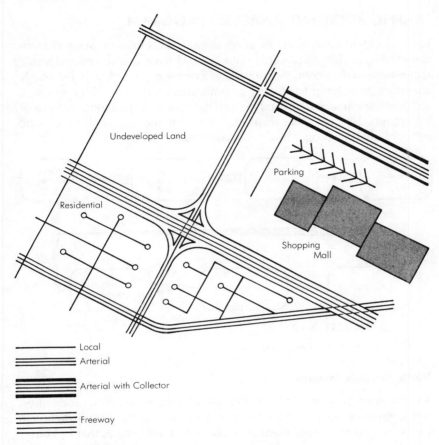

Undeveloped Land

Parking

Residential

Shopping
Mall

——————— Local

≡≡≡≡≡≡ Arterial

▬▬▬▬▬▬ Arterial with Collector

≡≡≡≡≡ Freeway

FIGURE 2-11

Street Class Configuration

Highway improvements and construction as a result of a systems approach would include geometric design and cross-section features that are correctly related to the street's function. Adhering to a basic formula for percentages of street class would provide a traffic environment that has greater efficiency and less conflicts. When vehicles are properly routed and channeled, traffic control devices strategically placed, and a balanced street class configuration maintained, we create a traffic environment in which travel corridors are better used. In this case there would be no congestion or clustering of vehicles funneled toward a common location. In contrast, vehicle platooning, space and gaps, and freedom of maneuver would result, thus eliminating many of the conflicts inherent in the movement of traffic over the highway system.

TRAFFIC ACCIDENT ANALYSIS PROGRAM

Traffic accident analysis relies upon compilations of accurate and complete traffic accident statistical data derived from a well-defined traffic accident record system. Accurate and complete reporting is extremely important. In helping to identify circumstances which combine to cause accidents, traffic accident analysis can determine, implement, and evaluate appropriate corrective measures. A systematic approach to a traffic accident analysis program is depicted in figure 2-12.

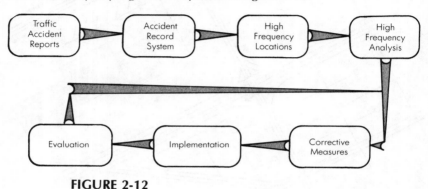

FIGURE 2-12

Traffic Accident Analysis

Traffic Records Systems

A traffic records system is the collection of documents, files, procedures, and summaries that provide a history of traffic problems in a jurisdiction in a way that permits assessment of overall cause and effect, that is, causes and effects of the traffic problem as a whole. It includes, but is far broader than, a system that embraces officer procedures for documenting accidents and traffic violations and the subsequent indexing and filing of these documents by the Records Bureau.

The traffic records system's major benefit is for planning activities. This planning can be directed toward preventing accidents and violations and to optimally allocate patrol resources so as to provide uniform and effective enforcement of traffic laws and response to traffic emergencies. A traffic records system provides the data base for studies of accidents and citations and, when automated, the capability for data handling necessary to reveal underlying trends.

Many types of traffic records systems have evolved to meet the needs and tastes of different traffic supervisors. Indeed, every traffic supervisor has some sort of a system, even if it is but a blotter record of accidents and citations. Most traffic records systems encountered in law enforcement agencies today would fit into one of the classes of systems enumerated below.

Pin Map Systems. One of the simplest of systems is to simply drive a pin into a street map at the location of the accident or citation. Over a period of time, patterns will be revealed by the buildup of pins in certain areas versus the virtual absence of pins in other areas. Pin maps have the advantage of being easy to understand and use.

Manual Tabulation Systems. In these systems tallies are maintained of accidents and citations by major characteristics, such as location, type of accident, time and day of week, criticality, and number of vehicles involved. Manual tabulations are frequently used in conjunction with, and to supplement, pin map systems. Manual tabulation systems provide numerical data for analysis that are lacking in pin maps.

Automated Systems. More and more jurisdictions are adopting these systems, particularly with the financial support of the National Highway Administration and the Law Enforcement Assistance Administration. In these systems the basic characteristics of accidents and citations, together with other relevant data to describe the street network and traffic beats, are fed into a computer operation where the data are organized and rapidly disseminated as computer printouts. The printouts may be available routinely in weekly reports, or they may be requested as needed for specific purposes. As an example, detailed summaries of accidents involving one or more drivers "under the influence" could be requested late in the year to help plan a holiday season campaign to detect drunken drivers and remove them from the streets.

The principal advantage of an automated traffic records system lies in its capability to sift rapidly and accurately through large volumes of data and then prepare meaningful summaries which can be utilized to improve traffic enforcement and control.

TRAFFIC OFFICER–TRAFFIC ENGINEER INTERRELATIONSHIPS

Both the traffic engineer and the police officer charged with responsibility for traffic control are necessary for the safe movement of traffic in any city, town, or village. The engineer may be a full-time traffic engineer or an engineer of the public works or other such department and only serve part-time in the role of traffic engineer. The police officer may be the only member of his department specifically responsible for traffic control, or he may be a high-ranking officer supervising several thousand officers in coping with the traffic problem of a large city. In any event, neither the police officer nor the traffic engineer alone can provide effective traffic control; one supplements the other. Police seek to prevent accidents under their basic obligation to the community they serve and in order to protect life and property. The traffic engineer studies the characteristic occurrence of accidents because they are a measure of failure in traffic design and operation.

The objective of traffic engineering is to *achieve efficient, free, and rapid flow of traffic, yet, at the same time, to prevent traffic accidents and casualties*. The objective of police traffic control is to *secure compliance with the law, expedite the flow of traffic, and promote the safety of motorists and pedestrians*.

The basic objective of police traffic control is the movement of traffic with safety. This is also the objective of any good traffic engineer, but engineers are also concerned with the planning and geometric design of streets and highways, and safe, convenient, and economical transportation of persons and goods over these facilities.

The police position is not to usurp the authority of engineers in the broad problems of research, technical design, or construction and mainte- nance of streets, highways, or traffic control devices. Responsibilities for traffic engineering assigned to other city departments will influence the police executive's decision as to what engineering techniques he or his staff may attempt to perform. However, the scope of police activity in this field should be extended to (1) locating and studying high accident frequency locations, (2) preparing collision and condition diagrams, and (3) develop- ing of accident patterns and simple engineering remedial action.

The one restriction on the role of the police in traffic control is that it stop short of major physical changes in the existing highway and street system. The responsible police official can set in motion through the appropriate authorities such remedial action as signs, signals, or pavement markings where accident experience indicates an intersection or traffic route is congested or accident prone. The role of the police in this field should include channeling traffic and reversing lanes as well as establish- ing alternate routes for use when heavily traveled roads exceed their capacity.

If the police recommendation is not approved by the authority con- cerned, then it is the duty of the police executive to determine the reasons for such lack of action and to take corrective action under his basic obligation to the community to protect life and property therein.

Traffic engineering and control techniques begin with the street and highway system of a community and the characteristics of traffic utilizing such roadways and encompass all the means used to accommodate and control such traffic.

SUMMARY

This chapter presented some of the many facets of the traffic engineering field. The field of traffic engineering is broad; therefore, the scope of this chapter was limited to measurements of demand and highway capacity, relationships between traffic variables, and application of corrective traffic engineering measures.

Essential to traffic investigation and control is an understanding of the different factors that cause conflicts in the traffic environment and the possible devastating effects on lives and property. If demands for the use of the highway system exceed the system's ability to handle it, traffic accidents will tend to increase. Demand measurements and highway capacity studies provide important information in decisions regarding improvement measures.

Determining the relationships of traffic variables helps to isolate specific hazards of traffic dynamics that lead to collisions. Studies of gap acceptance, conflict patterns, control device placement, and speed zoning provide important data needed to develop corrective measures.

Traffic accident analysis programs use accurate and comprehensive statistical data to identify problem areas and to implement and evaluate improvement efforts. If a systems approach for highway system improvement and construction is used, it can create a vehicle routing system designed for efficient service and traffic safety.

In this chapter, we also discussed the importance of the traffic officer and the traffic engineer. Understanding the function of each is extremely important to effective coordinated effort. In the final analysis, the motoring public benefits if those agencies responsible for different phases of the traffic engineering concept work together toward a common objective to make streets and highways safer and more efficient.

DISCUSSION QUESTIONS

1. Discuss why better roads and better automobiles did not supply the ultimate answer to the traffic problem.

2. Define and discuss the role of the highway traffic engineer.

3. Discuss the importance of highway demand and capacity measurements.

4.   Discuss the interrelationship between highway capacity and level of service.

5.   Discuss the importance of speed zoning in terms of improved highway service.

6.   Discuss the primary role of traffic control devices.

7.   Discuss the differences, if any, that exist between the role of a traffic officer and a traffic engineer.

8.   Discuss the importance of a traffic accident analysis program.

9.   Discuss the rationale for a systems approach to highway transportation system planning.

chapter

The Traffic Supervisor

In any organization, the supervisor occupies a position of critical importance. The way an employee values his job and even the organization as a whole is colored by his relationship with an immediate supervisor.[1] N.F. Iannone describes the role of the supervisor in police work:

> In the law enforcement agency, he is of special importance because of the great need for teamwork. Upon him rests most of the responsibility for providing the cohesive force which welds the working force into a well-functioning, smoothly operating unit.[2]

A traffic supervisor is called upon to perform varied duties, to possess different skills, and to be many things to many people. In this chapter, three areas of basic importance to the traffic supervisor will be discussed in detail: the traffic supervisor as a person; the traffic supervisor as a communicator; and the traffic supervisor as a motivator.

THE TRAFFIC SUPERVISOR AS A PERSON

The personality of the supervisor plays an important role in the development of the ability to supervise.[3] While research in this area makes it clear

---

1. Howard M. Carlisle, "The Bond Between You and Your Subordinates," *Supervisory Management* 16, no. 4 (April 1971): 12.
2. N.F. Iannone, *Supervision of Police Personnel*, 2d ed. (Englewood Cliffs, N.J.: Prentice-Hall, 1975), p. 1.
3. Ibid., p. 35.

that there is no such entity as an "ideal supervisory personality,"[4] there are some traits that both research and common sense indicate are of critical importance for a supervisor to possess.[5]

The purpose of this section is (1) to increase the effectiveness of those already in supervisory positions, or those who are aspiring to become supervisors, by helping them concentrate on some specific areas of personality development; and (2) to provide a frame of reference for those administrators and supervisors who are evaluating the suitability of candidates for supervisory positions.

Five personality traits are necessary in an effective traffic supervisor: honesty, trustworthiness, empathy, mistakeability, and assertiveness. Each trait is important and necessary in its own right. Even if a supervisor possesses four out of five qualities, he could still experience significant problems. But it also should be kept in mind that personality traits are not "all or nothing" entities. A supervisor could grade himself on the five traits, giving an "A" in trustworthiness, a "C" in assertiveness, and a "D" in mistakeability. So the question is not "Do I have this trait or not?" but "To what degree do I possess this trait and how can I consciously work to develop it more?"

Honesty

There are two ways in which a person can be honest. One is *morally,* and this deals with having a sound moral character that precludes lying, cheating, stealing, and other forms of misconduct. Obviously, moral honesty is a necessary trait in any police officer, and even more so in a supervisor. But an equally important type of honesty, and one that gets tested much more frequently, is *psychological honesty.*

Psychological honesty means sharing openly, clearly, and consistently what one truly thinks and feels. It means expressing *both* complimentary and critical feelings when they are felt. The supervisor should be an accurate mirror to those he supervises so that they can clearly see their own strengths and weaknesses. The supervisor must accept responsibility for his own ideas and feelings, e.g., if the sergeant is unhappy with an officer's work, he admits to this opinion and does not tell the officer that "the lieutenant is unhappy with your work."

---

4. See Lawrence I. Sank, "Effective and Ineffective Managerial Traits Obtained as Naturalistic Descriptions from Executive Members of a Super-Corporation," *Personnel Psychology* 27, no. 3 (Autumn 1974): 423, and Peter F. Drucker, *The Effective Executive* (New York: Harper & Row, 1967), pp. 21-22.

5. See W.H. Newman and C.E. Summer, Jr., *The Process of Management* (Englewood Cliffs, N.J.: Prentice-Hall, 1961), pp. 220-21, and Bernard M. Bass. *Leadership Psychology and Organizational Behavior* (New York: Harper & Row, 1960), p. 451.

An individual can fail to be honest in a number of ways. One is "selective honesty." The traffic supervisor may share only his complimentary thoughts, depriving officers of opportunities to become aware of their weaknesses and the chance to strengthen them. More commonly, the supervisor may express only critical feelings, leaving the officer to wonder if he can do anything correctly, and if so, who really cares. The supervisor also may communicate honestly with those who work for him, but less so with his peers, and almost never to those above him.

One basic obstacle to psychological honesty is fear. A person will often be afraid that if he is honest, he will get hurt or may hurt someone else. The supervisor may fear that if he says what he truly thinks or feels, some people may not like or respect him.

The fear of hurting another person is readily seen in excuses used by a supervisor to avoid being honest with his criticisms: "He's got enough problems." "It wouldn't do any good anyway." "It's not the right time." "What if I'm mistaken?" "It will only make matters worse." "It's not that important anyway." "She'll learn sooner or later." None of these rationalizations are valid. The more an officer is allowed to think that things are "fine" when they are not, the more ongoing damage is being perpetrated on him. Being "nice" by ignoring a situation that should not be ignored merely postpones facing problems that are incubating each day. A problem that might have been solvable six months ago may now have become unsolvable.

Sometimes the supervisor chooses not to express complimentary feelings because he is afraid it may give the officer a "big head," or cause the officer to think the supervisor is getting "soft," or trying to "butter him up." All human beings need positive support as well as criticism. Commending an officer, formally or informally, is likely to have five times the educational effect as a reprimand, even when the reprimand is a valid one.

Despite the obstacles involved, the supervisor should strive to be psychologically honest for three reasons:

1. If a person is emotionally stable and likes and respects himself, he should be able to present his ideas in such a way that others will like and respect him also. This does not mean that everyone will always agree with the supervisor, but disagreement does not preclude admiration or respect.

2. When the supervisor is dishonest, he divides himself into two parts: a real self, which is hidden, and an image which is revealed. It is then the *image* that is liked and respected and not the real person. This should be a hollow satisfaction to any self-respecting individual.

3. Sooner or later, the supervisor will suffer the consequences of his dishonesty. People will come to realize that he is a "phony" who is primarily interested in protecting his own interests at the expense of fellow workers and the department. The supervisor may also find himself placed in uncomfortable and unhappy situations. For example, a supervisor may allow others to think he is more knowledgeable about a particular subject than he actually is. On the basis of this image, he may be appointed as a teacher at the police academy, a position for which he is woefully ill prepared.

So, while moral honesty is important, it only encompasses all the things that should not be done. Psychological honesty deals with all the things a supervisor can and should do to keep fellow officers abreast of reality.

Trustworthiness

In addition to being competent in his work both academically and experientially, two factors comprise trustworthiness in a supervisor.

First, he keeps *in confidence* all communications that were intended, explicitly or implicitly, to be so. Unfortunately, it takes only one slip-up in this area to undo a supervisor's credibility for a long time.

Why do some supervisors break confidences? Sometimes it is done inadvertently. But this almost never happens with a supervisor who has a reverential attitude toward the privacy of those he supervises. He protects the privacy of others with the same resoluteness with which he protects his own.

Sometimes a confidence is broken out of good intentions. The supervisor feels that an officer will be understood better if his marital problems are known by a fellow officer. The minor and tentative good that may stem from sharing such information is undone a hundredfold by the damage inflicted on a once trusting and respectful relationship between an officer and his supervisor.

At other times, confidential information may be divulged to enliven a gossip session or to make the supervisor look better in one way or another. It should be remembered that when a supervisor violates someone's confidence, he is severely damaging two people: the other officer and himself as an effective supervisor.

Second, the trustworthy supervisor is not *hypocritical*. That is, he is never "two-faced," saying one thing to one officer and something quite different to another.

For example, Sergeant Smith tells Officer Jones he is doing an outstanding job. But when Jones' partner consults Sergeant Smith about a small problem he is having with Jones, Sergeant Smith shares with the partner his "real concern about Jones not making it through his probationary period." Eventually, the discrepant message filters back to Jones, who is both confused and appropriately angry.

People are two-faced for several reasons. If you tell each person what he wants to hear, everyone is happy (until they sit down and compare notes). Second, it is a "cheap" way to ventilate one's feelings. The supervisor can tell Smith what upsets him with Jones and vice versa, without ever having to experience the discomfort of facing them directly. And, sometimes, such deception occurs out of malevolence. It is a way of "getting back" at an officer who has been irking the supervisor.

As with broken confidences, deception becomes apparent to those involved sooner or later, and the effectiveness of the supervisor can be severely damaged, if not eliminated.

Empathy

Empathy means a "feeling with" another. It connotes trying to "get inside" another person to see things as he does and to feel as he is feeling. It should not be confused with sympathy, which is feeling pity for another and is seldom a healthy sentiment. Empathy does not mean we have to *agree* with how a person perceives or feels about a situation. It simply means we understand the other person's reactions or feelings.

Empathy is important, because without this in-depth understanding of another the supervisor is incapable of communicating with the officer in a meaningful way. In the absence of empathy, the officer becomes a foreign object and in times of conflict is seen only as the source of confusion, anger, and frustration. As long as these feelings persist in the supervisor, there is less chance for a successful resolution to a problem or to a misunderstanding.

Empathy can be a very difficult trait to acquire. Often, if the supervisor is upset with someone, he *does not want* to understand him; he just wants to be upset with that person. Or, the supervisor may be fearful that if he really understands the officer, he may have to change some of his own behavior, attitudes, and beliefs, and that may generate anxiety within the supervisor.

Empathy entails hard work. It takes a lot of listening and gentle questioning. It foregoes easy solutions to problems such as "Don't worry about it"; "I don't care if you understand *why* you are to do it, just *do* it"; "Don't let your partner get to you"; "I'm sure things will turn out all right"; or "Yeah, sure I understand what you mean, but. . . ."

The supervisor will know he has reached a point of empathy when, after he has paraphrased what the officer has been saying, the officer's face lights up and he says: "Yeah, now you've got it." It is only then that real understanding and communication can begin.

Mistakeability

Mistakeability is one of the true signs of a mature person. It is the virtue of allowing oneself to make a mistake, accepting the responsibility for that mistake, and admitting it to others, especially to those who were affected by the error.

People who lack mistakeability deny that they could have made an error; or they admit the error but present "good reasons" that "explain" how it came about; or they take great pains to hide the mistake from the very people who have suffered because of it.

Mistakeability is a rare trait because of two myths:

Myth I: If I make a mistake, I am a lesser person. In fact, it is not mistakes that detract from a person but his inability to admit to them and rectify them. A supervisor may well make more mistakes than any individual who works for him, because the supervisor's role is usually much more complex, stressful, and responsible.

Myth II: If I accept and admit my mistakes, I will have to accept those of others, and then everyone will be making mistakes all of the time. In reality, "accepting" mistakes does not connote approval of them. The supervisor does not proclaim: "I made a mistake so you all get to make one now." His attitude *should* be: "I made a mistake. Here is how I did it and what I am going to do to insure that I do not make the same error again. I hope we all can learn from this."

This attitude accomplishes two things: (1) it encourages people to admit to their mistakes instead of covering them up (which causes even greater problems at a later date); and (2) sharing the causes of errors can diminish the number of future mistakes because the errors are used as learning experiences for all members of the department.

People who work closely with each other are going to see the others' weaknesses. There are two options. The supervisor and officers can deny their weaknesses, which only adds another great weakness to the list; or they can admit to the flaws which adds a strength that far overshadows most weaknesses.

Assertiveness

Perhaps the best way to define assertive behavior is first to describe its extremes: nonassertive behavior and aggressive behavior. The nonassertive individual is often shy, timid, and reserved. He finds it very difficult to stand up for his rights and to act on his feelings. He easily gives in to any request made of him or feels guilty for turning someone down. When things go wrong he blames himself first.

As a supervisor, this individual experiences many problems. He is taken advantage of by both those above him and those below him. He lacks the strength to "back" his officers in conflicts with citizens and superior officers. He encourages them to "forget" injustices, which creates resentment among those he supervises. He and the people he supervises are passed over for benefits time and again because he fails to let the needs and hopes of his officers be known to those who could help them.

On the other end of the scale is the aggressive person. He "puts himself up" by "putting others down." The chief aim of the aggressive person is to get what he wants, no matter what others have to pay in terms of time, energy, money, pressure, or personal hurt.

There are two ways to be aggressive. One is on a physical level. This type of individual dominates his environment and demonstrates his toughness with bravado. But a more intellectually oriented person can be equally aggressive. He may dominate conversation — both by verbosity and loudness; belittle the opinions of others; and leave no doubt that he considers himself the final word on nearly every topic. He often confuses managing people's *work* with managing their *humanity*. Often this individual does not wish to be aggressive, but he has not learned responses that are appropriately assertive.

As a supervisor, the aggressive person is a threat to the people around him. People feel insecure in his presence because they realize that their best interests are not his concern. They feel, rightly, that they are expendable and dare not express to the supervisor's face what they say and feel behind his back. As a result, fear reigns and morale is low.

At a midpoint between the nonassertive and the aggressive supervisor is the assertive supervisor. This person is able to let others know who he is and what he wants without damaging people in the process. He respects his subordinates' human rights just as conscientiously as he expects others to respect his. He is fully in charge of himself in interpersonal relationships, displaying confidence and capability without arrogance or hostility. He realizes that as a supervisor he has no right to take advantage of his subordinates' natural rights to courtesy and respect as human beings.[6]

As a supervisor, this individual is respected because his respect for others is so continual and obvious. His ability to approach people openly and honestly invites others to approach him on the same basis. People feel

---

6. Robert E. Alberti and Michael L. Emmons, *Your Perfect Right* (San Luis Obispo, Calif.: Impact, 1974), pp. 24-25.

safe around him because they know he operates in ways that will be in their best interest as well as his own and those of the department.

THE TRAFFIC SUPERVISOR AS COMMUNICATOR

"For supervisors — the strength of an organization and its real men and women in the middle — personalized communication should be a primary professional goal," states John Brennan.[7] A large percentage of the problems in any organization can be traced eventually to faulty communication.[8] The price an organization pays for ineffective communication can be measured objectively in number of dollars lost and employee hours wasted.

A person is not, by nature, a good communicator or a poor communicator. Good communicators are people who have taken the time to learn communication skills and to practice them. Effective communication depends on skills that can be learned. This fact was brought out sharply by a study in which police officers trained in reporting their observations did better than Phi Beta Kappa college seniors who had no such training.[9]

Because communication is the supervisor's most important, yet most difficult responsibility, a number of factors in the communication process will be discussed. The principles noted in this section are, for the most part, valid for all types of communication. However, the emphasis will be on verbal communication. This is because face-to-face communication is superior, under most circumstances, to written orders, memos, or business letters.[10]

Effective Communication Means Listening

Listening is perhaps the most overlooked aspect of the communication process. The word *communicate* almost always connotes talking rather than listening. Yet, no matter how eloquently a person speaks, if no one is listening to him, no communication is taking place. As Roy G. Foltz states: "Everyone who communicates should spend at least half of his time listening, and professional communicators should spend even a higher

---

7. John Brennan, *The Conscious Communicator* (Menlo Park, Calif.: Addison-Wesley, 1974), p. 190.

8. Roy G. Foltz, "Communication: Not an Art, a Necessity," *Personnel* 49, no. 3 (May-June 1972): 63.

9. Frank W. Draden and John T. Trutter, "Why Communication Goes Haywire," *Supervisory Management* 12, no. 1 (January 1967): 10.

10. Leonard R. Sayles and George Strauss, *Human Behavior in Organizations* (Englewood Cliffs, N.J.: Prentice-Hall, 1966), p. 249.

percentage of time listening, particularly to to those things that are emotionally upsetting."[11]

To become an effective listener, the traffic supervisor should be aware of some of the barriers to effective listening and some of the aids that can help him become a more active listener. Some barriers to effective listening are:

1. *Internal noise.* This term indicates that there is so much inner "static" going on within the individual that it significantly drowns out the bulk of what is being said to him. This inner noise is typically caused either by anxiety or anger. The listener is so threatened or angered by the situation (either the content of the message, or the sender of the message, or both) that he "cannot hear."

The astute supervisor perceives this officer's "tuned-out" look, the fact that he asks questions that have been answered, or that he makes irrelevant statements. The supervisor then chooses to discontinue his primary message in order to deal with the "hidden agenda," that is, the smoldering feelings of the officer. Once the feelings are ventilated, there will be more receptivity to the original message. If the supervisor is experiencing internal noise, he should deal with it before attempting to continue the conversation.

2. *Judgmental listening.* Passing premature judgments, whether they are favorable or not, tends to restrict an employee's freedom of expression. Even a poorly timed positive evaluation can be inhibiting because it could make it difficult for the person supervised to talk about mistakes he has made. Premature criticism may ultimately turn out to be unjust and, in any case, can discourage the officer from continuing with additional parts of his story. A good listener sends the message: "Tell me *everything,* and I will react after you let me know you are completely finished."

3. *An authoritarian attitude.* If the supervisor feels that "what I have to say is more important than what you have to say," he will be formulating his next words instead of listening. Or, he may convey the message: "Tell me only what I want to hear." This results in a filtering or cover-up of real problems. Often, the information that the supervisor is protected from will eventually return to haunt him.

4. *Misunderstanding silences.* A supervisor who is a good listener realizes that when the other person stops speaking, it does not necessarily mean that he has stopped communicating. Often, a silence is a part of an ongoing communication during which the speaker is reevaluating to himself what he has just said, or formulating in his mind how he will present the remainder of his message. To interrupt at that time may demolish the

---

11. Foltz, "Communication," p. 62.

speaker's train of thought and emotional state. It is not when the speaker's mouth stops moving that conveys when he is finished speaking; it is when his eyes "rest" and say: "OK, now it is your turn."

What are some aids to effective listening?

1. *Listen actively.* The supervisor's whole demeanor should reflect that he is actively involved in the listening process. His attitude, posture, eyes, and facial expression should make it clear to the officer that he is "with" him all the way. The actively listening supervisor asks questions that draw out the officer's ideas and feelings. The supervisor also checks up on what he has heard by restating it the way he understands it to validate his perceptions.

If the supervisor's mind wanders, he feels free to say: "I'm sorry, I was distracted for a second, could you repeat that?" He encourages the officer by nodding his head and periodically reassuring him by saying, "I understand" or "I could see how you would feel that way." If the supervisor senses some confusion or contradiction in the officer's story, he patiently asks for clarification, e.g., "I think I missed a step back there," versus "Hey, wait a minute; you just contradicted yourself!"

2. *Listen with the "third ear."* A good listener has the ability to go beyond the spoken words to their *meaning* and *feeling* levels. For example, an officer may say to his supervisor: "I really need to get off 'swing shift'; it's creating havoc with my life."

The poor listener who is merely hearing words and not messages replies: "I'm sorry, Bill, but you have to take your turn with 'swing' along with everyone else — it's part of the game."

The supervisor who is an astute listener is aware of the possibility of other messages:

— Is Bill trying to tell me that he and his wife are having problems?

— Is he telling me he is under a great deal of psychological stress and that he is becoming worried about it?

— Are his kids developing behavioral problems because he does not see them much anymore?

— Is there something going on during the swing shift that is upsetting him?

These are all areas that a good supervisor will want to gently explore before making a final decision.

3. *Learn to read nonverbal communication.* Someone once said that the "loudest" kind of communication is the kind we cannot hear. What this means is that an important part of "listening" is done with one's eyes. Facial expressions, gestures, posture, and mannerisms may transmit a message that is not being sent verbally or may contradict a message that is being sent verbally. A smirk on someone's face, clenched fists, finger tapping, wander-

ing eyes, bored or upset looks, slouched or rigid posture, a smile — all may express messages that a good listener will perceive and pursue in a friendly way. A poor listener will either miss these nonverbal cues or purposely ignore them because he does not wish to "hear" what the messages are saying. As Bernard B. Beegle states:

> It is the supervisor's own interest to *observe* how his subordinates communicate through gestures and mannerisms and to acknowledge these signs as legitimate messages that demand attention. When employees communicate non-verbally, they are signalling you to get involved. They are asking you to take the initiative to talk to them, to find out if problems exist, and to take action to solve them quickly.[12]

4.   *Encourage honest feedback.* All three of these words are important. "Encourage" means that the supervisor, in a clear and nonthreatening manner, invites the officer to share his ideas and feelings. The supervisor's message is: "I'm really interested in what your feelings are on this — what you think about it is important to me." This is contrary to the supervisor whose message is: "Well, if there is nothing else, you may return to work."

"Honest" means that the supervisor conveys a sense of security that assures the officer that he can "take in stride" any reaction that the officer may offer. The message is: "There may be some things you agree with and don't agree with. I need to hear both because I want to understand what this means to you." This is in contrast to the supervisor who conveys: "Well, what I said makes pretty good sense, don't you think?"

Feedback, in itself, is important. Without it, the supervisor is deprived of information he needs to make good decisions. It also deprives the officer of feeling that his ideas are important enough to be considered in the decision-making process.

Listening pays off in three ways. The supervisor gets all the facts and feelings from his officers so that he feels confident of the situation. Second, the officer feels that the supervisor really cares about him. Finally, the officer is now willing to listen openly to what the supervisor would like to say.

Effective Communication Is Direct

When a supervisor wishes to share some information with an officer, be it a commendation, reprimand, or just general information, he should communicate it directly, preferably in a verbal message, but at least with a

---

12.   Bernard B. Beegle, "The Message That Is Sent Without Words," *Supervisory Management* 16, no. 2 (February 1971): 14.

written communication. This seems simple enough, yet it is one of the biggest causes of failure in communication.

Being *indirect* is often easier. One can be indirect by communicating "by inference." A supervisor protests: "Why should I have to *tell* Officer Smith she is doing a good job. If she hasn't been 'called on the carpet' recently, she should *know* she is doing well!" Or, "If Officer Smith can't tell she's got problems around here by the way I treat her, she's beyond hope anyway." In both instances, if the supervisor spent ten minutes with the officer, he could undoubtedly save hours of time at some later date.

The supervisor can be indirect by being subtle. Subtlety is employed mostly with unpleasant communications. The supervisor "drops hints," veiled suggestions, and innuendos that the officer's performance or behavior is unsatisfactory. The supervisor then says: "I hope he got the point." But there is no place for "decoding" messages in healthy communication. If the officer failed to "catch" the point, it is because the supervisor failed to *make* the point.

A third way of being indirect is for the supervisor to express his thoughts about an officer to a third party, hoping that the "word" will filter down to the officer. This is almost always disastrous because the message is often contaminated by the messengers, depending upon their involvement in the situation. The result is that by the time the communication finally gets to the intended officer it is often distorted in some way. This, in turn, creates a new set of problems.

Effective Communication Is Immediate

As little time as possible should elapse between feeling the need to communicate and the actual communication. Immediacy is important for two reasons. If the situation calls for the expression of unpleasant feelings (anger, disappointment, criticism), the longer the supervisor holds in these feelings, the more likely they will be overexpressed (because they incubate), underexpressed (because they wear off), or never expressed. In none of these cases will the officer benefit from knowing how his supervisor truly feels; hence, he may overadjust his behavior, underadjust it, or fail to adjust it.

Second, immediacy is important because the closer in time a person is rewarded or punished for his behavior, the stronger the linkage between the behavior and the consequences. This is essential for true learning to occur.

The two main barriers to immediacy in communication are procrastination and disturbed priorities. People often put off what will create anxiety within them; they are chronically awaiting the "right time" to convey the message. But in effective communication, there is only *one* right time, and that is the present. Disturbed priorities are evident when a supervisor is "too busy" to communicate issues while they are still "hot." He has letters to write and meetings to attend, which he thinks are more important than communicating with subordinates. The more a supervisor interposes other duties between himself and those he supervises, the more distance there will be between them.

Effective Communication Is Clear

Communication should be concise and lucid. Most people talk too much. This is done to camouflage their insecurity stemming from not knowing what they really want to say, or knowing but being reluctant to "get to the point." It is often helpful for a supervisor to phrase mentally the one or two thoughts that he wishes to convey. Then, when the time comes, the supervisor is better prepared to share those ideas in a simple and concise manner. The more words that are used, and the more decorative they are, the more cause for distraction, inattention, and confusion.

There are three common types of unclear messages. One is the ambiguous message. The supervisor tells an officer: "I want you to concentrate on the speeding drivers on Main Street, but I also want you to use your head." What does this mean?

An unclear message is an inconsistent one. A supervisor may tell his officers: "I don't want any more complaints from citizens about your hiding to catch drivers 'blowing' stop signs." Two weeks later the same supervisor tells the same officers: "You people are going to have to start enforcing stop signs. We've had three injury accidents this month at those intersections."

Third, an unclear message is a "double message." A supervisor says: "I want you to enforce the double-parking laws downtown, but I don't want the merchants up here complaining." These are "damned if you do and damned if you don't" messages.

A good communicator is secure enough in what he thinks and feels that he can afford to be to the point and lucid without being blunt.

Effective Communication Is "Pure"

A "pure" communication is one in which the *stated* purpose for the communication and the *real* purpose are identical. A "contaminated" communication occurs when there is a discrepancy between the real and stated purposes.

For example, a supervisor may advise an officer: "I'd like to talk to you about a few problems with your accident reports." If the communication is "pure," this is exactly what will happen. But perhaps the supervisor is using the officer's traffic reports as a pseudo-issue. The supervisor may feel that the officer has been "goldbricking" lately and is angry with him. So, while the supervisor's purported motive is to help the officer with his reports, the real purpose is to "stick it" to the officer.

The results of this contaminated communication are

1. The officer is confused because he *hears* what the supervisor is saying about the reports, but he *feels* waves of hostility and punitiveness which seem incongruous and inappropriate.

2. The officer may feel the supervisor's wrath but leaves the discussion not knowing the cause of his anger. Consequently, he will be unable to make appropriate changes in his behavior.

Other "hidden motives" can be seen in the following "double-plays":

— I want to talk with you about your reports (but I really want to impress you that I know more about your work than you do).

— I want to talk with you about your reports (but I really want you to know that I am your boss, which you do not seem to realize).

— I want to talk with you about your reports (but I really want to show you what a nice person I am so you will like me).

Most hidden motives could be legitimate issues for communication, but they should be dealt with as separate communications and not camouflaged by other issues.

Effective Communication Is Constructive

"Constructive" communication means that the purpose of the communication is to better the other person, not to tear him down or to destroy him. The message in a communication can be viewed, analogously, as a brick. A brick can be *thrown* at another person, but this will cause a "fight or flight" reaction in him. Either he will fight, i.e., throw another brick; or he will flee — neither of which creates an atmosphere for effective communication.

But a brick can also be used to build a bridge between the supervisor and the officer. A supervisor can express displeasure, disappointment, or frustration in a way that reflects on the individual's particular behavior but not on who he is as a person. For example, a supervisor may state: "I noticed that you have been late for our last three meetings; you seem like an irresponsible person."

"Throwing bricks" can be done in several ways. One is by the vocabulary we use. Referring to people with emotionally loaded labels such as "dumb," "lazy," "irresponsible," or "dishonest" accomplishes nothing except to increase the listener's defenses. The more defenses that are erected, the less real listening and thoughtful consideration will be given to what is being said.

"Brick throwing" can also be done by the use of sarcasm, which is a very ineffectual method for communicating. Sarcasm is belittling and hostile, and it precludes the mutual openness that is a prime requisite for effective communication.

Bringing up old or unrelated issues is another "brick." This is often prefaced by "Now that we are getting things off our chest. . . ." If the side issues are important, they should have been brought up when they were "hot"; if they are not as important, they should not be added to the main issue.

Embarrassing another person in front of others is also a situation that interferes with communication. The message gets lost in the inner static that is created by the feeling of humiliation the listener has.

Comparisons also are likely to interfere rather than to help the reception of a message. Suggestions such as "Why don't you watch Officer Smith; *she* knows what she is doing" are seldom helpful. The main effect of such a statement is that the officer builds up a resentment toward both the supervisor and Officer Smith.

Making inferences about behavior rather than focusing on observations can be destructive. For example, it is better to say: "I noticed you had a hard time keeping awake at the meeting, and I was wondering what it meant," than to say: "You were obviously bored stiff at the meeting — what's the problem?"

Attributing motives to an officer's behavior can be problematic as well. It is more constructive to say: "You seem to be having trouble with your accident investigations," than to accuse: "I suppose you think that if you create enough problems in accident investigation, I'll let you go back to routine traffic patrol."

Even the most severe criticism can be imparted without angry and denigrating words. The question the supervisor can ask himself is whether his aim is to destroy the individual or open up channels for communication.

In constructive communication, the main attitude of the supervisor should be one of support. One method of accomplishing this is to point out concrete examples of where the officer handled something well, so that the mistake may be put into proper perspective.

Another way to be supportive is for the supervisor to share the fact that he may have made the same or comparable mistake in the past and to elucidate the negative consequences that flowed from it. The officer who leaves a discussion with his supervisor feeling "I blew it" while still respecting the supervisor as a person and an officer is infinitely more likely to rectify a mistake than the officer who leaves feeling "He doesn't respect me anymore. Well, I don't care *what* he thinks." When mistakes are pointed

out in an atmosphere of realistic support and encouragement, better cooperation and more effective behavior will result in the officer.

THE TRAFFIC SUPERVISOR AS MOTIVATOR

"A supervisor's essential task is to create a climate in which employees
satisfy their own needs by working to fulfill department objectives," states
Howard P. Smith.[13] In attempting to accomplish this task, the supervisor
should realize three points:

1. In the last quarter century, it has become obvious that money (salary,
    financial rewards, and benefits) is no longer a significant motivation
    for most people.[14] Since individuals have become more educated and
    sophisticated, it is increasingly important for management to fulfill
    their *emotional* needs.[15]

2. Motivation, then, is not something that a supervisor does to his work-
    ers.[16] A supervisor cannot give motivation to his people. He can only
    create a work situation in which the workers can get their needs met
    both through the work they do and through their relationships with the
    supervisor.

3. There are two main reasons for a supervisor being committed to the
    fulfillment of his subordinates' emotional needs: (a) On a humanitar-
    ian level, it is intrinsically good to offer other human beings the
    opportunity for growth and happiness. (b) On a pragmatic level, a
    person who is getting good "emotional groceries" at work will con-
    comitantly develop good "psychological muscles." This enables him
    to rise above many of the conflicts that can plague an organization:
    petty jealousies and rivalries; suspiciousness that others are against
    him or getting more than he; gossip and backbiting; and a lethargic,
    uncommitted approach to his work. This officer is more resilient to
    stress, more adaptable, and more interested in the goals of the depart-
    ment.[17]

---

13. Howard P. Smith, "Keys to Employee Motivation," *Supervisory Management* 16,
no. 2 (February 1971): 41.
14. Clois E. Bristo, "Do You Motivate Your Subordinates?" *Supervisory Management*
16, no. 9 (September 1971): 12.
15. Vincent W. Kafka, "A Motivation System That Works Both Ways," *Personnel* 49, no.
4 (July-August 1972): 62.
16. John R. Hinrichs, *The Motivation Crisis: Winding Down and Turning Off* (New York:
Amacom, 1974), p. 44.
17. Saul W. Gellerman, *Management by Motivation* (New York: American Management Association, 1968), p. 50.

The Nature of Emotional Needs

The chief goal of the supervisor is to provide opportunities for the employee to *move* from being a less satisfied to a more satisfied human being, and, consequently, to being a more effective worker. We will discuss some of the theoretical and practical principles involved in emotional growth. We do not intend to provide a "cookbook" to be followed literally, but rather to present a frame of reference for understanding and relating with people in a work situation.

There are three categories of needs: maintenance needs, growth needs, and self-actualization needs.[18] These three categories represent a hierarchy, with maintenance needs at the base (see fig. 3-1). Once maintenance needs are met adequately, the person progresses to growth needs. When these are satisfactorily fulfilled, he then "graduates" to self-actualization needs. Because this hierarchy represents a growth process, there may be some overlapping between one level of need and another.

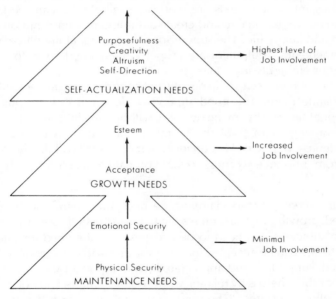

FIGURE 3-1

*Hierarchy of Emotional Needs and Their
Relationship to Job Involvement*

18. See F. Herzberg, B. Mausner, and B.B. Snyderman, *The Motivation to Work* (New York: John Wiley, 1959), and Abraham H. Maslow, *Toward a Psychology of Being* (New York: Van Nostrand, 1962).

When an individual progresses from a lower level need to a higher one, the lower need does not disappear. It will continue to exist, but its strength and importance will be replaced by the higher level need. For example, a self-actualized individual still needs to feel safe, accepted, and esteemed. But his main source of motivation stems from higher needs.

Maintenance Needs. This first level is comprised of two sublevels: the first is physical security (the desire for food, water, warmth, rest, health). When this stratum of needs is adequately met, the focus progresses to emotional security (money, working conditions, freedom from arbitrary decisions, freedom from threatening relationships with fellow workers or supervisors, job security). Research indicates that when maintenance needs are not met, workers are dissatisfied, and this creates poor morale and lowered production. *But, when maintenance needs are met, this does not produce job satisfaction – it only prevents dissatisfaction.*[19]

In traffic enforcement, the supervisor can help create an atmosphere in which maintenance needs are met. For example, he can see that work schedules are reasonable and create a minimum of hardship on personal health and family life. The supervisor can insure that the officer's vehicle and emergency equipment are properly maintained so as to avoid any unsafe or embarrassing situations for the officer.

The supervisor can help dissatisfied partners work out their differences or separate them. The good supervisor does not threaten his officers' emotional security by spying on them, withholding information from them, embarrassing them publicly, or threatening them with anger, unreasonableness, or power. He conveys the message: "I will do all I can to free you from 'nuisance worries' so that you can concentrate on the job you were hired to do."

Growth Needs. Once maintenance need fulfillment can be taken for granted, growth needs become salient. Growth needs are also comprised of two sublevels: the need to be accepted and the need for esteem.

The need to be accepted includes the desire to belong and to be liked, affirmed, supported, and appreciated. One important way the supervisor can contribute here is by relating *with* his subordinates and not *to* them. As Saul Gellerman states: "The most effective supervisor is a catalyst, not a drill sergeant. . . . The self-important, self-impressed supervisor with a passion for keeping his 'prerogatives' to himself and his subordinates 'in their place' may still be commonplace, but he is also obsolete."[20]

The good supervisor can allow his subordinates to feel they are friends without fearing that they will take advantage of his friendship. He realizes

---

19.   Hinrichs, *The Motivation Crisis,* pp. 91, 139-40.
20.   Gellerman, *Management by Motivation,* p. 39.

that being a friend also means being honest, strong, guiding, and, at times, corrective.

Supervisory attitudes that short-circuit the fulfillment of acceptance needs include:

— "I was hoping you wouldn't be transferred to my department, but now that you're here, let's make the best of it."

— "You're on your own, and God help you if you mess things up."

— "We can get along fine without you."

These attitudes are quite human and, at times, may even be appropriate. However, they are not helpful either to the supervisor or to the officer. Either the supervisor should try to understand better his own feelings and those of the officer to see if some rapport can be reached, or he should see to it that the officer is transferred.

Messages that convey acceptance are:

— "I'm glad I have you in my department."

— "I like you as a *person,* not just someone who issues a lot of traffic citations and investigates a lot of accidents."

— "When you are experiencing difficulty with anything, feel free to bring it up, and we'll work on it together."

— "I really appreciate the extra work you did for us the other day."

It is necessary to realize that *saying* these things is more helpful than not saying them. But, more importantly, they should not be just statements but sentiments; not manipulative devices, but genuine reflections of the supervisor's feelings and attitudes.

Esteem needs follow the successful fulfillment of acceptance needs. Esteem needs include the desire to achieve and have one's achievements recognized; to feel skilled, important, and rewarded. Officers should be allowed to achieve as far as their talents will take them. To assign a person with a new bachelor's degree in administration of justice to marking tires (putting chalk marks on tires to determine if the vehicle has been moved over a period of time) for overtime parking may be "starting him at the bottom, so he will know how it feels." But, if that is his eight-hours-a-day job for more than a few months, law enforcement will lose a good individual. Interested and talented officers can be encouraged to address service organizations, to give seminars both within the department and outside of it, and to publish and to teach.

A supervisor cannot *make* a person feel important. He only can allow the officer to be important. One way of doing this is to allow the officer to participate in the decision-making processes that affect him. Such individuals perform at a higher level than those who are not given such an opportunity.[21]

---

21.   Victor H. Vroom, *Work and Motivation* (New York: John Wiley, 1964), p. 267.

The supervisor can provide nonmaterial rewards. This includes allowing the officer to take on more responsibility; genuinely asking him for advice in an area with which he is particularly familiar; asking him to help out the supervisor on a particularly important project; and giving him full credit for his accomplishments. This attitude is in contrast to one that says: "You're doing a good job; aren't you glad you had me to teach you all these things?"

When the officer's growth needs are being met, the organization as a whole should benefit. As Adams states: "The employee is more likely to produce a better quantity and quality of service if he feels that he is understood, accepted, liked, and that his work is generally approved."[22]

Self-Actualization Needs.   When a person's growth needs have been met well for a good length of time, he transcends to the highest and infinite level — that of self-actualization needs. Among the more important self-actualization needs are self-direction, altruism, creativity, and the need to see a meaningful purpose in one's work.

The need for self-direction means a desire to be more self-determining and autonomous. It is manifested in the wish to make more decisions, to become individually responsible for one's work and more "on one's own." This need does not flow from needing other persons less but from a growth in self-confidence and an increased willingness to trust oneself and to accept the consequences for one's own actions.

Altruism or the need to give of oneself unconditionally indicates that the person wishes to give for the sake of giving, and not for ulterior motives (as might be seen in the need for acceptance). This officer enjoys teaching younger officers and sharing his experiences with them. He gives to the department and to the community in ways for which he could never be adequately rewarded.

The need to be creative is seen in the attempt to solve problems using new and unique approaches. The individual is willing to approach a situation from a new light, sometimes risking ridicule or failure.

Because of the need to find a meaningful purpose in one's work, the old reasons for working (money, fellowship, prestige) are still present but are no longer as compelling. The work itself has to make some sense; it has to have some perceived inherent value.

The officer with self-actualization needs is the greatest challenge to the department. It takes a self-actualized administration and supervisorial staff to provide adequate opportunities for this officer's growth. It means allowing the officer a high degree of self-direction instead of keeping him "under thumb." It requires providing opportunities for the officer to give of

---

22.   Thomas F. Adams, Gerald Buck, and Don Hallstrom, *Criminal Justice Organization and Management* (Pacific Palisades, Calif.: Goodyear, 1974), p. 129.

himself instead of restricting him to routine assignments. The officer should be given opportunities to try new approaches and allowed to enjoy his successes and learn from his failures. The supervisor must allow the officer to pursue facets of his work that are intrinsically meaningful to him in contrast to performing tasks merely to receive a paycheck, a pat on the back, or a promotion. The officer has to feel that a little piece of the world is going to be slightly better because of the work he performs.

There are a number of ideas that a supervisor should be aware of with regard to allowing his workers to meet their emotional needs:

(1)   The supervisor is not solely responsible for the emotional growth of his subordinates. The officer's family, friends, church, and social organizations also are influences. Moreover, the supervisor cannot assume responsibility for the total work situation. There are some factors over which he has little or no control, such as fiscal matters and major policy pronouncements. However, the supervisor should recognize that he is one of the most important influences in the officer's life. Hence, the supervisor has ample opportunity to create an atmosphere in which the officer can grow, stagnate, or regress.

(2)   The supervisor is in no way asked to sacrifice his own need fulfillment for those of his subordinates. What was said about the critical importance of need satisfaction applies to supervisors as well. If a supervisor is not seeing to it that his emotional needs are being sufficiently met at work, he will be unable or reluctant to meet those of others.

(3)   The supervisor can realize that once an officer's needs on any particular level are reasonably satisfied, they no longer act as motivators. For example, giving an officer a chance to make overtime pay (security need) is going to be ineffectual as a motivator if what the officer *emotionally* needs is to feel a sense of achievement in his work (growth need). When this fact is not understood it creates frustration for both the supervisor and the officer. The officer feels misunderstood. The supervisor feels confused because he has gone out of his way to do a favor for the officer who does not seem to be grateful.

So, a supervisor must know, at least generally, what each individual needs in order to provide appropriate opportunities for growth. He must realize that what motivates Smith does not motivate Jones and to confuse the needs might result in negative consequences. He must also realize that what motivated Jones two years ago (teaching recruits — an esteem need) has been traded in for a higher need (creating new procedures for accident investigation — a self-actualization need). Self-actualization needs, however, are infinite and are never totally met.

(4)   It is helpful for a supervisor to understand this relationship between complaints from his subordinates and their level of need fulfillment. The supervisor who dreams of the day when no one complains to or about

him is dreaming of the day when he is supervising angels and not human beings.

Complaints should not be viewed as criticisms to be defended but as clues to be interpreted. Psychologist Abraham Maslow writes:

> . . . we should, according to motivation theory, never expect a cessation of complaints; we should expect only that these complaints will get to be higher and higher complaints, i.e., that they will move from the lower-grumble level to higher-grumble levels and finally to metagrumble levels.[23]

Hence, as a supervisor is more successful in allowing officers to motivate themselves, their complaints will not diminish necessarily, but they will be of a higher quality. An officer may begin employment with his complaints centering around such topics as the cheap quality of the highway flares that were issued to him. Five years later the same officer may be complaining about not being given complete freedom in running his accident investigation team. If this is so, the supervisor can feel that both he and the officer are growing in their job situation. The nature of the complaint, then, is often a solid clue as to what level of need fulfillment the officer has reached and what he needs next if he is going to continue to grow.

SUMMARY

In summary, the traffic supervisor is the fulcrum of the traffic department. On one side is the administration, expecting him to meet their needs. On the other side are the line officers, expecting him to meet *their* needs. And, as a healthy human being, the supervisor is also trying to meet his *own* needs. He will never be able to always keep "all three balls" in the air. At one time or another, he is going to let someone down. He should expect that periodically this will occur, and he should neither berate himself for this nor blame others for expecting too much of him. This is merely a fact of life for supervisors.

A supervisor can significantly increase his effectiveness and decrease his chances for failure by trying to acquire some of the personality traits of a good supervisor. These are not inherent; they are learned. As in learning anything, it takes awareness of one's behavior and daily practice.

A supervisor can also learn to communicate in an effective way. He should realize that, as a supervisor, he is *always* communicating. The

---

question is whether what he is communicating is a destructive or constructive message.

The supervisor can understand what the true nature of motivation means. He must realize that his role is not to infuse motivation but to allow people to unleash their own intrinsic motivation.

So, the key to success for the supervisor is understanding human behavior and relating personally with people. As Harold Mayfield says of the supervisor:

> He establishes the climate of the workplace for the people under him. Simply by acknowledging that his workers are human beings and by treating them considerately, a supervisor can do much to erase the notion from their minds that large organizations are impersonal and inhuman. His hands are not often tied by higher authority when it comes to handling his personal relationships with subordinates. And rarely will someone higher up in the organization make up for his deficiencies in this respect. This is his responsibility.[24]

DISCUSSION QUESTIONS

1. "*Who* a supervisor *is* is often more important than what he does." What does this statement mean and what are some of its practical implications?

2. Of the five traits discussed in this chapter (honesty, trustworthiness, empathy, mistakeability, and assertiveness), which is the most difficult for you to "master"? Why is this so? What can you do to develop this trait?

3. In communication, listening is very likely the most difficult part of the process. Why is something that should be so very easy, so terribly difficult?

4. Comment on the following statement: "The question is not whether a supervisor is communicating or not, since he is *always* communicating; the question is, what is he communicating?"

5. Comment on the following statement: "If you tell people they are doing a good job, or tell them that you appreciate them, or tell them how important they are — this should adequately meet their needs."

---

24. Harold Mayfielid, "Who Is 'The Company'?" *Supervisory Management* 12, no. 3 (March 1967): 15.

chapter

The Traffic Officer in Court

Traffic officers learn early that issuing a citation or writing a collision report is the simpler part of their work. The more difficult and challenging task is testifying in court.

How effectively a traffic officer testifies in court is important for three reasons. First, if the officer does his job well, justice will be served, and that is important in itself. If the officer performs inadequately, justice may not be served, thus subverting the judicial process. From a practical standpoint, time, energy, and money may be wasted.

Second, if the driver is found guilty, it could be a learning experience for him that may prevent future accidents or injuries. The defendant who is found not guilty because the officer testified poorly may feel vindicated and repeat the violation, risking damage to himself and others.

Third, if an officer presents his case well in court, he will feel good about himself and be willing to go through the experience again. The officer who feels foolish as a result of his court appearance will be disinclined to enforce the law as diligently in order to avoid another unpleasant court experience.

When justice is not served, officers often blame the judge, attorneys, or the law. Certainly, any one or all of these can interfere with justice being served. However, reality demands that we consider a fourth cause for subversion of justice: the police officer who testifies ineffectively.

The basic principle for a traffic officer to understand is that he is a facilitator of justice. Justice alone is powerless. To the degree that an officer allows the truth to surface, justice will be served; to the degree that the officer is inept or has other priorities, justice will not be served. Some officers bring good cases into court, but the defendant is found not guilty because the officers expected justice to surface magically despite their poor performance.

In this chapter, we describe eight principles that can help traffic officers become more effective in court testimony.

PRINCIPLES FOR EFFECTIVE TESTIMONY

Be Reality-Centered

In every criminal trial there are three factors: (1) the viewpoint of the defendant; (2) the viewpoint of the officer; and (3) reality. Reality is comprised of the facts of the case that are untouched by the defendant's or the police officer's perceptions, interpretations, or judgments.

During the course of a trial, reality may "move around." At one point reality may reside in the defendant's viewpoint; at another time it is in the officer's viewpoint; and at still another time it is excluded from both viewpoints, and it is the responsibility of the judge and jury to rescue it. Justice is served when the reality of the event being adjudicated is clear enough that a judge or a judge and jury can make a fair decision.

The effective officer is reality-centered. Ideally, his viewpoint and reality are identical. But, because officers are human, reality can be tinted by personal needs, feelings, and honest mistakes. The two main needs that can cause an officer unconsciously to tilt reality in his favor are the need to be correct and the need to win. When the need to be correct is very strong, the officer will find it difficult to consider or accept a viewpoint or any part of a viewpoint other than his own. When the need to win is very strong, the officer will clutch his viewpoint with the intensity of a fullback clutching a football as he runs through the defense toward victory. Although these officers would deny it, they consider being correct and winning more important than justice.

The two feelings that interfere most with an officer's accurate perception of reality are anger and fear. When an officer feels strong anger toward the defendant, the officer may distort reality to the defendant's disadvantage. When an officer equates his self-worth or his competency as a police officer with garnering a guilty verdict, his fear of losing will color his perception of reality in his favor.

Honest mistakes are made by everyone and are caused by being distracted, by misunderstanding, and by normal errors in judgment. The attorneys for the prosecution and the defense, as well as the judge, may have their own strong needs, fears, and capacities to err. But it is incumbent on all of them to be aware of how they can distort reality and to work at controlling these forces. Recognizing these forces is a major step in the process.

Reality-centered officers present facts in a clear, unbiased manner. They do not perceive themselves as "winning" or "losing" in court, and they do not speak in those terms. Knowing that it is only justice that will win or lose, reality-centered officers understand that justice can win with a "not guilty" verdict and lose with a "guilty" verdict. To these officers, reporting reality takes priority and the verdict is of secondary importance and interest.

Tell the Absolute Truth

There is a difference between having an inaccurate viewpoint and lying. Thus, an officer may honestly testify that a vehicle was traveling at fifty miles per hour when, in fact, it was going forty miles per hour. Lying occurs when an officer testifies to what he knows is not true. For example, an officer may testify that he saw the barrel of a gun protruding from under a vehicle's front seat when actually he did not see it until he made an illegal search. He then indulges in some "creative report writing" to cover himself. The thought of police officers lying in court is an unpleasant one, but it does happen and therefore should be discussed.

How do officers allow themselves to lie in court, even though they may punish their children for lying and despise criminals for lying? They employ one or more of the following rationalizations:

— "I know the defendant is guilty, but the way the law and the courts are today, I could never prove it." This officer takes a vigilante approach and ensures that "justice will be done" in spite of the law and the courts.

— "The defendant will lie and be found not guilty unless I lie to counter his lies." This officer operates on the principle that the end justifies the means, even though he detests this attitude in criminals. The officer is not confident in his ability to convince the court with his honesty and does not believe that the judge and jury will be perceptive enough to realize that the defendant is lying.

— "The defendant should be punished whether or not he is guilty of this particular offense." This attitude usually stems from the officer's previous knowledge of the defendant, either personally or by reputation. The officer's attitude is that because the defendant has broken the law on numerous occasions and escaped punishment, it is time for his comeuppance whether or not he happens to be guilty in the current case before the court.

With all of these rationalizations, the officer perceives himself as a crusader for justice overcoming the obstacles placed in the way by the judicial process. Because the officer is so protected by his rationalization, he is incapable of viewing himself as a liar and a criminal as a result of his perjury.

On an ethical level, the officer who lies in court is violating justice and thereby violating all that he purports to stand for. He is no better and is perhaps worse than the criminals he arrests.

On a practical level, lying in court is often self-defeating for two reasons. One is that the officer's lies are unlikely to remain hidden after the attorneys, judge, and jury hold his testimony up to public scrutiny. Consequently, he may develop a reputation as an officer with doubtful credibility, which will taint every case he presents whether or not he is telling the truth.

Second, the officer who lies in court may be trapped by his own lie. For example, an officer observes a driver weave twice within a distance of a quarter of a mile. After the stop, the driver becomes increasingly abusive over a period of fifteen minutes at the stop and finally shoves the officer. Because of this, the officer also arrests him for battery. The officer feels that his testimony will be stronger if he states that he followed the driver for three-quarters of a mile and saw him weave several times. The following is an example of being trapped by a lie.

Defense Counsel: "Officer, you state in your report that you followed the defendant for a distance of three-quarters of a mile and observed him weave on several occasions. Is that correct?"

Officer: "Yes, sir; that's correct."

Counsel: "Officer, you allowed the defendant to drive a full three-quarters of a mile even though you had observed him driving erratically for some distance. Is it possible that you used the same kind of judgment in allowing a situation to develop at the traffic stop that a more seasoned officer would have prevented by taking appropriate action sooner?"

The defense counsel has skillfully planted a reasonable doubt in the minds of the jury regarding the officer's judgment. The officer may have allowed or perhaps invited the defendant to become so agitated that he could arrest him on the second charge of battery on a police officer.

If the officer had confidence in his judgment and the judicial process, he would have testified, "I followed the defendant for a quarter of a mile and observed him weave a half-car length to either side on two separate occasions. In my experience, such driving is often characteristic of an intoxicated driver. Because there was other traffic in the vicinity, I stopped the vehicle in order to prevent the driver from injuring himself or others."

Prepare the Case Well

An officer rarely has to ad-lib in court. If he has prepared well for court, he has anticipated all of the important questions he will be asked. There will be no surprises, and he will not get caught off-guard. The best way to prepare for court is to assume the role of the defense attorney. The officer should ask himself, "If I were trying to get a not guilty verdict for the defendant, what questions would I ask the officer, and what loopholes would I look for in the officer's testimony?"

There are three phases of preparation for a court appearance. The first phase occurs even before the traffic stop is made. As soon as an officer decides he is going to stop a driver for a violation, he should take a "stop action" shot of what is occurring for a distance of the twenty yards surrounding the vehicle at the point of violation. Included in this "perceptual snapshot" will be the amount of traffic in the immediate vicinity; its speed; its direction of travel; what vehicles are closest to the violating vehicle and what immediate or distant hazards are present; the number of people in the immediate area, especially the number of pedestrians and their position with regard to the violating vehicle; the number, positioning, and clarity of warning signs, stop signs, stop lights, and pedestrian crosswalks; the position of the sun (Is it shining in the driver's eyes?); and the driver's apparent attentiveness (How long does it take for him to notice the officer's emergency lights and to hear his horn or siren?). This may sound like a lot to observe in five seconds, but one can develop this skill, just as a quarterback develops the skill to diagnose the positioning of eleven scattered players on defense in far less time than five seconds.

When an officer has focused only on the driver and not on the surrounding area, the following can occur in court:

Defense Counsel: "Officer, you cited the defendant for going through a stop sign. Is that correct?"

Officer: "Yes, sir. That's correct."

Counsel: "Did the defendant tell you at the time that he was a tourist and didn't see the stop sign?"

Officer: "Yes, sir. I believe he did."

Counsel: "I see. Did you realize at the time you cited him that the sun was in a position to impair his vision?"

Officer: "I didn't notice where the sun was."

Counsel: "Did you notice that the stop sign was about two feet shorter than most stop signs so that drivers coming down the steep incline in smaller cars could see it?"

Officer: "I didn't especially notice that."

Counsel: "Did you notice the white van parked beside the stop sign, as shown in this photograph that the defendant took not five minutes later, and did you notice that it completely blocks the view of the stop sign?"

Officer: "I didn't notice it at the time I stopped him."

Counsel: "Did you notice that the limit line and the word 'Stop' on the street were so covered with oil and tire marks that they were virtually unreadable?"

Officer: "I didn't notice it."

Counsel: (to judge) "Your honor, I suggest that if the officer had noticed all of these extenuating circumstances and used reasonable discretion, my client wouldn't have had to lose a morning's wages to appear in court today. May I ask the court, in the interest of justice, that the citation be dismissed?"

Judge: "Case dismissed."

The second phase of preparation occurs during the traffic stop. The officer should notice the mental state of the driver; how many passengers there are in the vehicle; and how many sources of distraction there are, such as children, pets, or a loud radio. The officer should especially take care to record verbatim any relevant conversation with the driver or passengers. For example, a driver, out of earshot of his wife, may tell the officer that he had only two drinks with dinner, but the wife tells him that her husband is not intoxicated but only tired because he is taking tranquilizers. Verbatim quotes should be written on the officer's copy of the citation before leaving the stop.

Quotes that seem incidental at the time may be important, such as:

"I'm ten minutes late for work."

"I didn't see any other cars, so I thought it was safe."

"I had a fight with my boyfriend and I'm very upset."

Even the statement "Why did you stop me? I didn't break any laws" is important because it can be used to indicate the driver's inattention or ignorance of vehicle laws.

An officer also should be careful not to make statements to the driver that could be embarrassing to hear again in court. Some examples of "boomerang quotes" are:

"The officer said he'd seen me speeding a lot in town, and now he was going to make me pay for it."

"When I told the officer I was going to take him to court, he said, 'Anyone stupid enough to drive the way you do would be stupid enough to take it to court.'"

"The officer told me, 'I'm going to keep giving jerks like you tickets until you learn to obey the law in this town.'"

The third phase of preparation occurs between the citation and the court appearance. Some officers are not as aware of the relevant vehicle code sections as they think they are. For example, it is common to think that the offense is automatically felony drunk driving if an intoxicated driver is involved in a collision in which injuries occur. However, in many states there must be a third element present — namely, the intoxicated state of the driver must be the *proximate* cause of the accident and injury. The formula drunk driver + injury = a felony could be a faulty assumption that could catch the officer unprepared in court.

For example, a drunk backs his vehicle out of his garage and runs over a child in the street. The officer must be prepared to prove that the cause of the accident was the driver's intoxicated state and not that his view was blocked by a tree or that the child ran behind him in a way that the accident would have occurred with the most sober driver.

An officer should also be able to discuss intelligently the general principles of every procedure that he used in the case: e.g., chemical tests, statistical procedures, radar, determining speed by skid marks, rules of evidence, Miranda warnings, and legal aspects of line-ups.

The following is an example of an officer who did not adequately prepare himself during phase three:

Defense Counsel: "Officer, you said you clocked the defendant's speed on radar at fifty miles per hour in a thirty-five mile zone. Is that correct?"

Officer: "Yes, sir. That's correct."

Counsel: "What kind of radar is it?"

Officer: "It's an HR8."

Counsel: "What does HR stand for?"

Officer: "I don't know; that's just what it's called."

Counsel: "I see. Who manufactures the radar?"

Officer: "I don't know. I think some company in Minneapolis."

Counsel: "You said it was drizzling at the time of the alleged violation. Are you familiar with the research on the effects of drizzle on radar?"

Officer: "No, I'm not."

Counsel: "Do you know if the radar you have works on the Doppler principle or the Pascalian principle?"

Officer: "I was told that we don't have to know things like that."

Obviously, this officer felt that all he had to do was mention the word *radar* in court and the defendant would be found guilty.

An officer who prepares well through all three phases will find few or no surprises waiting for him on the witness stand.

Answer the Question

When an officer is asked a question in court, the officer should answer it directly, adequately, and succinctly. To do otherwise causes confusion and frustration and raises the suspicion that the officer is not on solid ground.

There are three mistakes that can be made with regard to answering questions in court. The first mistake is *over-answering,* that is, giving more information than is required. The following is an example:

Defense Counsel: "What made you think the defendant was under the influence of alcohol?"

Officer: "Well, for one thing he was weaving all over the road. He had a strong odor of alcohol on his breath, which I noticed when he shouted at me that he was a lawyer and that I didn't know what I was doing and that I would be sorry if I arrested him. All the passengers were drunk, and one of them tried to get away. The driver said he was diabetic, but that wouldn't account for the alcohol on his breath and his belligerent attitude. All these things led me to believe that the driver was under the influence of alcohol."

The officer's over-answering complicates matters by raising the possibility that (1) he was intimidated by the driver "pulling rank" on him and implying that the officer was incompetent and used poor judgment; (2) the officer was so angry at everyone in the vehicle that his judgment was clouded, preventing him from merely calling a cab for the driver — something the officer has done in the past in similar circumstances; or (3) the officer felt that he was capable of judging the effects of insulin deprivation on coordination, speech, mood, and breath.

A second mistake, illustrated in the following example, is *under-answering* the question:

Defense Counsel: "Why did you feel that the defendant was driving in a reckless manner?"

Officer: "Because he drove forty-five miles per hour through a crowded business district for three blocks, forcing pedestrians to leap out of the way."

Counsel: "And you feel that constitutes 'willful negligence' — the key element in reckless driving?"

Officer: "Well, no. He also passed a vehicle over a double yellow line and almost hit a school bus head on."

Counsel: "I would say that driving over a yellow line is *hazardous,* but it hardly qualifies as reckless driving, does it, officer?"

Officer: "Well, he also drove down a one-way alley the wrong way, hitting some shopping carts that knocked down and rolled over a supermarket check-out girl."

This officer's "shaggy dog" response will cause one or both of two reactions. People hearing his testimony will be so frustrated with him they will feel anger toward him, or they will be laughing so hard *at* him that the seriousness of his testimony will be lost.

A third mistake is *not answering* the question that is asked. Officers fail to answer the question that is asked because (1) they were not listening attentively to the question or (2) because they want to make a point not covered by the question being asked. The following is an example of the latter:

Defense Counsel: "Officer, your report states the defendant's vehicle left fifty feet of skid mark and that your skid index indicates that the vehicle would have been traveling at approximately thirty miles per hour. Because the defendant's vehicle is much lighter than the average vehicle, could it be that the defendant was traveling at a speed significantly less than thirty miles per hour?"

Officer: "Well, the defendant himself said he was going thirty miles per hour, and two witnesses stated he was going in excess of thirty miles per hour."

The officer's answer is correct if the question had been, "How fast did the driver and two witnesses say the driver was going?" But that was not the question. There are only two appropriate answers to the question that was asked: "Yes, it could be" or "No, it couldn't be." By giving the right answer to the wrong question, the officer gives the impression that he is trying too hard to make the defendant appear guilty.

It is better for an officer to answer only the question asked, even if the answer implies something that the officer does not mean. It is then up to the prosecution to ask the officer questions that will invite the officer to expand on his answers and to clarify areas that could be misinterpreted.

Remain Dispassionate

When a person communicates with ideas and not with feelings, we say that he is *dispassionate*. Although it would not be a mentally healthy way to live, being dispassionate is necessary for good performance in certain limited situations — in combat, in surgery, or in a courtroom.

In court the biggest enemy of dispassion is anger. Once an officer allows himself to feel anger, he has imperiled his position. Even the most naive juror knows two things about anger: (1) Anger is often the response of an insecure person who is threatened, and (2) anger clouds judgment. Next to being caught in a lie, the most damaging thing an officer can do in court is to become angry.

When a defense attorney causes an officer to become angry (upset, impatient, frustrated, sarcastic), it is analogous to a lineman in football causing the quarterback to fumble. That is, it is a big break for the defense. The following is an example of how this can happen in court:

Defense Counsel: "Officer, how big would you say the defendant, Mrs. Pixley, is?"

Officer: "Oh, a little over five feet tall, and she weighs about a hundred pounds."

Counsel: "And in your report how old did you state she was?"

Officer: "She's forty-seven years old."

Counsel: "I see. And how big are you, officer?"

Officer: "I'm six foot two and weigh about two hundred pounds."

Counsel: "I see. And could you tell the court your age?"

Officer: "I'm twenty-three years old."

Counsel: "Good. Now you have charged Mrs. Pixley here committed battery on you. Is that correct?"

Officer: (in a somewhat defensive tone) "Yes, that's what she *did*."

Counsel: "Well now, officer, when Mrs. Pixley told you that you were acting like a little boy and that she should take you over her knee and spank you, isn't it true that you found this upsetting?"

Officer: (in a louder voice) "No, it isn't."

Counsel: "And isn't it true that when she called you a 'moron' this offended you to the extent that you pushed your forefinger into her chest and told her to keep her mouth shut?"

Officer: (now speaking in a loud, pressured voice with reddened face) "Absolutely not! I don't go around poking ladies in the chest! I charged her with battery because she shoved me, and if a woman breaks the law she has to suffer the consequences whether she's five feet tall or ten feet tall!"

Counsel: "Thank you very much, officer."

The defense counsel *should* thank the officer. The officer himself did what the defense counsel could never have done alone. The officer demonstrated to the court that he has a "short fuse" and raised the possibility that the defendant merely held the overbearing officer away from her, which would have been reasonable and justified under the circumstances. If this officer had realized that the defense counsel was going to bait him in order to get him angry, the officer could have been prepared for it and fended off each jab.

Admit Ignorance and Mistakes

No one in a courtroom is perfect. Once this is understood, we can ask the question "Who is going to be honest about their imperfections, and who is going to try to hide them?" Secure people can make statements such as "I don't know the answer to that question" or "I believe I was in error." The principle of admitting one's ignorance or mistakes is in opposition to the one that states, "If you don't know something, bluff it so you won't look bad, and no one will know the difference anyway."

On an ethical level, failing to admit ignorance and mistakes is dishonest and, consequently, justice will be impeded. On a practical level, it is likely that the ignorance or mistake will eventually become obvious to those in court, and the officer's entire testimony will be suspect.

An officer who can admit to ignorance on a particular issue or to having erred will show himself to be a secure and honest person whose testimony is believable. The following examples show how this principle is applied or ignored.

Example I:

Defense Counsel: "Officer, do you recall if you Mirandized the defendant before or after you arrived at the jail?"

Officer: "I don't recall, sir."

The officer who cannot clearly remember the situation might give the following response:

Officer: "I think I Mirandized him as soon as we placed him in the patrol car."

Counsel: "So, does your testimony contradict that of your partner, who said *he* Mirandized him *at the jail?*"

Example II:

Defense Counsel: "Officer, in your report you wrote that the defendant's vehicle had faulty brakes. Yet later that day the defendant's insurance agent tested the brakes and found them to be functioning properly. How do you explain this?"

Officer: "Well, sir, there were multiple injuries at the scene and I was distracted. The defendant told me his brakes failed, so I wrote that down, but I forgot to go back and test them."

This is in contrast to the officer who replies as follows:

Officer: "Well, ah, I don't know. Sometimes the brake fluid can build back up after awhile and appear to be fine."

Counsel: "I see. So even though three people testified that you did not test the brakes and the brakes were fine two hours later, you still maintain that you personally tested the brakes?"

It is clear to everyone in court that the two officers who could not admit imperfection are bluffing. Although they may have had a strong case representing many hours of work, their cases now are suspect.

Be Aware of Nonverbal Communication

The messages an officer sends to others without uttering a word comprise nonverbal communication. The maxim "Actions speak louder than words" is often true. Thus, a traffic officer should be aware of the ways he can unintentionally communicate messages to the court.

Appearance. How an officer dresses for court makes a statement about what he thinks of himself and how seriously he views his court appearance.

If the officer testifies in uniform, the uniform should be pressed and clean and his shoes shined. If he testifies in street clothes, he should dress in the same manner as the attorneys. When attorneys are dressed in suits, dresses, or coats and ties and the officer appears in a leisure suit, pantsuit, or shirt, slacks, and boots, the message is "I'm not taking this trial as seriously as everyone else."

Vocabulary. Although vocabulary is verbal, the words the officer uses can convey a nonverbal message. The officer who uses poor grammar, slang, or street dialect gives the impression of being unintelligent, casual, or glib. The following is an example of how vocabulary can convey a negative message and distract from the testimony:

Defense Counsel: "Officer, what first brought the defendant to your attention?"

Officer: "Well, first off, I *heard* him before I seen him. By the sound of his car I *knew* he was smokin'. Then I *did* see him and he was doing eighty to ninety."

Counsel: "I see. Then you stopped him, and what occurred at that point?"

Officer: "Well, he started giving me a bunch a heat, and I would have hooked him up right then 'cept we was short that night, so I just wrote him."

In less than thirty seconds, this officer has presented himself as a less than credible witness.

An officer should use words that are clearly understandable to everyone in the courtroom by avoiding jargon and technical language and should talk neither above the jury nor below them. In short, the words that an officer uses should not distract from his testimony.

Tone of Voice. An officer's tone of voice tells something about him. Officers who speak in a loud voice in court appear to be overbearing; those who speak too quietly or unclearly appear insecure. The following is an example of the latter:

Defense Counsel: "When were you first advised that there was an injury accident, and what did you do?"

Officer: "Well, I was first advised by (unintelligible) that there was an injury accident involving a vehicle on (unintelligible). On arrival I told my partner, Officer (unintelligible), to radio for an ambulance while I treated Miss Smith for (unintelligible) injuries."

Counsel: "Ah, Officer, we missed several key words in your testimony. You'll have to repeat what you said in a louder and clearer voice so that everyone in the jury can hear you."

This type of interchange is frustrating to the court. In addition to wasting time, it raises some doubt about the officer's confidence in himself or at least in his case.

Voice tone can also communicate anger, which is often channeled into a sarcastic tone of voice. A sarcastic tone can evoke aggressive reactions from attorneys and judges that may surprise the officer. The officer then wonders what he said that upset them when it was not *what* he said but *how* he said it.

Posture. How an officer stands and sits in court will convey a definite message. Officers whose posture is stooped or who sit in a slouched position do not inspire confidence. On the other hand, those who have a military bearing give the impression of being authoritarian and rigid. The officer should stand and sit in a way that connotes that he is relaxed yet alert and that he is interested but not overinvolved.

A judge and jury often unconsciously form a general impression of the officer between the time he walks into the courtroom and the time he has spoken a few sentences. If the impression is positive, the officer has gained some upward momentum that may override some minor weaknesses in his presentation. If the impression is negative, a downward momentum results that may override some positive points in his presentation.

Help the Prosecution Prepare the Case

Even the most competent prosecutor is at the mercy of the officer when it comes to obtaining facts and assumptions. The officer has witnessed the violation, or, in a collision case, has interviewed drivers and witnesses and has written a detailed report. If he made an arrest, he knows the exact probable cause, the specific method of search and seizure, the nature of the physical evidence, and the dynamics of the interview. Even the most detailed officer's report can only contain half of the information needed to present a strong case in court.

An officer can help a prosecutor by writing a memo concerning the salient facts and his impression of the case and sending it to the prosecutor before he meets with him to prepare the case.

A memo differs from a formal report in several ways. A memo includes facts, educated guesses, hunches, impressions, questions, and predictions that would be inappropriate in a formal report. In general, a memo fleshes out a formal report in a way that gives the prosecutor more of a "handle" on the case. The following is an example of a memo.

TO: Prosecutor
FROM: Officer Jones
RE: State vs. Smith: Hit and run collision, resulting in one death and two injuries.

The following are some facts and impressions that may be of some help to you in understanding the case.

1.   Smith has been arrested twice before for drunk driving and once for leaving the scene of an accident.

2.   His wife phoned me to tell me he's been mixing barbiturates and alcohol against both his physician's and her warnings. She hopes that this will "teach him a lesson."

3.   From what his wife said, Smith is going to see a psychologist a couple of times before the trial to prove to the court his "good faith" in trying to straighten himself out. She says he won't continue therapy after the heat is off.

4.   When he is sober, he is a very likable person. He will appear in court as a very gentle man who loves his wife and four children. He will appear to be very cooperative, honest, and appropriately contrite. He will want to convince the court that he is a good candidate for rehabilitation and has learned his lesson well. Unless we stress the seriousness of his crime and his several maneuvers to avoid apprehension, the court may well overlook some pertinent facts.

5.   Apparently he has sent condolences to the family of the deceased and has offered to pay all medical bills of the injured party. This will undoubtedly be used to prove his acceptance of responsibility and repentance.

6.   Since he realizes that we have sufficient evidence to prove his guilt, he will likely testify that he had a "few drinks" and panicked when the accident occurred. He will likely state that he was going to phone the police just before they contacted him. However, because of the extent of damage to his vehicle, he had to park it five blocks away from the accident and call a taxi to take him home. He could have called the police instead. He told his wife that someone had stolen his car. His first response to the officer was that someone stole his car. It wasn't until the officers told him that witnesses gave an accurate description of him that he admitted to being the driver. Therefore, he allowed three hours to elapse without contacting the police, and when the police contacted him, he denied his guilt.

Testifying in court is a skill that can be developed and improved no matter how experienced the officer is. This skill can be developed by being aware of the principles discussed in this chapter and by learning from mistakes. Officers will make mistakes in court just as will attorneys and judges. But the officer who admits the mistake and understands how he made it is likely to avoid making the mistake again.

Depending on the skills of the officer, testifying in court can be a threatening and demoralizing experience or it can be a rewarding culmination of the officer's work, putting the importance of his profession into clear focus.

SUMMARY

The ability to testify effectively in court in an honest, clear, and professional manner is extremely important in modern police work. In this chapter, we have pointed out that the officer needs to understand clearly the purpose of courtroom testimony — the concept that he is a facilitator rather than a vindicator of justice.

Eight important principles add credibility and articulateness to testifying:

1. *Be reality-centered.* Reality and the officer's viewpoint of the incident should be identical.

2. *Tell the absolute truth.* Your professional credibility as well as your reputation suffers when you testify falsely. Perjury is never worth the risk.

3. *Prepare the case well.* Do not wait until your court appearance begins to review your case. Review your reports ahead of time. Play the role of defense attorney and ask yourself the questions you would ask the officer in order to present an effective defense. Thus, you can prepare your testimony from the facts of the case as you know them to be.

4. *Answer the questions.* Be sure to listen to the questions intently before you answer. Answer the questions directly, and do not elaborate unless either the prosecutor or defense counsel ask you to. The key is carefully listening to what is being asked of you — not what you think the court should hear. Always be sure to pause momentarily after hearing the question, and if you do not understand the question asked, then ask to have it repeated before giving your answer.

5. *Remain dispassionate.* Getting excited, angry, or sarcastic in your testimony only weakens the prosecution's case. If you remain calm, keeping your voice in a general conversational tone, you will be able to fend off attacks by the defense counsel.

6. *Admit ignorance and mistakes.* When you have forgotten a fact or made a mistake in your answer, simply answer that you either do not

recall those facts or that you believe you have made an error in your response.

7. *Be aware of nonverbal communication.* Your personal appearance should reflect a professional image whether you are in uniform or a suit or dress. In your testimony, use words that are easily understood by the jury. Keep general police jargon out of your testimony unless it is asked for to illustrate a specific point. Your voice should be kept in normal tones so as not to become overbearing, and your sentences should not be unintelligible. Erect posture presents good bearing and conveys a professional impression to the jury.

8. *Help the prosecution prepare the case.* Whenever possible, assist the prosecution by giving your candid impressions about the events surrounding the case. Sometimes a brief memo on an important case can be of valuable assistance.

Testifying in court is a skill that must be developed and continuously improved in order to make the most effective, professional delivery in court.

DISCUSSION QUESTIONS

1. Discuss the eight principles of effective courtroom testimony.

2. Discuss some ways in which officers can be trained to become more effective communicators in court.

3. What things can you do to improve your testimony in court?

4. Why is it not a good idea to give narrative answers to directed questions in court?

5. Discuss the following statement: "It shouldn't make any difference to a court *how* the officer presents himself. The only thing that should count are the facts that he presents."

6. Describe one situation that could occur while you are testifying that would severely tempt you to hedge on the truth.

7. Discuss the following statement: "One of the major mistakes that police officers make in testifying is that they don't answer the question that is asked." Give examples.

8. If your presentation in court was excellent but the defendant was found not guilty, how could this subtly affect your attitude toward testifying in the future?

9. An officer goes into court with the following attitude: "This defendant is guilty, and it's my job to see that the court understands this and punishes him appropriately." How will this attitude affect the officer's presentation? What would be a better attitude?

True-False

1. Relatively minor cases do not require preparation before the trial.

2. An officer's main objective in testifying in court is to bring about the prosecution of the offender.

3. Rationalizations on the officer's part are never an excuse for perjured testimony.

4. Professional conduct in a courtroom in many cases may aid the officer in winning the jury's support.

chapter

Enforcement Tactics

Public support for the enforcement of traffic violations is of utmost concern to law enforcement agencies today. The success of the police in reducing traffic accidents hinges on the methods employed in traffic enforcement. The police have the responsibility to move traffic in the most expeditious yet safest manner possible. The accidents that are largely created by the thoughtless motorists who violate the law by speeding, cutting in and out of traffic, following too closely (tailgating), and so on will continue to be a problem. Although there are presently many types of enforcement programs being employed throughout the country, only a few of them are having a deterrent effect. One of the most effective methods to reduce these high accident exposure areas is the use of selective traffic enforcement. This is a somewhat negative tactic as far as the public is concerned, because it employs maximum enforcement in a concentrated location. The purpose is to take enforcement action on those traffic violations that are causing or tending to cause traffic accidents. The public, however, feels that the police are being overzealous in their enforcement. This has had some detrimental effect on the public's support of its local police agencies. It should be pointed out that it is really not the tactics generally utilized by the police that bring the charges of "extremism," but rather their failure to inform the public as to the reasons for the use of such tactics.

The need to "sell" highway safety to the public is an ongoing challenge to American law enforcement agencies. Various highway safety programs and the education the public derives from them will, in turn, increase public support and at the same time bring about accident reduction. With this end in mind, we shall explore in this chapter the problems, possible alternatives, and hopefully the rationale for the use of sound traffic enforcement tactics. We will not present the one best way to deploy personnel and equipment to reduce accident severity, but rather a number of considerations useful for the methodology of traffic enforcement.

First, let us consider the two individuals whom we will focus on in order to obtain a clear understanding of the actual problem — the traffic violator and the traffic enforcement officer. The driver (and all of us fit into this category at one time or another) of any motor vehicle has both a legal and moral responsibility to drive in a safe, reasonable manner. This of course must also include all law enforcement personnel assigned to mobile enforcement and/or patrol. Drivers may be placed into one of three main classes: (1) the defensive driver, who seldom commits a traffic offense; (2) the occasional offender; and (3) the chronic offender.[1] It is the last two classifications to which our second individual, the police officer (hereafter referred to as the "officer"), will direct most of his attention. While we realize that a large number of drivers fall into the classification of the "occasional offender," there are still far too many drivers who are chronic offenders. Both warrant selective discussion.

The occasional offender, in some thoughtless moment, may take a chance at beating the traffic light that is just about to change from caution to stop. Perhaps the individual may be late for work or school and so speeds up a bit to reduce the amount of time it will take to get from home to his destination. He does not normally drive this way, but circumstances have caused the driver to modify his driving behavior to meet the problem of tardiness.

The chronic offender is a socially maladjusted individual who regards our system of social order, which is a series of regulated legal statutes, as being unworthy of his attention. The chronic offender feels the law was made only for the other person and not to provide guidelines for an orderly and civil society. This driver, although he has received numerous traffic summons or citations (depending upon the particular part of the country), continues to violate the law, thus becoming a mobile threat to the safety of the motoring public.

The officer's job is to protect society from the drivers just identified. In reality, the officer finds himself in a quandary trying to establish some type of human balance between enforcing the law by the spirit rather than by the letter of the law. This man or woman is highly trained, works under rules and departmental guidelines, obeys the law, and has a code of ethics. It is this individual to whom the major emphasis of this chapter is geared.

---

1. Paul B. Weston, *The Police Traffic Control Function* (Springfield, Ill.: Charles C Thomas, 1969), p. 41.

OBJECTIVES OF TRAFFIC PATROL

Although there has been little written on some of the very basic police methods and techniques otherwise referred to as "knowhow," experience has provided some guidelines. The patrol officer assigned to a line or area beat learns continually from those who are older and more experienced as well as from fellow officers. The advice that he receives and the skills he develops are the result of observation and analysis.

The learning ability of officers and, for that matter, people in general may be divided into three types: (1) those who learn by others' experiences; (2) those who learn by their own experiences; and (3) those who never learn.[2]

There is a great deal of statistical evidence to validate the fact that many officers have had a tendency or have in fact fallen into the second and third groups. The everyday business of issuing traffic summons or citations, as well as making physical arrests, provides the best type of field instruction for other officers. There is really no one best way to perform these duties, as circumstances will vary from jurisdiction to jurisdiction and from state to state. Some guidelines may, however, be provided to assist the officer in safely and efficiently carrying out these tasks.

First of all, one must be mentally prepared. The officer must be in the right frame of reference, that is, "knowing that I am a police officer — I have a duty and a responsibility to the public for which I serve." Enforcement is not just a job assigned to an individual, but a professional undertaking that involves judgment, skill, and a high degree of training.

Second, the officer must be provided with the necessary tools with which to work. These include but are not limited to: state traffic or vehicle code statutes, departmental guidelines for proper enforcement, technical and legal training, and authority and responsibility within which to function. In addition, the officer needs the hardware (i.e., patrol cars, cruisers, motorcycles, motor scooters, helicopters, fixed wing aircraft, radar units, and so on) from which he must operate. These tools are the basis by which the more technical methodology is developed.

The officer through observation mentally checks the actions of his fellow officer and determines whether a certain procedure employed is good or bad. He then has the responsibility to incorporate, as a positive trait, that which is good and reject that which he finds to be bad.

A symbolic purpose of American law enforcement is reflected in this quotation from Abraham Lincoln: "The first intent of our American government is not to compel people to do certain things and restrain them from

---

2. *Enforcement Tactics Manual* (Sacramento: California Highway Patrol, 1965), p. 1.

others, but rather to make the right life and the useful life the natural and easy one to live." Officers should strive to mirror this example and support its ideal. The officer is the voice of authority and not the authority, for that rests with the people.[3]

The last main ingredient to the formation of good sound traffic enforcement is the support of the motoring public. This does not necessarily mean that the general public should enjoy the mass issuing of traffic summons or citations. Rather, it means that the public understands the need for highly professional traffic enforcement and helps by complying to a greater degree with the various traffic statutes of each state. Although the basic role of police and traffic patrol is to reduce the opportunity to commit unlawful acts, it is incumbent upon the general public to follow the rules and guidelines of highway safety.

The intelligent officer, through careful patrol methods, is the final line of defense against accidents. The omnipresence, or the impression of it, is created by frequent and conspicuous patrol around the clock. Adequate patrol succeeds in effecting immediate apprehensions and building a reputation for quick, courteous, and professional enforcement that is passed on through the media and from person to person.

There are other duties that the enforcement officer must perform while on routine patrol. For instance, there are numerous types of public services: removal of traffic hazards such as rocks, broken glass, tree limbs, spilled loads, and animals on the roadway; directions, travel information, and other similar types of aid; assistance to disabled motorists; and checking and removal of abandoned and stolen vehicles.

The public obtains a picture of the type of law enforcement agency present within the community based on what it sees in the daily activities of the patrol officer. It is the basic patrol function that occupies so much of the individual officer's time; therefore, he must employ both efficient and effective enforcement tactics.

By patrolling, officers are better able to provide better services, but they also are in a position to give greater protection to the driver. There are four primary purposes for patrolling: (1) observation, (2) apprehension, (3) deterrent effect, and (4) assistance to the public. Also, through setting an example officers encourage safe driving practices. Officers should always drive or ride in their cruisers or patrol vehicles in such a manner as to present the impression that they are "on patrol." Being alert and available while on a tour of duty is an officer's continued responsibility. By doing this, the officer indirectly instills in every driver six fundamental beliefs:

1.   It is the driver's responsibility to know and understand the law.

---

3.   *Enforcement Tactics Manual,* p. 1.

2. He must believe in the law.

3. He must have the feeling that the traffic officer is everywhere.

4. If the driver violates the law, he will be caught.

5. When a driver is apprehended, he will be arrested.

6. Finally, upon arrest and conviction or adjudication there will be punishment.

TECHNIQUES OF TRAFFIC PATROL

Visible Enforcement

One of the most effective methods of reducing the opportunity for suspected wrongdoing is through visible traffic enforcement. The potential violator is deterred from committing a hazardous violation by the very fact that a uniformed officer, in a distinctively marked patrol unit, is moving or at rest upon the highway. An open, active, and visible patrol affords better supervision of traffic and, since a greater area is covered, a deterrent effect results.[4] There is no deterrent effect when an officer places himself and his unit in an area where he is virtually in hiding. There are some cases, however, where the traffic problem is so great and the hazard is of such a degree that an officer should be in a position of advantage in order to observe those accident-causing violations. The fact still remains that where there is a high degree of officer visibility and the public is very conscious of his presence, there is a definite reduction in accident-causing violations.

What is the traffic enforcement officer actually doing while on routine patrol? He is in a position of readiness, waiting for a call (a request for service from the public) and observing (looking for those conditions that may require service or enforcement). The former is *reactive* in that the call for his services stems from a source to which he must respond. The latter is *proactive* because the patrol officer is seeking to initiate remedial action to solve a particular problem. The major function of a patrol officer is observation. Clearly, the officer's effectiveness is dependent upon that which he observes and evaluates. The scope and sureness of his observation has an influence upon his ability to detect problems of varying degrees. He is able to detect offenders, remove hazards, and provide for general services.[5]

The officer must plan his daily tour of duty. This means that he carefully evaluates the problems that have occurred from the time he went

---

4. *Enforcement Tactics Manual*, p. 9.
5. Paul M. Whisenand and James L. Cline, *Patrol Operations* (Englewood Cliffs, N.J.: Prentice-Hall Essentials of Law Enforcement Series, 1971), p. 10.

off duty until his return. He must read the daily log, teletypes, special broadcast memorandums, departmental directives and orders, and so on. During the role call or briefing session the officer should pay particular attention to those occurrences that will have some effect upon his patrol operation. Those things that his supervisors identify as being of utmost importance should be noted in written form in a pocket notebook for future reference. Just before going out on patrol, the officer should check with the beat officer just coming off duty who had been assigned to the same area of responsibility. The officer should determine any unusual problems or hazards that may not have been passed on to him through the briefing session. It is always wise to get a general feeling of how the activity has been on the previous watch or shift. If there has been an extremely busy time just handling traffic accidents or "crashes" (a new term that is replacing the words *collision* or *accident*), then the officer should plan to cover this area first upon going out on patrol. Finding out what type of traffic violations have been causing these accidents may warrant him to perform some diligent type of enforcement in these areas.

Although some departments sanction the use of off-street parking for observation while others do not, there is a need for this activity at times. It is possible that there is no other area immediately available or the potential hazard to the officer may be too great to maintain a fixed post upon the surface street. A check with the department's policy and/or the supervisor should determine if this is an allowable method of fixed observation. If the method is used, there are some cautions to keep in mind. It is important that the officer always park the patrol vehicle legally. The patrol unit is never parked on the wrong side of the street, headed in the wrong direction. This creates a hazard to both the officer and to other drivers in the area. Citizens may feel that the officer is attempting to hide and, therefore, it becomes a kind of game with them. Drivers also resent deliberate violations of the law by patrol officers. This tarnishes the very image of professionalism that officers are trying to create.

Officers should avoid becoming too set in their patrol procedures. By varying their activity through careful planning, they become more alert and eager to perform their daily tasks. The very reason for their presence is to reduce the potential crash. The officer who becomes so methodical in his day-to-day patroling procedures diminishes his effectiveness proportionately. It is always a good practice to reverse the patrol, for example, by stopping the vehicle at times in conspicuous locations, holding back from the entrance to an intersection at a red signal to observe cross traffic, circling the block and approaching the intersection from a different location, and operating in the extreme right-hand or outside traffic lane, so as to be readily available when the need arises. By changing the pattern of patrol, other drivers cannot predict an officer's presence and, therefore, the effect of *omnipresence* is established (the officer appears to be everywhere). It may be that someone is waiting for the officer to pass by in order to commit some unlawful act (other than a traffic offense). Another effective technique is to approach an area of concern slowly, then pull up and stop at a location where the officer can observe carefully without being seen too easily and wait for a few minutes. This may fool even the most cautious deliberate violator or criminal. Remember that the deliberate violator likes nothing better than to know where the patrol unit is. By maintaining a methodical type of patrol, drivers soon learn to anticipate an officer's presence at a given location and will regulate their conduct accordingly. This, however, may be a positive factor at times. For example, the problem of drivers passing a stopped school bus with its flashing red lights operating and children exiting or entering the school bus is deadly. When this comes to an officer's attention, he should take positive and immediate steps to deter it. Placing himself at the various locations along the school bus route during the time of its operation and apprehending those violators that pass the stopped school bus may greatly curtail the hazard. If an officer is observed in the area routinely enough, that in itself may all but completely eliminate the problem.

Speed of the Patrol Unit

The proper speed of an officer's patrol vehicle has a great deal to do with the quality and quantity of his apprehensions. While the speed of the officer's patrol vehicle may vary with the type of enforcement being used, or the location (city streets versus expressways and freeways) and the traffic with which he must contend, there are some fundamental principles to be considered.

It it not uncommon for an officer to fail to observe traffic violators while driving at high speeds. This is due in part to the fact that at higher speeds one's vision periphery tends to narrow to the point of tunnel vision. In fact, tests have proven that at speeds in excess of 80 to 90 miles per hour one is no longer steering a vehicle but aiming in excess of 4000 pounds of hurtling steel. The chances are far less at high speeds of being able to negotiate a vehicle should a sudden emergency arise. Furthermore, high speeds appear to the public as an abuse of an officer's immunity to speed regulations. Although each department's recommendations for normal patrol speed may differ slightly, it is suggested that a speed of five miles less the normal flow of traffic be maintained. This allows the officer the greatest opportunity to observe other drivers, while at the same time operating his patrol vehicle at a speed which will afford the best maneuverability should a violation be observed. It must also be pointed out that driving too slowly may impede the flow of traffic, thereby creating a hazard as well as possibly violating the law. The patrol unit should always be driven in the extreme right-hand lane during routine patrol duties. However, when using emergency lights and siren, the unit must be driven in the far left-hand or inside traffic lane. This gives the emergency vehicle the safest portion of the highway upon which to operate. When operating on narrow or two-lane roadways, the officer should frequently pull over to the right-hand curb or edge of the roadway and, in some cases, actually stop momentarily to allow traffic to pass.

Apprehending the Traffic Offender

Once a traffic violation is observed, the officer must be in a position to effect an arrest, thereby taking some type of positive enforcement. The officer has a responsibility to apprehend the offender as quickly as possible for several reasons. It reduces the opportunity to evade arrest or to create additional exposure to other drivers who could very well be involved in a traffic mishap with the violator as well as prevents the offender from forgetting about the traffic violation and possibly developing some type of alibi. It also affects other motorists, who may have witnessed the violation, by assuring them that violations of the law will be dealt with swiftly and positively. This instills in other drivers that law enforcement is for the protection and safety of all upon our streets and highways. This in turn generates public support for all law enforcement.

Before discussing the techniques of apprehension, some background factors should be covered. The first and most important consideration is the officer. Has he been properly trained in the operation of an emergency vehicle? This should be a combined classroom (about 20 percent) and actual driver training (about 80 percent) type of emergency vehicle driving course (see figs. 5-1 and 5-2). Most states having large police agencies have their own Emergency Vehicle Operations Course (E.V.O.C.) such as those of the California Highway Patrol, Michigan State Police, Ohio Highway Patrol, New York State Police, Los Angeles Police Department, and the Los Angeles County Sheriff's Department. There are also privately owned and operated defensive driving academies. These are usually instructed by former police officers and race drivers, all well qualified in the skills of defensive and emergency driving techniques. Most of these private organizations are in some way associated with various law enforcement agencies in the basic driver training of new police officers. One such organization is the Academy of Defensive Driving in Irvine, California. This school has been set up by retired and in-service law enforcement personnel, all of

FIGURE 5-1

Classroom Instruction

FIGURE 5-2

Field Training and Testing

whom are experts in the field of emergency vehicle operations and defensive driving techniques. For example, this school meets the high standards for police driver training as required under the Peace Officer Standards and Training (P.O.S.T.) in the state of California. There are a number of such schools, both public and private, to which a police department can and should send each officer for training. The minimum recommended course should be no less than three days (twenty-four hours) of actual contact time.

The officer should be familiar with the provisions of his respective state's vehicle code to determine the limitations of criminal and civil liability as they pertain to the operation of an emergency vehicle. An officer must also be well acquainted with his individual department's orders, policies, and standard operating procedures as they may pertain to the operation of a police emergency vehicle. We must point out that governmental agencies are no longer exempt from civil liability and responsibility resulting from the negligent operation of any emergency vehicle while operating under code three (traveling with visible, distinctively colored emergency warning lights, and an audible, operating siren).

The second consideration is the type of high-powered police vehicle being used. Most law enforcement agencies provide specially equipped vehicles for use in apprehending law violators. Each officer must respect and operate such a vehicle as if it were his private vehicle. This is not to say that when the need arises he should not effectively use the power provided to rapidly overtake an offender, but he should do so with good, sound judgment. It is very important that the officer make a complete inspection of his police patrol car before going out on duty. This includes both the exterior and interior: all lighting equipment, both regular and emergency; the siren, tires, brakes, and steering; and any special emergency equipment that may be provided for his use in addition to that which is a permanent part of the police car. It is his duty and responsibility to report any malfunctions, damage, or missing items from the patrol car before turning it over to the next officer for his tour of duty.

Now that we have discussed the two considerations significant to the successful operation of a police emergency vehicle, let us look at the particular techniques for apprehending a violator.

The officer must be well acquainted with his beat and should know those areas where a violator can be stopped safely and clear of traffic. He should select the proper place to stop the violator, keeping in mind both his safety and that of the violating driver. At night it is best to make a traffic stop within a well-lighted area whenever possible. This practice will materially reduce the chances that the occupants of the violator's car will resist the officer or endeavor to overpower him. Likewise, there may be other persons in the area who will serve as witnesses to what transpired during the physical arrest or issuance of a citation.

After having selected the location along the roadway at which the officer desires to stop the violator, he should check other traffic around him, particularly that to the rear. He should use rear emergency warning lights to advise drivers following the patrol unit that a traffic stop is about to take place, at least until the hazard no longer exists. (This of course may vary by department policy and the needs of the officer—his safety—at that moment.)

The officer uses emergency warning lights to the front and sounds the horn or siren (if needed) to gain the attention of a violator. As soon as the violator responds to these signals, the officer starts braking the patrol vehicle, bringing it to a stop between ten and fifteen feet to the rear of the violator (see figs. 5-3 and 5-4).

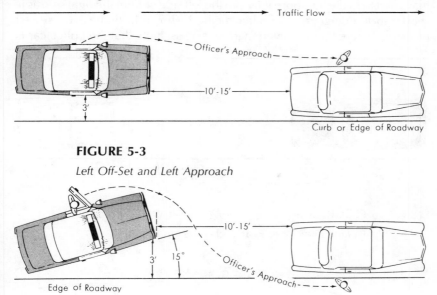

FIGURE 5-3

Left Off-Set and Left Approach

FIGURE 5-4

Left Angle and Right Approach

The single officer approach to the violator's vehicle may be either from the left or right side. If made from the left side, the officer should always check the condition of traffic approaching from the rear before exiting on the driver's side. Many officers have been seriously injured and some even killed while alighting from their patrol cars on the left side. On the other hand, the right-hand approach by the single officer has proven a very effective method of making an enforcement contact. It gives the officer that extra margin of protection from the oncoming traffic, the element of surprise, a better point of observation, and a somewhat more accessible place from which to contact the violating driver. In figure 5-3 a single officer approach is shown, left off-set and to the rear of the violator. Figure 5-4 is similar, but in this case the police car is parked at a 15-degree angle and the officer now makes a right-hand approach rather than a left-hand approach.

Two other methods of single officer traffic or other type of enforcement stop are shown in figures 5-5 and 5-6. In figure 5-5, the traffic stop is made in the conventional method, probably on a city street or other similar location. The police car is parked directly to the rear of the violator's vehicle, leaving a safety space of between ten and fifteen feet. The officer may elect to make his approach from the left side or from the right side as is shown in the diagram. The other method, shown in figure 5-6, is used primarily where there is a very narrow access. Note that the police car is

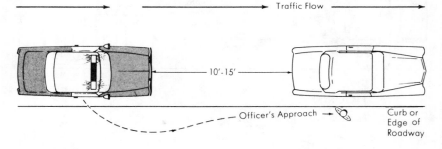

FIGURE 5-5

Parking Directly to Rear–Right Side Approach

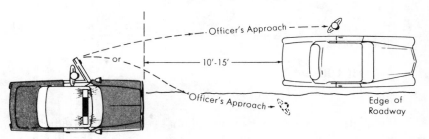

FIGURE 5-6

Narrow Access–Right or Left Approach

parked off the road slightly. The left side of the police car is almost in line with the right side of the violator's vehicle. At this point the officer may use either the left or right side approaches.

When there are two officers working together in the same police car, the method of stopping the traffic violator and the approach may vary from department to department. The following two diagrams illustrate methods for making high-risk and/or felony stops. Figure 5-7 shows the police car parked straightaway or directly to the rear of the violator's vehicle with a safety space of between ten and fifteen feet. As the driver of the police car makes his left-hand approach, the passenger-officer alights from the right side of the police car, hesitating momentarily behind the right passenger's car door. After the officer making the left-side approach makes contact with the driver of the violating vehicle, the passenger-officer moves to a position at the right front fender of the police car. The passenger-officer should stand about one foot to the right of the right fender so that he may be in the best possible position of observation. It may be necessary in some cases for the passenger-officer to move up to a position along the right-hand side of the violator's vehicle. Caution should be used in this circumstance as it leaves both officers without any protection. Should an emergency occur, the passenger-officer has considerable distance to travel in order to return to the police unit. This last method, illustrated in figure 5-8, uses the left off-set technique of parking the police car.

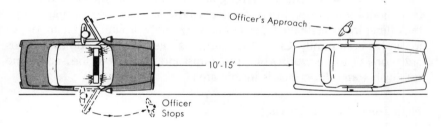

FIGURE 5-7

Straightaway–Two-Officer Patrol Unit

Upon making verbal contact with the violator, the officer should explain the purpose of the stop and request that the driver's license and vehicle registration be presented. He should briefly discuss the conditions surrounding the violation and explain the type of enforcement about to be employed (verbal warning, written warning or citation, or physical arrest). The officer should then terminate the contact in a professional manner, allowing for any questions from the driver. The officer also should explain

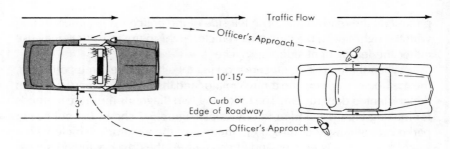

FIGURE 5-8

Approach of Two Officers with Left Off-Set

how the driver is to take care of the summons or citation, by appearance or by mail, and so on. Remember, the officer is not only enforcing the law but also selling highway safety. He should allow the driver to merge with traffic safely before proceeding on. The officer should also remember to always verify the driver with his license and the registration or title with the vehicle he is operating. Many automobiles are stolen each day of the year and part of an officer's sworn duty is the apprehension of these criminals.

The officer often uses other forms of traffic regulation to accomplish his purpose. One is through hand traffic direction (see chapter 7 on traffic direction). Another is through the promotion of pedestrian, bicycle, and motor vehicle safety education programs. Neither time nor space provides us an opportunity to explore and discuss these programs, so we suggest that the officer investigate the types of highway safety programs that are ongoing in his community. Class discussion may generate the numerous pros and cons of these worthwhile programs and perhaps at the same time establish some direct needs in this area.

High-Speed Pursuit Driving

Pursuit and emergency driving involve the same driving skills that the field officer must master for normal routine patrol operation, with an additional emphasis on good sound defensive driving skills. Pursuit driving requires that the officer be at peak efficiency and extremely alert, a condition that is actually enhanced by the increased activity of the nervous system and other body functions that are stimulated by the excitement of the situation.[6]

Of prime importance to the officer in making the decision whether to go into a high-speed pursuit, or a "code three run," are the circumstances. If the officer feels justified in going into pursuit, then it is he who must

6. Thomas F. Adams, *Police Patrol Tactics and Techniques* (Englewood Cliffs, N.J.: Prentice-Hall, 1971), p. 236.

shoulder all responsibility for his actions while on the emergency run. Deciding to pursue is always a process of weighing the hazards presented by the pursuit as opposed to those hazards created by allowing the violator to escape arrest. Although there are varying degrees attached to each circumstance, it is the officer who must rely on his good judgment to make the final decision. The degree of hazard in which the officer must place himself and others is dependent upon the degree of hazard in which the violator threatens other traffic.[7]

High-speed chases often begin with a simple traffic violation. The officer, while attempting to stop the violating driver, finds to his amazement that not only is the driver not stopping, but he is also actually trying to evade a lawful arrest. While in pursuit, it is always a good idea to reevaluate the situation to determine if it may be wiser to obtain more information about the fleeing suspect and the automobile he is driving, to follow up with an investigation, and then to file a complaint in the local court. Officers have lost their lives while in pursuit of a traffic violator who initially ran a red light or a stop sign.

Experience has shown that use of the siren and red light does not always assure an officer of immediate right-of-way. Conflict occurs many times because a motorist is unable to hear the siren. The human element is always present and under emergency conditions motorists and pedestrians will react differently. Certain techniques in the use of the siren and in driving will compensate to some extent for the shortcomings of persons who are excited or inattentive to their driving.

The siren should be operated throughout its entire tone scale, fluctuating from a high to a low pitch. Where the possibility of traffic conflict is present, the siren should be activated sufficiently in advance so that pedestrians and motorists may have adequate warning of the approach of an emergency vehicle.

A patrol vehicle using a siren should pass traffic on the left even though it is necessary to drive across a center line of the roadway. A motorist will often swerve to the right at the approach of an emergency vehicle. Therefore, an officer should cautiously pass on the right *only when no other course is open.* Sudden use of the siren immediately behind another vehicle should be avoided as it may cause an excited motorist to stop so abruptly that his car will be struck by the patrol vehicle.

The purpose of the red light and siren is to minimize traffic delay. Speed above the posted speed is seldom necessary or justified. The red light and siren are not protective armor; the officer can still be involved in an accident and never reach the scene of the emergency.

---

7. Donald O. Schultz, *Police Traffic Enforcement* (Dubuque, Iowa: William C. Brown Co., 1975), p. 48.

The following safety rules during emergency vehicle operation should be observed:

1. Do not follow immediately behind another vehicle and then suddenly blast the siren. The motorist may rapidly apply his brakes.

2. Do not pass on the right when using the siren unless no other course is available and then only when reasonably sure that the car being passed will not drive to the right as you go by.

3. Do not sound the siren at its highest pitch continuously; fluctuate its sound throughout the tone scale.

4. Do not lead or escort an emergency vehicle.

5. Drive with due regard for the safety of all persons using the highway.

6. When driving at high speed with red light and siren, keep near the center of the roadway so oncoming vehicles can see the red light approaching.

7. Increase speed between intersections and approach intersections with extreme caution. Use of second gear is sometimes of benefit at speeds less than 75 miles per hour.

8. Make a habit of using your safety belt at all times.

9. The law gives you the right-of-way when the siren and red light are in operation, but you must give motorists and pedestrians the opportunity to yield to you.

10. Check your beat first each day for changes and hazards. An intimate knowledge of your beat and your (and the car's) limitations are to your advantage.

11. Do not be ashamed to ask for assistance. We are a *team*. Radio gives us mobility. Use it! Advise your route, speed, and describe your suspect and vehicle.

12. Maintain a safe distance when observing for violations of following an emergency vehicle too closely to the rear. A motorist may yield to the emergency vehicle and, after it has passed, pull directly in front of you.

13. If involved in an accident, notify your sergeant and do not talk unnecessarily.

While the law provides some legal protection, the officer will find that real protection lies with his personal judgment and defensive driving habits rather than with a reliance on emergency equipment. A large portion of the driving public can hardly cope with normal driving problems; we therefore take on added responsibility and must use extreme care when operating an emergency vehicle.

The officer will perform his duty best if his driving is based upon the following principles, proven by experience to be sound:

1. Get there as quickly as possible with safety.

2. Keep your speed at a level which will enable you to avoid hazards, which you anticipate by being alert and exercising due care.

3. Keep your vehicle under control at all times.

4. *Allow motorists and pedestrians an opportunity to yield the right-of-way.*[8]

AUTO THEFT INVESTIGATION

The economic loss due to auto theft would stagger the imagination of most individuals. Each year the unrecovered property loss of automobiles reaches figures in excess of 60 million dollars. About half of all motor vehicles stolen in the United States are taken from residential areas, and almost 60 percent of these are taken right off public streets. Two-thirds of these thefts occurred at night after 6:00 P.M. In the past few years nearly 35 percent of all vehicles stolen are for commercial purposes, such as chopping up and stripping for parts. Nearly 53 percent of the autos stolen each year are by persons under eighteen years of age. Approximately every 32 seconds, 24 hours a day, 365 days a year, some type of motor vehicle is stolen. In other words, there is one in 143 chances that your automobile could be stolen.

Statistics have shown further that about 55 percent of America's auto thefts are the direct result of the key being left in the car or the ignition left unlocked. Of all the vehicles stolen, about 59 percent are actually recovered. Even more significant is that the number of auto theft cases being solved has dropeed from 24.3 percent in 1967 to 14.1 percent in 1978. The economic cost of auto theft has reached a figure in excess of 4 billion dollars annually; this includes the stolen vehicle, higher auto insurance premiums, police protection, and trials.[9]

What do these statistics mean to the traffic or patrol officer? They mean that there is a great likelihood that an officer will stop someone in a stolen

---

8. *Enforcement Tactics Manual,* pp. 71-75.
9. Federal Bureau of Investigation, *Uniform Crime Reports* (Washington, D.C., 1978) and U.S. Department of Justice (Washington, D.C., 1979).

vehicle at least once or perhaps twice in his career. It is therefore imperative that the officer understand some of the basic characteristics of auto theft.

Strict traffic law enforcement is the most effective weapon with which the officer may combat the auto theft problem. Often a violation committed by a criminal fleeing the scene of a crime or by a thief driving a stolen vehicle will provide an officer with the opportunity to stop the car and apprehend a wanted person who might otherwise escape detection. For this reason, the officer must remain constantly alert for the minor violations and irregularities which will lead to an interrogation of the driver and a thorough examination of the vehicle. The more vehicles stopped and drivers checked, the greater is the chance of apprehending an auto thief or other wanted person. The following signs should be watched for and investigated.

Damage Indicating Forced Entry.   Broken wind wings, damaged door handles or locks, damaged trunk compartment door, ripped convertible top, and a wired ignition system are all irregularities which may indicate that the vehicle has been stolen. Vehicles displaying these signs should be stopped and the driver questioned closely regarding the reason for such damage.

Suspicious Behavior of Driver.   Many drivers will display symptoms of nervousness or odd behavior upon being stopped by a police officer. This is a normal reaction and should not be interpreted by the officer as an indication that every driver acting in an unusual manner is a criminal. However, there are certain actions which should arouse suspicion:

1.   Extreme nervousness or bluster.

2.   The driver who, upon being stopped, jumps from his car and hurries back to the patrol car. There may be a reason for his not wanting the officer to see the inside of the car.

3.   Drivers who attempt to divert the officer's attention or give evasive or hesitant answers to routine questions.

4.   Drivers or occupants who do not fit the car, such as poorly dressed persons in a new car or exceptionally young persons in a late model family-type car.

5.   Drivers or occupants who constantly watch the officer.

6.   The driver who attempts to evade arrest for a minor violation.

7.   An extremely reckless driver.

8.   Drivers who turn into the first available side street when being followed by a patrol car or when approaching one from the rear.

9. The driver who does not seem familiar with the operation of his car.

10. Driving without lights.

11. Cars stuck off the roadway due to unfamiliarity or lack of skill on the part of the driver.

Registration and License Plate Irregularities.   The registration card on all vehicles with which the officer comes in contact should be checked for alterations, erasures, or other discrepancies. All such irregularities demand an immediate investigation, including a careful examination of the engine and/or vehicle identification number.

The license plates will often reveal valuable information to the observant officer. He should watch for the following:

1. New plates on an old car or old plates on a new car.

2. Plates loosely attached with wire or cord.

3. One plate attached over another.

4. Plates dirty, obscured, or bent.

5. Plates altered through the use of black tape or paint.

6. Plates on front and rear that do not match.

7. One plate.

8. No plate.

Investigation of Suspected Stolen or Wanted Vehicles.   A careful search should be conducted of all abandoned vehicles and those suspected of being stolen or wanted. The extent of the investigation and search will depend upon the circumstances present at the time and place that the vehicle is located. However, the following steps can normally be followed and will often reveal important information to the officer:

1. When a car is suspected of being stolen and is licensed in a state where the license stays with the vehicle, close attention should be paid to the holes in the plate normally used to affix the license to the vehicle. If the plate shows that it has been attached to other holes in addition to the ones being used at the time of observation, there is a strong possibility that this license has been attached to some other vehicle. This is easily detected in a distinct marking around the holes previously used. In states that require the license to remain with the original owner, who has several cars throughout the year, the plates will have been attached and detached several times.

2.   It is always good practice to check all cars on which the license plate appears to have been disturbed. The officer should be especially aware of late-model vehicles when the license plates are attached with wire or material other than the normal bolt. In many cases, the suspect has stolen a license plate and attached it to the stolen vehicle by means of a piece of wire. Special note should be made as to the location of the plate on the suspected vehicle. In haste, the suspect may attach the plate to the grill of the vehicle or other locations not commonly used by the average car owner. This is an outstanding clue on new cars, since it would be unlikely for the dealer to attach the plate to any place on the vehicle other than the one designated. The vehicle may also be suspect if the old plates or dirty plates have new and clean bolts used to attach them to the vehicle.

3.   A broken wind vent may be a clue as to whether a vehicle has been stolen, as the thief frequently uses this means of entry into a locked vehicle. The glass is generally broken near the lock release button and the hole is often plugged with cloth or cardboard. After theft, in cases where the keys are not available to the suspect, the only means of entry to other areas of the vehicle is by force. Close note of the trunk lock should be made. This is especially true with new cars. The punched-out trunk lock may lead to the arrest of a car thief and the recovery of the car.

4.   Not often is the dealer's nameplate a factor, but it certainly should not be overlooked. Sometimes a suspect will remove the dealer's nameplate from the trunk lid to disguise the stolen automobile. This is done by removing the nameplate completely, leaving nothing but noticeable holes in the lid. The suspect may also attempt to hide the nameplate by using spray paint, blending it in with the body of the vehicle. In regard to new vehicles, this nameplate should, in most cases, indicate the town or city of the dealership. Generally, this location will not conflict with the state license plate.

5.   The service record, usually located on the door casing, will sometimes lead the officer to the origin of the theft if he does not know where the car was stolen. Most of these tabs bear the name of the city where the gas station is located and the service was performed. This can be used to question the suspect as to when and where he had the car last lubricated, how many miles ago, or the approximate date of purchase, if he insists the vehicle is his.

6.   Check the radiator for heat and the surface of the ground near the tires for evidence that would indicate how long the vehicle had been parked at its present location.

7.   Are the doors locked or the ignition key in the switch? Check under the hood and dashboard for a jumper wire or similar device.

8.   Check I.D. numbers for evidence of alteration or tampering.

9.   Check the outside of the vehicle for damage or bloodstains which would indicate a hit-and-run accident.

10. Check the inside of the vehicle for bloodstains, burglary tools, firearms, narcotics, or other evidence which may indicate its use in the commission of a crime.

11. Check for possible mechanical failure. This may be the reason the vehicle is unattended.

12. Search the vehicle thoroughly for any evidence that would indicate the identity of the owner, occupants, or driver. Letters, envelopes, matchbook covers, road maps, lubrication tabs, newspapers, and other seemingly unimportant material can often provide the evidence necessary to solve a vehicle theft or other crime. This search should include the trunk compartment, with special care centered under and behind the spare tire. The absence of a spare tire or other accessories, especially on a late-model vehicle, will often indicate that the vehicle has been stolen, as a thief without funds will usually sell them at the first opportunity. The glove compartment, under the dashboard, and the underside of the seats and floor mats should all be closely examined.

13. Request information about the stolen car, including registration, license, and vehicle identification numbers.

If the vehicle is parked well off the roadway, in a driveway, or in front of a residence and the doors have been locked and the ignition key removed, it often indicates the driver is nearby and will return soon. If the vehicle under observation is believed to be stolen or the driver wanted, a stakeout should be set up to await the suspect's return, first taking the precaution of removing the spark plug wires.

If the investigation reveals that the vehicle is stolen or wanted and the location or the length of time it appears to have been abandoned indicates that the driver is not going to return, or if a stakeout has proven fruitless, the vehicle should be impounded with care taken to preserve any evidence or fingerprints that may be present.

If there is no stolen vehicle report and no evidence that the abandoned vehicle has been involved in another crime, it should be observed at regular intervals by the beat officer and removed to a place of storage after a reasonable length of time has elapsed. It is a good policy to check for a stolen vehicle a second time if the vehicle remains in the same position for longer than twenty-four hours, as the stolen vehicle report may not have been filed at the time of the first request.[10]

SUMMARY

Tactics used in traffic enforcement may vary from agency to agency and state to state; however, they all have the objective of making the streets and highways safe. This is one of six objectives that should be implemented. The other objectives are to eliminate actual or suspected opportunity for wrongdoing, to regulate traffic, to provide the many necessary services that will aid the motoring public, to prevent accidents, and to determine the problems an officer faces on the beat.

All traffic enforcement units carry out various functions, such as the enforcement of traffic laws and regulations, control of the flow of automobiles and pedestrian traffic through the means of direction, and the investigation of traffic accidents. Other traffic duties may be performed that are essential for advancing the objectives of an officer's particular department traffic control program.

In order to have efficient patrol, officers should be required to keep up with constant changes in the law. Enforcement methods require that officers maintain reasonable on-view patrol. Observation techniques should be employed so that officers can readily view accident-causing violations and thereby take the necessary enforcement action.

The quality and quantity of enforcement must be maintained by good planning. Communicating with the public and providing education for them are important. Selective enforcement is predicated upon the fact that the people must know the law and that the law is everywhere. A citizen should know that if he breaks the law, he will be caught. If apprehended, he will be arrested and upon adjudication will be prosecuted.

Officers alert for those accident-causing, moving violations should take some type of immediate enforcement action. Enforcement may be in the form of a written notice to appear (citation or summons). It may be a written or verbal warning or perhaps a physical arrest. The officer must use sound judgment when taking any type of enforcement action. He should be courteous but firm and explain the violation.

The quantity of enforcement also varies. A good guideline to follow is one enforcement contact or action for every hour worked. It is a known and proven fact that when citations are up in a critical area, traffic accidents are down. How can we determine just how many citations to issue? This is

10.   *Auto Theft Manual* (Sacramento: California Highway Patrol, 1969), pp. 32-40.

usually a departmental problem; however, through the use of good selective enforcement over certain designated periods of time, guidelines can be established. Selective enforcement requires that an officer first determine three things: (1) the time of day that accidents are the highest, (2) the locations where accidents are occurring most frequently, and (3) the types of violations that are most prevalent. When all three of these have been determined, the officer can then apply direct, selective enforcement to those problem areas.

We looked at the various problems regarding auto theft and explored some things to watch out for and techniques of investigation to be applied. In order to cover fully the spectrum of enforcement, the next chapter deals with enforcement psychology. The student should also consult the portion dealing with establishing traffic accident violations in chapter 10. These are good tools to aid the enforcement officer. When properly applied, they can work to effectively reduce the accident problems in a community.

DISCUSSION QUESTIONS

1.   Identify the various methods presently used by law enforcement to reduce traffic accidents in your city.

2.   List some possible guidelines that a police agency might use in developing a good traffic enforcement program.

3.   Discuss the positive and negative values of selective enforcement.

4.   Identify the various techniques used by auto thieves in stealing motor vehicles.

5.   What are the methods used to locate and identify a possible auto theft?

chapter

The Traffic Stop: Some Psychological Considerations

The purpose of this chapter is to help traffic officers recognize some of the factors that contribute to the success of a traffic stop. A successful traffic stop is one in which an officer does all in his power to provide a learning opportunity for the driver. The learning opportunity is comprised of the officer informing the driver that he committed a violation and what the consequences will be — a warning, a citation, or an arrest. Drivers who are open to the learning opportunity will realize immediately, or upon later reflection, that what they did was wrong and that the consequence was appropriate, even if unpleasant. Some drivers are unable or unwilling to be open to the learning opportunity. Officers cannot be responsible for the reactions of these drivers any more than a quarterback who throws a perfect pass can be responsible for the receiver who drops it.

The main obstacle to a successful traffic stop is conflict. The more conflict there is in any situation, the less learning will occur. There can be two kinds of conflict in a traffic stop: avoidable and unavoidable. Avoidable conflict is caused when an officer mishandles parts of the traffic stop. Unavoidable conflict stems from the driver's inability to react to the situation appropriately. When an officer prevents avoidable conflict, he substantially increases the chances of effecting a successful traffic stop.

In this chapter, we will discuss three principles that can help officers reduce the amount of avoidable conflict at a traffic stop, thus making traffic enforcement more effective and rewarding.

107

PERSONALITIES OF OFFICER AND DRIVER

The first principle in reducing avoidable conflict at a traffic stop is as follows:

> *What occurs at a traffic stop is largely determined by the personalities of the officer and the driver.*

If one knows the main personality characteristics of the officer and the driver, it is possible to predict with 80 percent accuracy what will occur at a traffic stop. While it is true that each person is a unique individual, it is also true that each of us has a typical way of behaving, especially under stress. In this section, four types of officers and four types of drivers will be discussed as well as the likely interactions between them at a traffic stop.

The Officer

The Helpful Officer.   Helpful officers enter law enforcement motivated by the need to be helpful to others. Through the years, they temper their ideals with reality but never lose sight of their basic motivation. Officers specializing in traffic enforcement want to help people stay alive. They realize that there are two and a half times as many people killed in vehicle accidents than are murdered each year.[1] This statistic alone is enough to motivate them and make them proud of their specialty.

At a traffic stop, the helpful officer's main objective is to educate the driver by explaining that he committed a violation, thus reducing the possibility that the driver will commit the same violation again. The officer may decide that issuing a warning is adequate or possibly more instructive than issuing a citation. Or, if the nature of the violation and the driver's inability to understand its hazardousness warrants, the officer may issue a citation. In either case, the helpful officer's motive is not contaminated with the need to be right, the need to be liked, or the need to punish.

These officers' basic motivation to be helpful is seen in their behavior toward motorists at traffic stops. Their attitude is understanding and fair and is reflected in observable behaviors: a relaxed facial expression, a calm voice, and a posture that is alert but nonthreatening. The content of what is said to the motorist is instructive and respectful. If conflict does arise on the traffic stop, it is unlikely that these officers initiated it or contributed to it.

---

1.   *Accident Facts,* published by the National Safety Council (1978), states that 49,500 persons were killed in vehicular accidents in 1977; while the *Uniform Crime Report,* published by the Federal Bureau of Investigation, reports 19,000 murders for an equivalent period of time.

The Authoritarian Officer.   Officers with authoritarian personalities normally have three common traits. First, they regard the law and justice as synonymous instead of viewing the law as but one instrument of justice. Their attitude is "The law's the law," and they enforce it even when such enforcement violates the other instruments of justice — reason, prudence, and understanding. They leave discretion to the courts. Consequently, these officers sometimes enforce the law to the detriment of justice.

A second trait of authoritarian officers is that they identify with middle-class values to such an extent that they take violations of the law as a personal affront. Thus, they are seldom dispassionate in their enforcement and often become personally incensed with violators, especially those who question their authority. They cannot recognize that they are often more interested in exercising their authority than in enforcing the law. They tend to pontificate rather than communicate with violators.

A third trait is a tendency to be prejudiced toward anyone who is different in race, religion, socioeconomic status, sex, or lifestyle. Although they insist that they treat everyone equally, they often do not.

Because authoritarian officers respect the law (at least as they perceive it) and tend to handle situations "strictly by the book," the citizen complaints they receive deal mostly with poor judgment and very seldom with illegal or abusive behavior.

The Aggressive Officer.   Aggressive officers have a good deal of pent-up anger stemming from the frustration of wanting much more from life than they are getting. Some aggressive officers are able to control their anger most of the time, but they explode periodically. Others seethe with aggression, which seeps out almost continually. These officers unconsciously use their authority as an instrument of their anger instead of the law and, in fact, can bend the law to make room for their anger. Their anger can cause them to ignore sound law enforcement procedures and to violate drivers' rights.

Sometimes aggression helps these officers make a good arrest and perform heroic feats. The problem is that *they* do not control their own behavior, *the situation* controls it. If a situation invites them to react heroically, they will. But if a situation invites them to react abusively or unconstitutionally, they will do so. These officers, sometimes dubbed "cowboys," rationalize such behavior as "good aggressive police work."

The Placating Officer.   Placating officers are "professional nice guys" whose basic need in life is to be liked and accepted. As individuals, they are liked not for who they are but for how much they do for others. Because they are unable to say "no," they have many fair-weather friends. However, as police officers, their basic need to be liked and their secondary need to enforce the law often come into conflict.

These officers hate to be seen as a "bad guy," and some citizens perceive any officer who gives them a citation or arrests them (or their relatives) as "bad guys." Hence, under the rationalization of "good public relations" and "the best interests of justice," these officers fail to enforce the law even when it is appropriate and necessary.

Unfortunately, such officers are often liked in the community because they look the other way when violations occur, typically issue warnings instead of citations, and drive drunken drivers home rather than arrest them. The affirmation they receive from the community reinforces their belief that they are good police officers. Sometimes even police administrators like these officers because they never "make waves" and often receive commendations from local businesses and residents.

The problem is that these officers fail to realize that conscientious law enforcement is the best form of public relations. Allowing drivers to circumvent the law may lead to personal acclaim but not to genuine respect.

The Driver

There are four basic types of drivers that officers will meet at a traffic stop. Each will interact differently with the various types of officers described above.

The Cooperative Driver. Cooperative drivers know what they did wrong and admit it, or they are unaware of what they did wrong but take the officer's word for it. These drivers are upset primarily with themselves and not with the officer. They often honestly lament, "I'm ordinarily a very responsible driver. I don't know what got into me to do something so stupid." Their attitude toward the officer is either positive or neutral, and they will often assure the officer, "You're just doing your job." One such driver said to the officer, "I'm glad that my fifteen-year-old daughter is with me, because she will be driving soon and it's good for her to see what will happen if she breaks the law." Traffic stops with cooperative drivers sometimes end with the driver apologizing for inconveniencing the officer.

When a cooperative driver is stopped by a helpful officer, the traffic stop can actually be a pleasant experience or at least a painless one. But when the cooperative driver is stopped by an authoritarian officer or an aggressive officer, the officer may succeed in destroying the cooperation and converting it into righteous indignation. Officers who complain that they never get cooperative drivers on *their* stops may get them, but they turn them off by the first sentence out of their mouths. Placating officers, on the other hand, will cite cooperative drivers more than other drivers because they are "easy" and do not threaten the officer.

The Blameless Driver.   These drivers are insecure people who always perceive themselves as blameless. If they cannot admit mistakes at home or at work, it is unlikely that they can admit a mistake at a traffic stop. Blameless drivers who are stopped for going through a red light protest that it was still amber; those who are stopped for following too closely blame the driver in front of them; those who are stopped for speeding blame their speedometer; and those who are stopped for going through a stop sign blame the officer for having been too far away to see the situation clearly. These drivers have maintained their self-esteem by calling other people wrong throughout their lives.

The helpful officer recognizes this personality trait and does not try to argue the driver into admitting guilt, knowing that such an attempt would be both fruitless and inflammatory. He listens politely to the driver's protestations and, after the driver has sufficiently vented his wrath, calmly advises him as to what action the officer believes is appropriate. This does not mean that the driver will magically turn into a cooperative driver, but it does mean that the officer did his best to minimize any conflict at the stop.

Authoritarian officers are frequently unable to restrain themselves with a blameless driver. They believe that no one is going to escape responsibility for breaking the law and absolutely no one is going to tell an authoritarian officer that he is wrong. These officers will lecture at length, prosecuting the driver and defending themselves. To authoritarian officers, this type of traffic stop represents a contest that will be won or lost. The tactics they use to convince the driver that he is in error are based on logic, experience, authority, sympathy — anything that might cause the driver to finally admit, "Well, officer, after listening to you, I must admit that I am wrong." Of course, the chance of this happening is miniscule, but not so small as to deter the officer from pursuing the same tactics at each traffic stop.

Aggressive officers secretly like to stop blameless drivers because it gives them a chance to vent their hostility. Under the guise of being angry because the driver "could have killed someone," the officer launches a personal attack on the driver. If one were to interrupt the officer in the midst of the barrage and ask what the driver did wrong, the officer would probably have to stop and think for a minute. This is because the attack is focusing less on the violation than on the officer's anger. The officer's attack only makes the blameless driver more defensive. As a result, both individuals are reduced to childish statements, threats, and epithets. Both the driver and the officer leave the traffic stop muttering to themselves, "What a jerk."

When the blameless driver is stopped by a placating officer, the driver is likely to escape with a mere warning because the officer does not want to face the tension created by issuing a citation. After the driver is told by the officer that he will not receive a ticket, this driver usually responds, "Well, thank you very much, officer. You know, you could be right — maybe I didn't stop at the sign. I'm sorry for getting so upset with you." The placating officer congratulates himself for doing a marvelous public relations job and looks forward to a letter of commendation. The fact that he was scared off by the driver's defensiveness never occurs to him. Contrary to what the placating officer thinks, the driver respects police officers no more as a result of getting a "break" and is likely to commit the same violation again because he escaped its consequences.

The Nonchalant Driver.   Nonchalant drivers have a very casual attitude toward life, which extends to their driving habits. They can be fifteen minutes late for an appointment and not give it a second's thought, and they can drive fifteen miles per hour through a stop sign and think nothing of it. When they are confronted with their transgressions, they respond with surprise, "What's the big fuss?"

An example of such a driver is a woman who is late picking up her children at school and tries to compensate by driving fifteen miles per hour over the speed limit. When the officer stops her, the woman explains irritably, "Yes, I know I was going a little fast. But if I'm late picking up my kids, they will be very frightened, and I want to prevent that." She fully expects the officer to reply, "Oh well, in that case, go ahead. I'm sorry I delayed you." When the officer issues a citation, she is incensed. She cannot believe that "an officer of the law" would be so insensitive and uncaring as to allow her children to become terribly frightened because the officer delayed her. She will often threaten the officer by saying that she will tell the school principal the "exact reason" for her delay and may even talk to the police chief about it.

The helpful officer realizes that it is not his responsibility to cure this person's nonchalant attitude toward life. He patiently listens and then explains what action is going to be taken and why. Whether a citation or a warning is issued, he hopes it will make the driver a little less casual about his driving.

Authoritarian officers become the most upset with the nonchalant driver because this driver's attitude is "I know what the law is, but my needs are more important than your laws." Because this attitude undercuts the very foundation of the authoritarian officer's personality, he is likely to lecture the woman in the example that it is her responsibility to leave the house on time and that it is her fault — not his — if her children are frightened. He will tell her that if she kills someone else's kids because she does not want her kids to be frightened, she will have more to worry about than she does now. Of course, *none* of these statements will be helpful, and *all* of them will be inflammatory. The authoritarian officer is likely to say some things that will be regretted when they are repeated in court or in the chief's office.

Aggressive officers who stop the nonchalant driver will likely use sarcasm as a way of getting the driver to see the seriousness of the violation: "If you run over somebody else's kids on the way to pick up your own, I'll just tell their mother that you were late, and I'm sure she'll understand." This approach only reinforces the driver's opinion that police officers are mindless and petty people.

Placating officers are unlikely to issue a citation to the nonchalant driver. They will rationalize the inaction by convincing themselves that there were "extenuating circumstances" (which there *always* are with nonchalant drivers) and that "it's not worth the hassle."

The Hostile Driver.   Hostile drivers look for trouble the way most people look for fun and have a great deal in common with the aggressive officer. These drivers have large amounts of pent-up anger and are always looking for an inviting target — a "bulldozer" approach to life which extends to their driving. Because they view traffic laws as needless restrictions on their freedom, they ignore laws half the time and purposely flaunt them the rest of the time. Secretly this driver wants to be stopped by an officer because it will provide an excellent opportunity to unload some anger.

The hostile driver's first words at a traffic stop are often "What do *you* want?" By this opening challenge, it is clear that he does not want to solve a problem but to start a fight. His idea of "winning" at a traffic stop is not so much to avoid getting a citation but to force the officer to say or do something foolish that the driver can describe in detail to friends, the police chief, the court, and perhaps even to the local newspaper. If he succeeds in baiting the officer, it is worth the price of the citation.

Helpful officers who stop the hostile driver realize it would not be helpful to themselves or to the driver to jump at the hostile bait, no matter how tempting it is. They realize that the two ingredients for being successful with this driver are silence and a calm firmness. The silence says to the driver, "I'm too secure to let you get to me," and the calm firmness says, "I'm going to do what I think is appropriate despite your attitude."

Authoritarian officers will find it almost impossible to ignore the bait. They will plug in their "you can't talk to me like that" tape, and the hostile driver will prove to the officer that he can and will. The conversation will deteriorate quickly, usually ending with both the driver and the officer looking foolish.

Aggressive officers meet a mirror image of themselves in the hostile driver. They don't even *try* to resist the bait but lunge at it daringly. Their "you don't scare me one bit" tape will incite this driver to near violence.

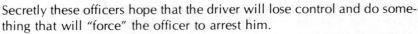

Secretly these officers hope that the driver will lose control and do something that will "force" the officer to arrest him.

Placating officers play their "hey, calm down, Mr. Smith, all I want to do is talk to you" tape and terminate the stop in less than two minutes. They rationalize that "giving a ticket to a guy like that is only going to make him worse."

Summary.   Officers cannot control the types of personalities they will encounter at a traffic stop, but they can control their own attitudes and behaviors and remain consistently helpful regardless of the driver's reactions. Anyone can be nice to cooperative drivers and aggressive toward hostile drivers. The mark of an effective officer is that he remains helpful under all circumstances and does not get forced out of the role by any driver.

COMMUNICATION

The second principle an officer should remember during a traffic stop is:

*How the officer communicates will affect the success or failure of
a traffic stop.*

In this section, we will discuss four dimensions of communication: verbal communication, nonverbal communication, levels of communication, and irrelevant communication.

Verbal Communication

Verbal communication is comprised of the words and phrases officers use to explain the nature of a traffic stop to the driver. There are five pitfalls that officers can avoid in their conversations with a driver.

(1) *Being abrupt.* An officer who approaches a driver and says, "Sir, you went through a stop sign at the last intersection, so I'm going to have to issue you a citation" and immediately walks back to his patrol vehicle is being abrupt. It only takes an extra minute to explain the situation to the driver; to ask the driver if he was aware of the infraction; and to listen to how the driver responds. This allows the driver to feel that he is being treated like a human being and not like a number. Moreover, the driver's response will give the officer some information on how to decide an appropriate course of action.

(2) *Being overtalkative.* An officer should be succinct, which lies between being abrupt and overtalkative. Many officers talk too much on a traffic stop, prolonging it to the point of diminishing returns. For example,

an overtalkative officer might say, "Mr. Smith, the reason I was parked watching cars approach the stop sign is that we've been getting a lot of complaints from the residents. They say that drivers have been ignoring the sign, which makes them and their kids jump out of the way. I notice that you live only two blocks from here, so you must be aware of the sign and how dangerous it is if you don't stop. Part of our law enforcement duty is to see to it that . . . etc."

The problem with overtalking is twofold. First, it is unlikely that the driver is listening because he is too distracted by his own feelings about the situation. Second, what the officer is actually doing is "sandbagging" the driver with reasons for the driver to feel guilty and wrong. A natural reaction would be for the driver to "fight for air" to maintain some semblance of self-esteem. When this occurs, a needless argument ensues with each sandbag. All a driver needs to know is that he violated a law and that he may respond to enable the officer to make a decision regarding the violation.

(3) *Being judgmental.* This means that the officer uses words or phrases that demean the driver's motives or abilities. The following are examples of judgmental statements:

"You are obviously late and trying to to make up for it by speeding."

"You slowed down only because you saw the patrol car."

"You obviously are unconcerned about everyone else on the road."

"If you didn't have the dog on your lap, you wouldn't have been distracted."

"You were so involved in conversation that you didn't see the stop sign."

None of these statements will enable the driver to learn from his mistake. A normal person would react to any of them by denying the allegation and taking offense.

Officers will be most successful if they stick to the facts of the violation and the elements of the vehicle code; the personality of the driver should never be a topic for conversation. The officer can state matter-of-factly, "Mrs. Evans, I observed that you drove through the stop sign at about fifteen miles an hour, and the vehicle code states that a vehicle must come to a complete stop at the limit line." Any other embellishments are likely to diminish the potential for a positive learning experience.

(4) *Using a negative tone of voice. How* officers say something is often more important than *what* they say. While the words themselves may be

polite, the tone with which they are said can inject a negative connotation. One negative tone of voice stems from anger. For example, an officer may say, "Sir, I just clocked you doing sixty-five miles an hour in a forty-five-mile zone," in a tone that says simply, "This is why I stopped you," or in a tone that says, "You idiot, you almost got five people killed, including me, and I just hope you give me some lip because I'll nail you good." It is *normal* to feel like getting that message across, but it is a temptation that officers should learn to overcome.

A second negative tone of voice is authoritarian. An officer can say to the driver, "Sir, please remain in your vehicle until I'm through writing the citation," in two very different ways. One way implies that it would be safer and more expedient for the driver to stay in the car. The second tone can say, "Hey, I'm in charge here, and you won't make a move without me telling you to."

Officers are sometimes unaware of their tone of voice and, when presented with a citizen's complaint by the chief, insist, "All I said was 'Would you please wait in your car?' What's wrong with that?"

As much as possible, an officer's tone of voice should be conversational. In most circumstances, one's tone of voice should be that which the officer just used in speaking to his partner before the stop.

(5) *Using a poor choice of words.* The words we use will be perceived by the driver as an invitation or as a demand. It is always better to begin with invitations and hope that they will accomplish what we want. If invitations are not accepted, then the officer may shift into demands. It is helpful to remember the difference between an invitation and a demand. The following are some examples that show the difference:

> Demand: "I *told* you to remain in your car until I returned."
> Invitation: "Sir, the traffic's loud and you probably didn't hear me, but I would appreciate it if you could remain in your car. It would be much safer for you, and I'll return and explain the situation shortly."

> Demand: "I think you'd better get out of the car and do a roadside sobriety test for me."
> Invitation: "Sir, I have some reasons to believe that you've been drinking. It would ease my mind and it might be to your advantage to go through a few simple tests with me over here on the side of the road."

> Demand: "Sir if you *don't* sign the citation, I'll have to take you straight to jail, so sign it."
> Invitation: "Well sir, unfortunately, if you don't sign the citation, I am commanded by law to bring you to jail. I think it would be to your advantage to sign it. If you feel that you are innocent, you can ask for a court date, which would accomplish more for you than being arrested."

Nonverbal Communication

Nonverbal communication is comprised of the messages our bodies send without us uttering a word. An officer should be particularly aware of two types of nonverbal communication when on a traffic stop.

(1) *Facial expression.* The facial expressions most likely to make the traffic stop a learning experience are a friendly expression or at least a neutral one. An officer who regards a driver as "a law-abiding citizen who is very likely a good person who made a mistake" is more likely to have a pleasant facial expression than the officer whose attitude is "This jerk almost killed a carload of people." While it would be unrealistic for an officer to meet each driver with a smile, it is equally unrealistic to meet each driver with a scowl or a sneer. Under most circumstances, the first messsage that a driver receives comes from the look on the officer's face and that can set the tone for the entire stop.

(2) *Stance.* How an officer stands can communicate a message that is helpful or inciting. The officer who uses a combative stance, thumbs hooked into the front of the belt and leaning toward the driver, could be perceived as hostile and threatening. Sometimes officers are unaware that they are sending such messages; for example, an officer who has an unconscious habit of adjusting his holster as he talks may be scaring the life out of the driver. Officers who stand relaxed yet alert do not allow their stance to be threatening.

Levels of Communication

The psychiatrist Eric Berne postulated that all of us have three parts that are necessary for us to function effectively: the Adult, the Parent, and the Child.[2] The Adult part of us has three characteristics: it collects data in an objective manner; it estimates the probability that a certain behavior will work or not; and it keeps emotional expression appropriate. The Parent part of us is judgmental. It tells us when we are "good" or "bad," and it helps us judge others similarly. If it is healthy, it will keep us out of trouble and make life easier. If it is overbearing, we shall be overly harsh on ourselves and overly judgmental of others, behaving in an authoritarian and condescending way. The Child, if it is healthy, helps us behave in spontaneous, pleasurable, humorous, and creative ways. If it is unhealthy, it leads us to behave in "bratty" ways — stubborn, argumentative, selfish, and aggressive.

In general, the most appropriate and productive transaction between a police officer and the driver at a traffic stop is an Adult-to-Adult transaction, which is diagrammed in figure 6-1.

2. Eric Berne, *What Do You Say After You Say Hello?* (New York: Bantam Books, 1973), pp. 11-20.

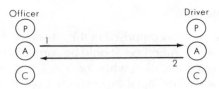

FIGURE 6-1

One example of an Adult-to-Adult transaction would be the following:

Officer: "Good afternoon. I observed you going through the stop sign at the last intersection and wanted to call it to your attention."

Driver: Either "I really didn't see the sign. I was so distracted by those boys fighting on the corner that I didn't see it," or "Well, I did see the sign, but figured I slowed down pretty well and thought it was safe enough to proceed."

The officer, his Adult still "plugged in" with a little healthy Parent added, responds with one of the following statements:

"Well, I saw those kids, too, and they were a distraction. Since you don't live around here and aren't familiar with this sign, and since you know you made a mistake, let me remind you that your main responsibility is to keep your eyes on the road. Seeing a stop sign and obeying it could save your own life or that of someone else."

"Well, I can understand your thinking on the matter. However, the law does state that a vehicle must come to a full stop, and it's important that people can make that assumption of each other. It's for that reason that I am issuing a citation, hoping that it will help you to remember to stop in the future."

The driver may respond in an Adult way: "Well, I don't like getting a ticket, but you're right. I knew what I was doing and took the chance, so I should take the consequences."

Less ideal transactions, however, can occur. For example, when a police officer "comes on" Parent, he can expect one of two types of response. One transaction occurs if he engages the Child of the driver, as diagrammed in figure 6-2 and described below.

Officer: "I don't know what's wrong with people like you. You obviously saw the stop sign and shot through it to beat that yellow Dodge through the intersection. Obviously you feel that where you are going is more important than other people's lives or property."

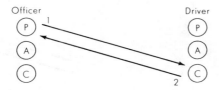

FIGURE 6-2

Driver: (coming on Child) "What are you so upset about? I'm helping you meet your quota of tickets for the month, ain't I?"

At this point, the officer will continue his Parental approach, only creating more of a Childlike reaction in the driver, or he will switch to his Child and enjoy a good verbal skirmish just as he did when ten years old.

When the officer in the situation comes on Parent, he also may activate the Parent of the driver, as shown in figure 6-3.

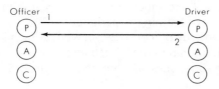

FIGURE 6-3

Officer: "You didn't stop at that sign back there, and being a father with all those kids in the car, you'd think you'd be more aware of what can happen when people don't stop at signs."

Driver: (coming on Parent) "Well, officer, I happen to be an attorney and am not used to being addressed as if I were a delinquent child. I happen to know quite a bit more about the law than you do, and it's too bad you had to bring up my children as an attempt to gain some leverage in this discussion."

At this point, the officer may respond by coming on even more Parental or by plugging in his Child to see if that will work better for him.

The officer may begin a transaction by using his Child. In so doing, he may hook the Child or the Parent of the driver. This will result in one of the two situations diagrammed in figure 6-4 and described below.

Officer: "Well, Speed, you just passed eight cars in the last eighth of a mile at seventy miles per hour. You won the race and here's your prize — a nice fat ticket."

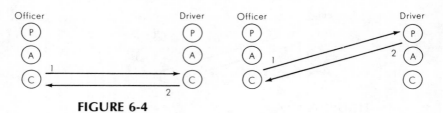

FIGURE 6-4

Driver: (responding with his Child) "Thanks, Ace, but if I was going seventy, you had to be going ninety to catch me. You were driving more dangerously than I was. How are you going to explain that to the judge?" Or,

Driver: (responding with his Parent) "It just so happens, officer, that I am a nurse responding to an emergency in the intensive care unit, and if you weren't playing your silly little game of hide and seek, I'd be there by now saving a life!"

In neither case is there much hope for salvaging this situation and turning it into a positive learning experience.

In many situations, the officer starts out well, using his Adult. But if the driver responds with his Parent or Child, then the officer slips into his own Child or Parent. One situation is diagrammed in figure 6-5 and described as follows:

Officer: (using Adult) "Good afternoon. I observed you go through that stop sign back there and would like to speak with you about it."

Driver: (responding with Child) "Like hell you did. I came to a full stop!"

Officer: (slipping to Child) "Well, I'm glad neither I nor my kids were standing in front of your vehicle when you made your full stop — we'd all be in the morgue by now!"

The continual challenge to the officer is to leave his Adult "plugged in" regardless of whether or not the driver is reacting to him in Parent or Child ways. The officer, because his Adult is operating, sticks to objective data that he observed; makes his judgment on all the data in the situation; and makes his Adult emotional responses to the *situation* and not to the driver.

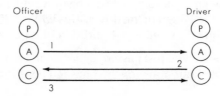

FIGURE 6-5

Imagine what would happen if a surgeon allowed his liking or dislike of his patient to influence his surgery. The officer cannot control completely how the driver will respond to him, but he can always control how he responds to the driver.

Irrelevant Conversation

Often when drivers are stopped for a violation, they will bring up irrelevant issues to place the officer on the defensive. In doing this, the original purpose of the stop becomes obscured and almost secondary to the irrelevant issue. The following are some typical ploys:

"Our house was burglarized two months ago, and instead of looking for the crooks you guys are out giving tickets for minor traffic violations."

"We have drivers speeding by our house all day almost running over our kids. How come you're never around when that's going on?"

"Why aren't you ever at the school crossings in the mornings when you're needed?"

Officers who bite at the bait and enter into long, heated arguments about such issues are inviting avoidable conflict.

On issues that the officer can do something about (e.g., speeding vehicles on his beat), he can answer, "I'm glad you called that to my attention. I'll see that the area gets extra patrol." Regarding issues that the officer has no control over (e.g., the competency of the burglary detail), the officer can respond, "Sir, the best person to speak with about that is Detective Smith, who is the head of Burglary."

These answers are polite, helpful, and should close the issue. If they do not close the topic, further baiting should be ignored, and the officer should continue with what needs to be done to complete the stop.

STANDARD PROCEDURE

The following is the third principle an officer should follow on a traffic stop:

The more an officer has a standard procedure to follow on a traffic stop, the more successful each stop will be.

This section will cover three topics: a model for a traffic stop; discretion and the traffic officer; and special problems that can occur at a traffic stop.

A Model for a Traffic Stop

The *specifics* of each traffic stop are different, so no one can give a traffic officer a recipe book to follow. However, the *nature* of all traffic stops is similar, and a general model can be offered as a way to limit avoidable conflict and to ensure more successful traffic stops. The more an officer can work from a general model, either the one described here or another one of his choice, the more confidence the officer will have in approaching and handling traffic stops.

When developing a model for a traffic stop, the officer must be aware of the true purpose of any traffic stop: to explain a violation and to cite or warn the driver. Any other purpose for a traffic stop will be likely to cause problems. The following are some examples of unsuitable purposes for a traffic stop:

(1) *To "sell" a traffic citation.* Police administrators often are fond of the idea of "selling" a traffic citation because supposedly everyone ends up happy. But, in reality, a traffic citation costs a driver an average of thirty dollars, the possibility that his insurance will be increased, and a half-day of lost wages if the driver contests the citation. To attempt to manipulate a person into feeling good about receiving a citation is dishonest. On a practical level, it is a waste of time. If the driver realizes he was wrong and deserves a ticket, there is no need for "selling"; in fact, it is abrasively redundant. If the driver is antagonistic and feels wronged, attempts at "selling" only open the way to more frustration and argument. An officer can be polite and professional without being a salesperson.

(2) *To get the driver to admit that he violated the law and deserves a citation.* Many people realize that they made a mistake but are not secure enough to admit it. Attempting to force these individuals into an outright admission of guilt will only result in avoidable conflict. It is better to hope that after reflecting privately on the situation the driver may entertain at least the possibility that he was at fault. Even if this does not occur, the driver is likely to be more careful in similar situations in the future. While it may be more satisfying to the officer to have the driver say, "I was wrong, and I'm willing to accept the consequences," it is not the purpose of or a necessary requirement for a successful traffic stop.

The officer who persists in trying to get the driver to admit guilt may only succeed in starting an argument. As a result, the driver may feel personally challenged and ready to seek retribution either in court or by complaining to the department.

(3) *To lecture the driver on the hazardousness of his driving.* It is important to distinguish between explaining and lecturing. Explaining is nonjudgmental and descriptive, such as, "Sir, you violated the pedestrian's right-of-way at the last intersection by driving in front of him and causing him to stop abruptly." An example of lecturing is "Sir, I'm sure you've been driving for at least twenty years, and it seems that by now you should realize the danger involved in driving so close to a pedestrian that the

pedestrian has to leap backward to avoid being hit." For the average motorist, a traffic stop is a semitraumatic experience during which he is so nervous, angry, or embarrassed that he is incapable of truly listening and hearing what the officer is saying. The driver is much more likely to remember the attitude of the officer than specific words. The officer may feel better after the lecture, but no overall good is accomplished.

(4) *To punish the driver.* Punishment is the court's responsibility — not that of law enforcement. By issuing a citation, the officer merely states that he thinks the driver violated the law. Whether or not the driver is found guilty and punished is not within the purview of the traffic officer. Consequently, any attitude or talk of punitiveness is inappropriate and very likely to evoke avoidable conflict.

Once the officer is aware of the purpose of the traffic stop — to explain a violation and to cite or warn the driver — he can develop a general framework to follow on a traffic stop. One such procedure, "Five Sentences, Plus One," is outlined below. To the extent that an officer remains in this type of framework, avoidable conflict will be reduced.

Sentence One: "Good afternoon, sir (ma'am); may I see your driver's license?"

Most drivers will present a license without comment. If such is the case, there will be no conflict stemming from Sentence One.

Conflict can arise when the driver, while presenting the license, asks in a hostile way, "Why are you stopping me?" In this case, the officer explains in a matter-of-fact, nonhostile way, "Sir, I stopped you because I observed that you failed to stop at the stop sign at that last intersection."

A very hostile driver may reply to the request to see a license, "I'm not going to show it to you until you tell me why you stopped me." Here the officer may enter into a power struggle by demanding to see the license before another word is spoken. But the purpose of the traffic stop is not to assert power; it is to warn or cite a driver in the smoothest way possible. Since this is the case, the officer can calmly and clearly explain why he stopped the driver. Ninety-five percent of the time the driver will then hand over the license so that the officer can continue.

Sentence Two: "Do you know why I stopped you?"

If the driver has asked the officer to explain the reason for the stop in Sentence One, this question has already been answered. But even in Sentence One, it is better for the officer to respond to the driver's question with the question, "Do *you* have any idea why I stopped you?" The very hostile driver will emphatically say, "NO!" Drivers who are less hostile or just scared will often respond, "No, unless it was for not coming to a complete stop at that stop sign back there."

The point is that it is always better to have the *driver* tell *you* why you stopped him. This is so because it is an admission of guilt and because it will be helpful to record the response in case the citation is contested in court. Even if the driver insists that he does not know why the stop was made, this should be recorded, too, because this driver's response indicates inattention or ignorance of the law.

In any case, after the officer has explained the reason for the stop in *one or two sentences,* he is ready for the next sentence.

Sentence Three: "OK, sir (ma'am), I'll be back shortly."

There are various points of view on this statement, but it seems better for the officer not to tell the driver that he is going to be cited at this point. When the driver is told that the officer will issue a citation, the driver may become upset and argue with the officer both before and during the writing of the citation. This is distracting for the officer and is one of the main causes for errors on citations. After the officer returns to the driver upon completion of the citation, the officer can proceed to the next sentence.

Sentence Four: "Sir (Ma'am), this is a citation for not making a legal stop at the stop sign at Third and Main Streets. Could you please put your signature here? It's not an admission of guilt, but . . . ."

If the driver signs without comment, there is no source of conflict. If the driver vents his anger, it will be when signing the citation or just before signing it. The officer is only interested in getting the citation signed, and any response to the driver will only prolong the situation and have no positive effect.

If the driver replies, "What if I don't sign it?" or "I *won't* sign it," the officer can politely reply, "Sir (Ma'am), it really would be in your best interests to sign it because the law commands me to arrest you if you don't." This statement is made with an attitude of educating the person to the law rather than with the attitude that says, "I hope you *don't* sign it, so I can take you to jail."

Sentence Five: "Thank you, sir (ma'am). Good afternoon."

It is better if the officer does not say, "Have a nice afternoon," because it could sound sarcastic or, "Drive safely," because it could sound as if the officer is "rubbing it in."

The "Plus One" sentence can be used at any time during the stop. It is used when the driver insists that he did not commit the violation or still does not understand the nature of the violation.

It is possible that a driver will not understand the officer's first explanation of the situation. For this reason, he should patiently offer a second explanation. If the person fails to understand the second explanation, he either cannot or is unwilling to understand it. It is at this point that the "Plus One" sentence is appropriate: "Sir (Ma'am), I have done my best to explain clearly the nature of the violation. I'm afraid I'm unable to do any more than that."

If the driver continues with "baiting" behavior (i.e., hostile questions, demands for further explanation, implied or explicit threats), it is best for the officer to ignore them. If the officer jumps at the bait by engaging in lengthy and repeated explanations, verbal duels, or exchanges of sarcasm, the officer is talking too much. And, when the officer talks too much, he is playing directly into the hands of the hostile driver. The hostile driver wants the officer to display something in demeanor or speech that will take the focus off the driver's misdeed and put it on the officer. Then the driver can tell his friends, the judge, and the police chief, "Sure I was going a little fast, but you know that *that cop* said. . . ." So the driver ends up having been a "little inattentive," but the officer is tagged as a "dumb cop."

Discretion

Another ingredient of a sound plan of action includes the traffic officer's willingness to use discretion. If an officer approaches the traffic stop with a compulsion to issue a citation, the number of successful traffic stops will be significantly reduced. When an officer has discretion as one of his instruments of education, he can approach a traffic stop more relaxed and can leave a traffic stop more confident that justice was accomplished.

Discretion is defined as "the freedom or authority to make decisions and choices." Some traffic officers are leery of the idea of discretion because the term has been misused by drivers. For example, "Come on, officer, can't you use some discretion here?" translates as "Can't you let me get away with this without giving me a ticket?" But discretion does not mean giving somebody a break. It means considering the relevant factors in a situation, with the result that the officer may issue a citation or a warning.

Some people in law enforcement think that discretion is up to the judge and not to the police officer; that is, they believe that the officer's job is to issue a citation for every violation and let the judge decide if it was just or not. This thinking implies that justice is the sole job of judges and not of police officers. However, no judge would feel that his power is being usurped by an officer who handles a situation reasonably and prudently on the street, preventing it from taking the court's time.

Discretion as Standard Procedure

Discretion for a traffic officer means that he considers three factors as a standard procedure:

(1) *Should the driver have known that what he did was illegal?* Some vehicle laws (e.g., it is illegal to drive through a red light) are well known. Other laws are little known; for example, in many states it is illegal to make a "U" turn in a business district. Some laws are unclear to the average driver; for instance, when a pedestrian in a crosswalk stops and signals the driver to pass in front of him, is it legal for the driver to proceed or must the driver enter into a contest to see who is more polite? In some states a pedestrian can waive his right-of-way, while in others he cannot.

The reasonable officer weighs this factor in his decision and judges whether the driver violated a law that the average driver should know or whether there was some legitimate confusion surrounding the circumstances of the violation.

(2) *What was the extent of the violation and the hazards it created?* One driver may slide through a stop sign at an otherwise vacant intersection at four miles per hour, and another through a crowded intersection at fifteen miles per hour. Both drivers violated the law, but will justice be served equally well by citing both drivers? In one set of circumstances the answer could be "yes," while in another it could be "no."

For example, the driver who goes through a stop sign at fifteen miles per hour may state casually that he was in a hurry and did not want to waste time stopping. An officer may choose to cite this driver because the driving was hazardous and the driver seemed unconcerned about it. Another person may go through the same stop sign at fifteen miles per hour but when stopped will apologize, stating that he is ill and trying to get home or is a physician responding to a legitimate emergency. In this case, the officer may choose not to cite him, warning the driver about the hazardousness of the driving but appreciating the presence of extenuating circumstances.

(3) *What was the driver's intent?* One driver may be a tourist with a spotless driving record who was distracted looking for a street and failed to see a stop sign. A second driver, a resident of the town, fails to stop at the sign because he is late for work or thinks it is a "stupid sign." The reasonable officer weighs what action on his part will be the most educational experience for each driver.

There are no obvious answers to any of these three situations. The officer must take all three factors into consideration when making a judgment.

Lack of Discretion

Officers who do not use discretion tend to have one or more of the following traits:

1. They are authoritarian personalities who can only think in terms of right or wrong; there is no in-between. To them, the law is the law and is synonymous with justice. They fail to realize that the law is only one instrument of justice and that reason, prudence, and understanding are coinstruments.

2. Because they are lazy, they find it easier to write a citation or just to issue a warning, not wanting to expend the energy that a discretionary process requires.

3. They think that the only way to teach somebody a lesson is to make them pay. They fail to realize that "overkill" can teach a lesson that is opposite to the one desired. For example, the tourist with a spotless record who is issued a citation possibly would learn only that police officers are "robots" without much reason or understanding.

The reasonable officer who uses discretion at a traffic stop will find work more rewarding and his self-concept more positive.

Specific Problems

There are two traffic stop situations that require the officer's special attention: the presence of passengers and the intoxicated driver. When officers have a preconceived plan of action, they are better equipped to handle these situations. The following discussion of some considerations and principles can help an officer formulate some general guidelines for such a plan.

The Presence of Passengers. Passengers in the vehicle often intrude upon the communication between the officer and the driver on a traffic stop. It is helpful for officers to be prepared should this occur.

The intrusion may be merely inquisitive, such as "Officer, what did he do wrong?" Depending on the situation, the officer might reply politely, "Sir, I think it would be easier for all concerned if I explained the situation to the driver, and he can explain it to you later," or he might briefly explain the situation to the passenger. However, giving explanations can invite the passenger to argue with the officer, even when the driver is being cooperative.

At other times passengers intrude in belligerent ways. For example, a wife may come to the defense of her husband by leaning over and shouting at the officer, "He most certainly did stop at that stop sign! Why, I was just thinking to myself, 'Harold certainly made a beautiful stop at that sign;' when all of a sudden I saw your red lights."

The best tactic is to ignore belligerent remarks by passengers as if they were not heard. The officer who gets involved with belligerent passengers is forced into a "no win" situation. No matter what the officer says or how he says it, it will only add fuel to the fire.

It helps to understand that passengers intrude because they are embarrassed for the driver and want to prove their loyalty, whether or not the driver violated the law. It is the passenger's way of saying to the driver, "I still think you're a good person." If the officer can understand this situation, he is less likely to take the intrusion personally.

Sometimes the driver with passengers will be defensive with an officer in an attempt to save face in front of family or friends. If the officer can understand that this is not a personal affront but merely the driver's way of saying to the passenger, "I want you to view me as a responsible person who would not violate the law," the officer can deal with it more easily. To respond to the challenge will create a negative exchange that will not be resolved.

On the officer's part, he should not unduly embarrass the driver in front of friends. If it is a routine stop and the driver seems comfortable remaining in the vehicle with his passengers, the officer should not act in a way that will demean the driver in front of friends. The attitude that says, "I'm afraid you made a mistake, and I'll have to issue you a citation," is the officer's best approach. If he feels it is appropriate to discuss the violation at length with the driver, it is better to invite the driver to step out of the vehicle and outside the passengers' hearing range.

When the driver has his small children in the vehicle, the officer should never make the parent look bad in front of them. An officer can issue a citation to a parent in a matter-of-fact way, just as a cashier at a store can say, "Oops, you're a dollar short." Because children are very impressionable, the way the officer acts and the way the officer treats the parent may leave an imprint on the child's mind. Even when the driver assails the officer, the officer can manage a smile to the children that says, "Your mom and dad are upset with me, but everything is going to be all right."

Intoxicated Drivers.   Because the behavior of many intoxicated drivers is erratic, they pose a special problem to traffic officers. While officers cannot predict the behavior of intoxicated drivers, they can learn to predict *their own* behavior when they work from a standard procedure. If both the behavior of the intoxicated driver *and* that of the officer are unpredictable, the traffic stop will be chaotic.

The following considerations can be helpful in creating a format for dealing effectively with intoxicated drivers:

(1) Because the thinking of intoxicated drivers is often impaired, using logic with them is both futile and frustrating. Some officers waste a lot of time trying to use logic to convince intoxicated drivers of their erratic driving or intoxicated state. These officers harbor the unrealistic expectation that the eighth or tenth explanation will sink in and the driver will become agreeable. A point should be explained twice when necessary, and if the point is not understood, the officer should take the appropriate next step. Intoxicated drivers often understand nonverbal communication better than verbal communication.

(2) Intoxicated drivers are often unpredictable, so an officer cannot make accurate assumptions about their behavior at first glance. Sometimes officers size up such a driver and make judgments that they regret. For example, it is not uncommon for an officer to think to himself or to say to a partner, "Ah, this guy looks harmless"; "This guy's cool; he'll play ball with us"; or "This guy's so drunk he can't move." One wonders how many dead or injured officers made this type of diagnosis a minute before they were struck.

An intoxicated person can be cooperative and even jovial for ten minutes and instantly lose control. This is why officers should never turn their backs on intoxicated drivers, even when they seem mellow, or allow an intoxicated driver to remain in the vehicle with the key in the ignition, even when the officer is standing next to the driver. In addition, officers should never allow an intoxicated driver out of their immediate control. Immediate control means that the officer is carefully watching the driver and is within one arm's length. Officers working alone sometimes make the mistake of allowing the intoxicated driver to stand by his own vehicle, to wander around the scene, and to approach and talk with bystanders. These officers naively think that the intoxicated driver will not drive off, fall in front of traffic, or assault a bystander who may make a ridiculing remark. If the intoxicated driver does any of these things, someone will get hurt and the officer and the department will be civilly responsible for the damages.

(3) When their thinking is impaired, intoxicated drivers cannot make good decisions even though they may momentarily appear lucid and sensible. An intoxicated driver may suggest that his wife, who may appear totally sober and be willing to cooperate, be allowed to drive. Yet the wife may have had more to drink than the husband and be five blocks away from lapsing into a stupor. The same driver may suggest that he take a taxi home, yet be five minutes away from assaulting the next person who angers him. After carefully evaluating the situation, the traffic officer must assume that his ability to make appropriate decisions is better than that of the driver. The officer must trust his own feelings and conclusions and not allow himself to be talked out of them, no matter how persuasive the driver is. The

officer's decision does not require a consensus with the driver and the passengers.

(4) Sometimes intoxicated drivers become belligerent, assuming the attitude "You can't tell *me* what to do!" Because of the anger and power that has been released by their drinking, intoxicated drivers sometimes successfully wrestle control of the traffic stop from the officer. Soon the intoxicated driver and the officer are negotiating solutions, with the driver holding the upper hand. When this occurs, it is already too late to salvage the success of the traffic stop.

Intoxicated drivers should be treated as any other driver, with the officer listening to and talking with the intoxicated driver as they would anyone else. But it is generally a mistake to make allowances for intoxicated drivers that an officer would not make for any other driver. Intoxicated drivers, and especially alcoholic drivers, are masters at manipulating, confusing, and shifting the focus from themselves to gain leverage in a situation. The more allowances the officer makes for this behavior, the more he is creating a problem that could have regrettable consequences.

(5) The best attitude for officers to take toward intoxicated drivers is a *friendly* but *firm* one. It is best to be friendly because intoxicated drivers often look for trouble; if they sense a ridiculing or hostile attitude in an officer, it could easily trigger a difficult situation. Friendly means being good-natured, helpful, and understanding. It does not mean that the officer thinks the intoxicated driver is comical, because that can create another set of difficulties.

Firm means that the officer explains everything twice (when necessary) and then takes action. An officer who is firm shows no indecisiveness. He should reach a point very soon in dealing with the intoxicated driver where he knows whether the driver is intoxicated or not and what action he is going to take. As soon as the officer knows what must be done, he should do it. Being firm also means that the officer does not change his mind. Once an intoxicated driver sees that he can get the officer to change his mind on one point, it opens the door to more manipulation and negotiation. It is better for the officer to appear inflexible than indecisive.

If the officer has decided to arrest the driver, the driver should be immediately handcuffed and escorted into a patrol vehicle. Any necessary conversation can be conducted within the safety of the patrol vehicle. Perhaps the biggest mistake officers make with intoxicated drivers is that they prolong the situation, with every unnecessary minute creating a new and different opportunity for problems to arise.

A related consideration is the indecision that an officer may experience with the "borderline drunk." For all practical purposes, there is no such thing as "borderline drunk." If an officer has to expend energy assessing whether or not a driver is sober enough to drive, then the driver should not be allowed to drive. It is perilous to allow such a driver to continue to drive, praying that he will make it home safely. If the driver does not arrive safely, the officer and the department will be civilly liable. Each police department should have a general policy dealing with so-called borderline drunk drivers that is sensible and clear.

In summary, officers can approach a traffic stop in one of two ways. They can approach the stopped vehicle with a "blank tablet"; that is, they will have no plan and necessarily will be *reactive* to whatever occurs at the stop. By being forced to react, they are at the mercy of the situation and may never gain control. Or, the officer can approach the stopped vehicle with a general plan of action that enables him to be *active;* that is, the officer will take control during the traffic stop. The officer with a plan of action approaches each stop more confidently, which significantly increases the chances for the stop to be successful.

SUMMARY

At each traffic stop the officer should have two goals: (1) to educate the person as to the hazardousness of his driving and (2) to control the traffic stop so that avoidable conflict will be prevented or at least minimized.

Whether or not these goals are satisfactorily met depends upon the personality of the officer; how effectively the officer communicates; how well the officer follows a plan; and whether or not he uses discretion. The officer cannot dictate the driver's reactions, but if the officer controls his own behavior, he will have control of the situation.

DISCUSSION QUESTIONS

1.   Because officers are human, no one is a "helpful" officer at every traffic stop. Knowing yourself, which of the three unhelpful roles would you be likely to slide into under stress?

2.   Which of the three problematic drivers would you personally have the most difficulty dealing with? Why?

3.   Respond to the following statement: "My job isn't to *communicate* with people who break the law. My job is to issue citations — that's all the communication people need."

4.   Why is it so difficult not to "bite" at irrelevant communications, such as, "Officer, don't you have anything better to do?" Officer: "Sir, I don't tell you how to do your job; don't tell me how to do mine."

5.   Of the four nonlegitimate purposes for a traffic stop (e.g., to sell a citation), which would you tend to use?

6.   What do you least agree with in this chapter? Why?

chapter

7

Traffic
Direction

The maintenance of a free and orderly traffic environment is of primary concern to any traffic enforcement agency. Among the functions of traffic control, the importance of traffic direction cannot be overemphasized. Ordinarily, traffic control devices and signals are sufficient to handle most traffic situations. Their primary function is to regulate, guide, and warn traffic along with the assignment of rights-of-way. Occasionally, predictable and unpredictable variables occur that are disruptive to the normal traffic flow (i.e., major sporting events, electrical failures, traffic signal failures, traffic accidents, and highway blockages). Events such as these may necessitate manual traffic direction and control.

SIGNALS AND GESTURES

When an officer has to direct traffic it is his job to tell people how, when, and where they may move in vehicles or on foot. Therefore, the officer must pay attention to cars, pedestrians, and bicyclists and see to it that they are given a chance to proceed. There is a natural tendency to overlook pedestrians and bicyclists. Actually, what the officer does is tell them how to behave. If he were not on hand to make decisions and direct movements when traffic is heavy, drivers and pedestrians would foolishly try to move at every chance. This causes repeated traffic jams. Motorists would also, without realizing it, get into dangerous situations that they did not anticipate.

The officer's most important job while directing traffic is to let drivers and pedestrians know what he wants them to do. If they do not understand him, they will have trouble and so will he. The instructions that follow were

133

developed to facilitate the communication process between the traffic director and the highway user. That is, they show the officer how to make his meaning clear to drivers and pedestrians.

Drivers are not often where they can hear an officer when he wants them to respond, so the officer cannot just talk to them. He has to use a type of sign language that is clearly understood by everyone. The officer could, of course, motion drivers to stop, start, or turn in many different ways. Suppose that he does it in a way that is entirely his own and different from all others who direct traffic. Perhaps some of the drivers approaching the officer's corner would catch on, but most of them would be puzzled. Since they have never come across such motions before, they would probably fail completely to understand the directions and ignore the officer. Therefore, it is important in directing traffic for *all officers to do it the same way.* Equally important, the gestures should be made where the driver can see them from a reasonable distance.

Directing Traffic by Hand

When directing traffic by hand the officer must let people know that he is in command. To project this image the officer must stand where he can be seen and as though he means business. To combat fatigue and be able to stand for sustained periods, he should stand straight with weight distributed equally on each foot. When not signalling, his hands should hang easily at the side (see fig. 7-1). He should not face vehicles he has authorized to move but stand with his side toward them. This stance conveys a message that tends to be less disruptive of normal traffic movement.

The assignment of right-of-way to cross traffic is accomplished by first stopping through traffic. To stop traffic the officer extends an arm, points a finger, and looks straight at the driver he wants to stop. The officer holds this position until the driver sees him, then with arms extended the officer

Businesslike   Casual

FIGURE 7-1

Stance

exhibits the palm of the hand toward the driver until he stops (fig. 7-2). When traffic is flowing in both directions, the officer stops one side and then the other (fig. 7-3). He should not lower either hand until both directions stop.

To start traffic that is stopped, the officer must decide which side of traffic is to be started first. Then he extends an arm and points a finger toward the car he wants to proceed. After gaining the driver's attention, with palm of hand facing upward, the officer swings his hand up and over to the chin (fig. 7-4). This motion involves bending the elbow. If traffic is to be started from both directions, he starts one side, drops the arm, then starts the other side. The officer may emphasize the same signal to proceed for timid or slow drivers.

Right turns require the least direction and signalling. The arm the officer signals with will be determined by the car's direction in relation to his position at the time it approaches. When a vehicle is approaching from

Point   Exhibit Palm

FIGURE 7-2

Stopping Traffic

Stop One Side   Then The Other Side

FIGURE 7-3

Stopping Traffic from Both Directions

FIGURE 7-4

Starting Traffic

FIGURE 7-5

Right Turns

the right, the officer points toward the driver with the right arm, then swings the arm toward the direction of the intended turn (fig. 7-5).

Left turns require more effort on the officer's part. He must be constantly aware of opposing traffic. When appropriate, he halts opposing traffic with the right hand and holds it. Then with the left hand, the officer points to the driver desiring to turn left and gives the signal to turn (fig. 7-6).

Positioning of left-turning vehicles is important, especially when cars are holding up traffic while waiting for an opportunity to turn (no left turn lane available). The officer points to a spot on the highway near him where a car can wait, thus clearing the traffic lane for through traffic. This procedure works best when only one car is trying to turn left. When a larger number are present, there may be a need to assign the right-of-way to the left-turning vehicles.

Two Officers Signalling.   The magnitude of a traffic problem may be such that more than one officer is needed to control the situation. When two officers are working together at one location, one of the two must originate

FIGURE 7-6

Left Turns

all signals and gestures. The reason for this is obvious. When two originate signals, conflicts will occur and occur quickly. The net effect could be total chaos rather than a smooth operation. One officer should always be in charge. It would be wise to assign responsibilities with regard to who will be responsible for each traffic entrant. For example, one officer should direct all north- and westbound traffic including turning movements, and the other all south- and eastbound traffic including turning movements.

Signalling Aids

Signalling aids consist of whistles, flashlights, and voices. The whistle, when used, should make sharp and distinct sounds. The following signals with the whistle are universal: go — two short blasts; stop — one long blast; and attention getter (daydreamer) — several short blasts.

The voice is seldom used in directing traffic. Arm gestures and the whistle are usually sufficient. Verbal orders are not easy to give or understand. However, some talking may be necessary, and if used, the officer must be polite and brief. Simple and concise statements are a must. Conversation should be avoided unless time permits brief explanations to insistent motorists.

INTERSECTION CONTROL

The officer's responsibility is to regulate crossing traffic. He should determine whether east-west or north-south traffic will move and for how long a period of time without interruption. He must control turning movements; coordinate vehicle movement at the intersection with adjacent intersections; detour traffic when necessary; supervise signal obedience and, if necessary, direct traffic to disregard signal indications; protect pedestrians and prevent them from illegally crossing the highway; prevent illegal parking and vehicles from stopping at locations that will interfere with traffic movement; provide for the safe passage of emergency vehicles; assist persons seeking information or assistance when time permits; and handle accidents within the area of his control until an accident investigation unit arrives. This list of responsibilities is not all-inclusive; however, it is a representative sample.

Positioning at intersections is important for efficient traffic directing. It was pointed out earlier that the officer should stand where he can be seen. Some common positions are center of the intersection, corner of the intersection, and center entrance to the intersection (see fig. 7-7).

The best position within a controlled intersection may be any one of these positions, depending on the type of intersection and prevailing traffic condition. Within the uncontrolled intersection the corner position is usually the best. As far as irregular intersections, multilane intersections, and divided highway intersections are concerned, the officer will have to

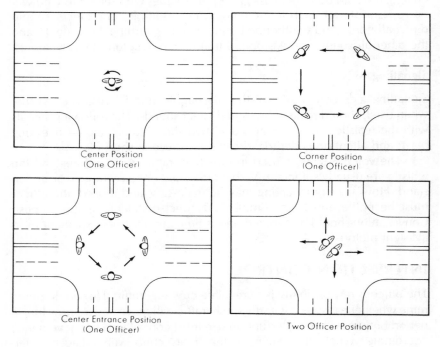

Center Position
(One Officer)

Corner Position
(One Officer)

Center Entrance Position
(One Officer)

Two Officer Position

FIGURE 7-7

Intersection Positions

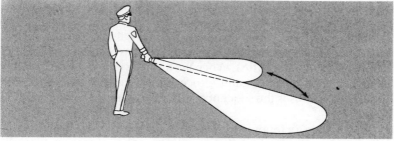

Direct Light Across Path

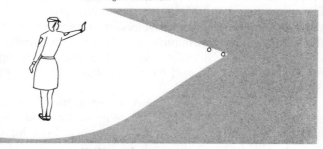

Use Normal Signals

FIGURE 7-8

Flashlight Use

adjust to the situation. More than one officer may be needed to adequately control the intersection.

Any time a position other than the center position is used, a systematic pattern should be developed. Ordinarily, one criterion is that movement should be unidirectional (moving in the same direction to reach each position).

The flashlight is intended for nighttime use. Several techniques have been developed and adopted for effective use of the flashlight. To stop traffic, the officer slowly swings the flashlight at arm's length across the path of approaching traffic. When headlights illuminate the officer, he reverts to the regular hand signals and gestures (fig. 7-8). The main purpose of the flashlight is to attract the attention of drivers. Its directional effectiveness is limited. However, when some lighting is present, the officer can signal to keep traffic moving. It must be recognized that a too rapid flashlight movement will decrease its effectiveness.

Traffic can be overregulated. Needless regulation will cause motorists to wait to be directed. At signalized intersections it is recommended that traffic be directed in a manner that is familiar to drivers. This means that at a particular intersection traffic direction should follow the same sequence as the traffic signal. This is recommended whether controls are functioning or not functioning. The former is obvious; however, the latter may not be so obvious. For instance, a signal customarily assigns the right-of-way to the left turner in left-turn lanes first. When the turning vehicles have cleared the intersection, then through traffic proceeding from the same direction is allowed to go. If this is the sequence, then this is the way traffic should be directed.

The rationale for following customary patterns is that drivers are prone to follow patterns with which they are familiar. Directing them in familiar paths eases the communication process. Typically, the traffic stream has a high concentration of repeat travelers and the ease in which they follow an officer's direction helps minimize traffic conflicts. Further, no decision is necessary on the officer's part as to how he will assign the right-of-way. If he knows the intersection and the signal sequence, he simply follows the sequence.

An officer may, on occasion, direct traffic in conjunction with a functioning signal. The traffic situation is such that the signal is not adequate to control traffic by itself. This may be a high-volume traffic situation with frequent demands for left turns and few turning opportunities. In most cases, the signal will do most of the work; however, action on the officer's part will be required from time to time. He will be afforded more time to be alert for symptoms of jamming. At the same time he must anticipate signal changes.

All exits of the intersection must be watched. If the intersection starts to fill up, the officer must try to prevent complete blockage. The officer should check the traffic stream and allow cross traffic to cross when practical. He can anticipate congestion and attempt to prevent vehicles from entering the intersection unless they have ample exit space.

The officer must be alert for blockage between intersections. Double parking, unauthorized loading, and minor accidents may be the cause for blockage. He determines the reason for mid-block horn blowing and, if necessary, leaves his post and clears the obstruction.

The officer can prevent tie-ups by making certain that motorists trying to make left turns do not hold one or more lanes of traffic up. He may have to use "no turn" signs or resort to detours.

A list of general rules for smooth operation during intersection control include:

1.   Use uniform signals and gestures.

2.   Try to break traffic at natural gaps whenever possible.

3.   In the absence of normal breaks, try to break the line behind slow-moving vehicles such as large trucks.

4. Keep stragglers and daydreamers alert and rolling and in their proper lane.

5. Do not get excited.

6. Do not leave a position just to bawl out a driver.

7. Look cheerful; be cheerful, but be firm.

FLARE PATTERNS

Highway flares (fusees) are used temporarily to control traffic for a relatively short period of time until the situation requiring their use can be corrected or until other devices have been installed and maintained by the appropriate agency responsible for maintaining the particular highway. Of the many events requiring the warning of oncoming traffic, the most prevalent is the traffic accident.

When an officer arrives at an accident scene, he should do several things. First, he should immediately assess the situation. The officer should visually check the scene and take notice of hazards and blocked lanes. He decides whether a flare pattern is needed, and if so, what pattern to use. Occasionally, passing motorists will have placed flares at the scene. If flares are already placed on the roadway upon the officer's arrival, it may be necessary to rearrange the pattern to get the desired channeling. Assessing the situation aids in establishing priorities. The handling of emergencies according to relative importance is essential.

When two officers are present, one should immediately establish a flare pattern if the obstruction cannot be readily moved and the other should handle other emergencies at the scene. A single officer should immediately establish a flare pattern unless first aid is urgently needed. In some situations he may have to utilize the aid of the public. Usually they are very willing to help. When the officer is alone at the scene, he places flares in a criss-cross pattern or stack so that when the first flare has burned out, it will light the next flare (figure 7-9).

Thought should be given to the proper location of flares to give approaching drivers a chance to slow down before coming upon the obstruction and to channel traffic into a safe path around the accident. Where the officer places the flares will vary depending upon the accident, the roadway, weather conditions, and what the officer wishes to accomplish. When investigating accidents near curves and crests, he should always put flares out on the other side of the curve or crest to warn the oncoming drivers that a hazard is present just around the corner or just over the hill (see figures 7-10, 7-11, 7-12, and 7-13 for flare positions).

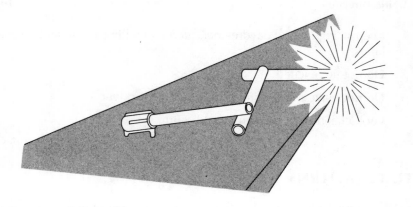

FIGURE 7-9

Stacking of Flares

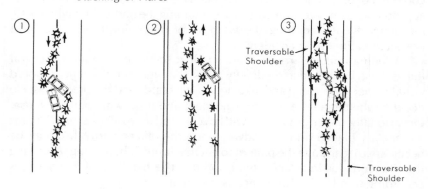

④ STOP AND GO—SINGLE LANE
TRAFFIC DIRECTION

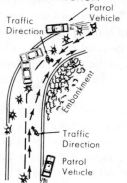

⑤ BLIND CURVE—
ONE LANE BLOCKED
TWO-WAY TRAFFIC
DIRECTION

Flares placed in both directions,
distance determined by sight
distance. They should be placed
ahead of the curve and should
gradually divert traffic away from
and around the blocked area.

FIGURE 7-10

Flare Positions on Two-Way Roadways

142

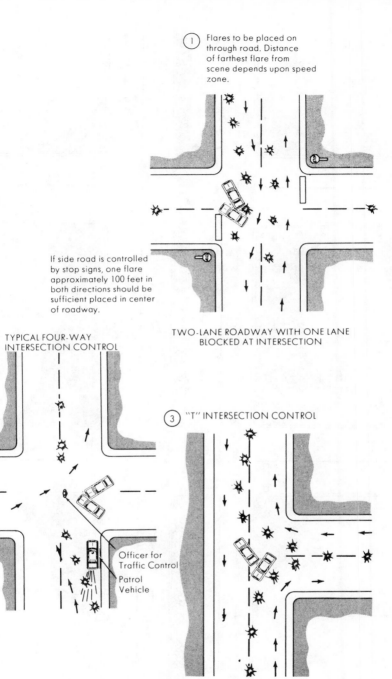

① Flares to be placed on through road. Distance of farthest flare from scene depends upon speed zone.

If side road is controlled by stop signs, one flare approximately 100 feet in both directions should be sufficient placed in center of roadway.

TWO-LANE ROADWAY WITH ONE LANE BLOCKED AT INTERSECTION

② TYPICAL FOUR-WAY INTERSECTION CONTROL

③ "T" INTERSECTION CONTROL

Officer for Traffic Control
Patrol Vehicle

FIGURE 7-11

Intersection Flare Positions

143

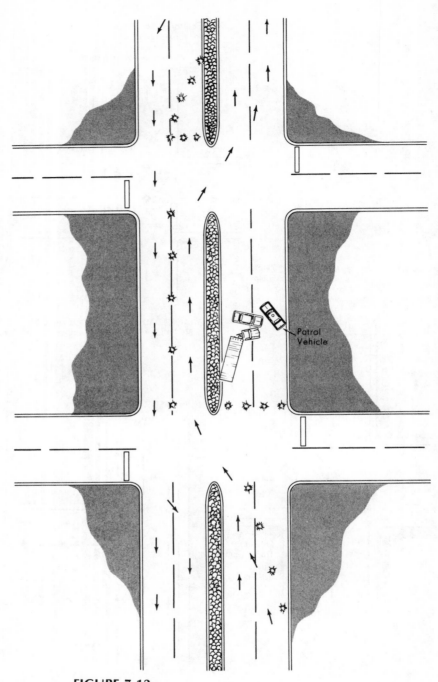

FIGURE 7-12

Expressway Flare Position

144

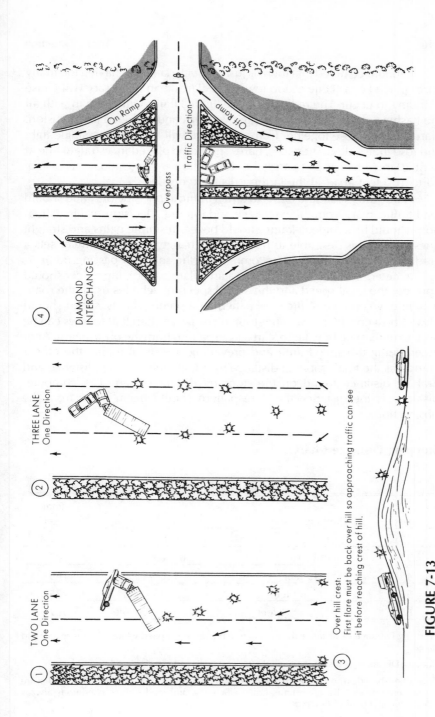

① TWO LANE
One Direction

② THREE LANE
One Direction

③ Over hill crest:
First flare must be back over hill so approaching traffic can see it before reaching crest of hill.

④ DIAMOND INTERCHANGE

On Ramp

Off Ramp

Overpass

Traffic Direction

FIGURE 7-13

Freeway Flare Positions

It should be noted that there is just as much danger in having too many flares placed at a scene as too few. More flares than necessary will cause blending to occur. The red glow of the lighted flares will blend in with all the flashing red taillights of stopping vehicles and will lead to confusion. Flares set too close together from a distance will blend into a single light and lose their value. Therefore, flares should be placed in a straight line at least 20 to 25 feet apart nearest the obstruction with a gradual increase of 50 to 100 feet apart at the farthest distance needed.

Flare patterns should be set to direct traffic to one side only and should lead traffic away from the wreckage and injured. Decision-making situations should be avoided. Traffic should be led in simple paths and straight lines. When it is desirable to have traffic change lanes, the officer sets a gradual alignment that will accommodate the speed of passing traffic.

In determining how far away to start a flare pattern, the officer should consider the legal speed and the actual speed of vehicles using the roadway in developing a traffic flare pattern at a scene. That is, speed should always be a consideration. The stopping distance chart that follows can be used to determine how far to start a flare pattern from the obstruction. After ascertaining the speed limit and prevailing speeds of traffic, the officer computes the total stopping distance by adding the thinking distance and braking distance found on the stopping distance chart. The computer distance is the distance the flare pattern should begin away from the obstruction.

Stopping Distance Chart

PASSENGER CARS ONLY

Speed	Thinking Distance	Braking Distance	Total Feet
25	27 feet	34.4 feet	61.4
35	38 feet	67 feet	105
45	49 feet	110 feet	159
55	60 feet	165 feet	225
65	71 feet	231 feet	302

Thinking Distance — distance traveled before brakes are applied while driver is reacting to danger.

Braking Distance — distance traveled after brakes have been applied.

This table is based on an average reaction time (0.75 second) and passenger car brakes that are 60 percent efficient. Reaction time, brake efficiency, and road surface conditions always affect total stopping distances.

Hazards Associated with Flares

The greatest danger associated with the use of flares occurs during the lighting process. Simple safety rules to be observed are:

1. Ascertain if there is a fire danger before lighting flares such as leaking gasoline, butane, and other flammable substances.

2. Turn head and eyes away before striking flares because they have a tendency to pop when struck.

3. Keep flares away from your body by extending your arm. Dripping molten material can cause serious burns.

4. Stand upwind from flares and hold them downward when using to direct traffic. The toxic fumes being emitted can be harmful if breathed for prolonged periods.

5. Grasp the flare by the end away from the flame and gently tap the burning end on the pavement. Snuff out the flame when the flare is no longer needed.

6. When placing flares at an accident scene, always walk toward oncoming traffic.

Techniques for Lighting Flares

1. Wax sealed cap type
   a. Pull black tab to break the seal and to expose the striking surface on the cap.
   b. Twist the cap off and remove to expose the igniting device of the flare.
   c. Point flare down and away.
   d. Hold cap with striking surface in the weak hand and flare in the strong hand.
   e. Strike the striking surface of the cap downward and away against the device.

2. Plastic cap type
   a. Twist plastic cap off to expose igniting device.
   b. Remove small cover from cap to expose the striking surface of the cap.
   c. Continue the same steps as with the wax sealed type.

3. If on a grade, in high wind conditions, or if the movement of traffic will make the flares roll, use the cap from the flare.

a. After lighting the wax sealed flare:
   (1) Stuff the loose end of the black tab into the cap, forming a loop with the tab. (This should be a reverse loop so that the black top is exposed.)
   (2) Place the cap on the rear of the flare (see fig. 7-14).
b. After lighting the plastic cap type flare, place the plastic cap on the rear of the flare and the extended tip will prevent the flare from rolling (fig. 7-15).

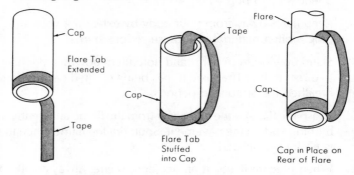

FIGURE 7-14

Wax Sealed Type Flare

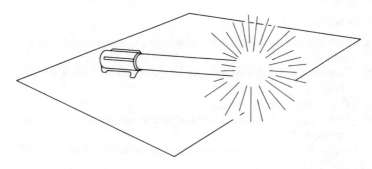

FIGURE 7-15

Plastic Cap Type Flare

SUMMARY

In this chapter, traffic direction was approached on a practical basis rather than a theoretical one. We stressed the importance of using uniform signals and gestures for starting, stopping, and turning traffic. The use of signalling aids such as the voice, whistle, and flashlight was explained along with their relative benefits and limitations.

Intersection control can be simple or complex depending upon the intersection type, location, and traffic therein. The officer should be aware of his important responsibilities associated with intersection control and important traffic variables. Control is exercised when the officer follows traffic signal sequences at signalized intersections and takes the proper position within an intersection.

Although accidents are not the only events requiring flare patterns to warn oncoming traffic, they are the most prevalent. An officer at the accident scene should establish priorities so that he is able to handle emergencies.

Officers should be instructed in the proper placement and alignment of flares. Aids for establishing flare distance requirements, such as the stopping distance chart, were presented as well as a method for computing thinking distance or reaction distance.

DISCUSSION QUESTIONS

1. Discuss the importance of uniform signals and gestures.

2. Discuss the reasons why traffic direction at signalized intersections should follow the normal signal sequence.

3. Discuss why the voice as a signalling aid is seldom used.

4. Discuss the importance of avoiding decision-making situations when laying flare patterns.

5. Discuss why speed should always be considered when developing a flare pattern.

chapter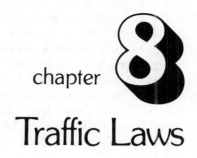

Traffic Laws

Traffic laws evolved with increased use and complexity of automobiles and highway service at the turn of the century. Prior to the development of the automobile, people were accustomed to vehicles being drawn by animals. Maximum speeds were about six miles per hour. The relatively slow speed and animals that instinctively avoided contact with other animals and vehicles provided a relatively comfortable traffic scene. Since then, the traffic scene has changed rapidly. From about 1900 until the present time highway speeds, not necessarily legal speeds, have increased to over 100 miles per hour, and the animal with its instinct for self-preservation has been replaced as the source of power. The increased speed and the loss of an inherent protective system have contributed to the creation of a devastating traffic environment.

EARLY TRAFFIC LAWS

The capacity for greater speed developed faster than people's ability to contend with it. Thus, speed became the focus of controls and restrictions early. Nationally, during the early 1900s speed restrictions were among the first traffic laws enacted. The first state to have a statute regulating speed was Connecticut. In 1901, its speed was limited to twelve miles per hour in town and fifteen miles per hour outside of town.[1] Along with speed laws came the enactment of traffic laws that applied to vehicles meeting, passing, signalling, and operating with specific safety equipment.

---

1. Edward C. Fisher, *Vehicle Traffic Law,* ed. Robert L. Donigan (Evanston, Ill.: The Traffic Institute, Northwestern University, 1970), p. 39.

In contrast, speed was not among the first laws pertaining to the use of vehicles in California at the turn of the century. Those laws in existence stated that all vehicles meeting on a roadway must pass on the right and that one vehicle should give one-half of the roadway to the other vehicle. Later, around 1905, laws were enacted to regulate vehicle registration, drivers' licenses, and speed. A seal two inches in diameter was issued to be displayed on each registered vehicle. A small badge was issued to every chauffeur (operator for hire) who was required to have a driver's license. Speed limits of ten miles per hour were set for in-town travel and twenty miles per hour for out-town travel.

NEED FOR UNIFORM TRAFFIC LAWS

With the mass production of automobiles by Henry Ford (1917-1918), the status of automobiles quickly moved from being a pleasure item to an item of necessity. Since that time the need for traffic laws has become progressively greater. To meet this need, traffic law legislation was provided by various governmental bodies at local and state levels. All too often the laws enacted were not representative of or did not have direct application to the traffic problem. At best, attempts to resolve the traffic problem through legislation were fragmented. Invariably, these fragmented approaches were not comprehensive enough to deal with the real issues. In addition, many of these laws lacked uniformity and were in conflict with each other geographically. Local laws conflicted with state laws, and state laws conflicted with other state laws. This situation created havoc for the motorist crossing geographical boundaries. Further complicating the situation was the lack of uniformity of traffic law enforcement.

UNIFORM VEHICLE CODE

It was soon recognized that uniform traffic laws with national application were sorely needed. What people did not need were laws so binding or rigidly structured that local problems could not be resolved. To deal with this need, a National Committee on Uniform Traffic Laws and Ordinances was formed. In 1926, after much hard work, the first issue of the Uniform Vehicle Code was published. Many states adopted this code as a guideline for state laws. Two years later the Model Traffic Ordinance was published.[2]

The design of the Uniform Vehicle Code was to provide a comprehensive guide and standard for state motor vehicle and traffic laws. It reflected the need for uniform traffic laws throughout the United States. The concept

---

2. National Committee on Uniform Traffic Laws and Ordinances, *Uniform Vehicle Code and Model Traffic Ordinance* (Alexandria, Va.: Michie Company, 1968), p. v.

of uniform laws did not mean that all laws must be the same in all aspects of the highway traffic environment. However, similar situations should be treated with a high degree of consistency as to the type of action contemplated.

The Uniform Vehicle Code's purpose was to provide a guide for the establishment of reasonable and comprehensive traffic codes within each state. The philosophy of the National Committee on Uniform Traffic Laws and Ordinances can be found in their motto, *Salus, Libertas, Lex* — Safety with Freedom Through Law.[3] Traffic legislation is enacted not to impose unnecessary or unreasonable restrictions on highway traffic but to insure that traffic shall flow smoothly, expeditiously, economically, and safely. Furthermore, all highway users should have reasonable protection from being killed, injured, or frustrated by the improper driving practices of others.

RIGHT TO REGULATE TRAFFIC

Needless to say, the issue of states' rights to regulate traffic was raised. In due time this issue was clarified and now the states' power to regulate public highway use is quite clear. The burden of legislating reasonable traffic laws and providing a traffic environment where the drivers can reasonably anticipate how to behave has become the responsibility of most states. Today, all states have reasonably comprehensive traffic codes.

State traffic codes patterned after the Uniform Vehicle Code, except as otherwise expressly provided, are applicable and uniform throughout the state and in all counties and municipalities therein. No local authority can nor shall enact or enforce any ordinance that is in conflict with the state code unless it is expressly authorized. It has been generally accepted by most states that municipalities may legislate on the same subject so long as the municipal ordinance does not conflict with the state law, and if there is no conflict between them, both laws may stand.[4]

However, California is one of the few states limiting municipal authority to enact laws. Local authorities cannot enact or enforce any ordinance on matters covered by the California Vehicle Code unless expressly authorized therein. This means that ordinances substantially similar and those designed to clarify state laws are invalid. Local authorities can enact laws that are supplementary to or in addition to state laws, but they have no power to legislate on matters which are not purely local in nature or on traffic control that is not a local matter.[5] Similarly, statutes in Indiana and

---

3.   Ibid., p. vii.
4.   Fisher, *Vehicle Traffic Law,* p. 126.
5.   *Abbot* v. *City of Los Angeles,* 53 Cal. 2d (Adv) 679, 3 Cal. Rptr. 158, 349 P.2d 974 (1960).

New Jersey prohibit enactment of ordinances covering offenses defined by state law. The Supreme Court of Georgia in *Hannah* v. *State,* 97 Ga. App. 188, 102 S.E. 2d 6214 (1958), held that municipalities do not have the right to duplicate provisions of state laws. The rationale of this case was that ordinances are "local and special laws."

CRIMINAL LAW IMPLICATIONS

For traffic laws to become operative they must be consistent with the principle of criminal law. Criminal law criteria vary among states; however, the degree of differentiation is not that great. In most states violations or offenses take place when prohibited acts are committed or when required acts are omitted. In essence, a crime is committed when one or the other occurs.

Crime is defined as the commission or omission of an act for which there is a prescribed penalty. In most states no act is criminal unless expressly provided by statute. In support of this requirement, the Supreme Court of Nebraska in *Dutiel* v. *State,* 135 Neb. 811, 284 N.W. 321, 324 (1939), ruled that "no act is criminal unless the legislature has in express terms declared it to be so, and no person can be punished for any act or omission which is not made penal by the plain import of the written law." Yet there are some states which operate under the concept of "common law," which consists of doctrine that is not set down in any written statute or ordinance and depends merely upon time-honored usage.

Traffic law statutes consist of various elments *(corpus delicti)* that must be present in each circumstance before an offense is complete. When all the elements are present, the offense is complete regardless of the state of mind of the violator. That is, no specific intent is required of the violator to break the law unless it is specifically expressed in the statute as an element of the offense.[6] Most traffic laws are formulated to make an act or omission unlawful regardless of whether there was intent to violate the law or to do wrong.

Classification of Offenses

Most states have codified provisions for the classification of crime for each law violation. The most common classifications of crimes are felonies and misdemeanors. Some states pattern their classification after federal statutes. Federal statutes identify three categories of crimes: (1) felony, (2) misdemeanor, and (3) petty offense. In the area of traffic laws some states, along with California and New York, classify some traffic offenses as traffic

---

6. *State* v. *Sonoderleiter,* 251 Iowa 196, 99 N.W. 2d 393 (1959).

infractions. In Pennsylvania violations of traffic laws and regulations relating to the rules of the road are designated as "summary offenses" and are not considered crimes.[7]

Generally, a felony is a crime which is punishable by death or imprisonment in a state prison, and every other crime or public offense is a misdemeanor except those offenses that are classified as infractions. A traffic infraction is not a crime, and the punishment imposed should not be deemed for any purpose a penal or criminal penalty or punishment. For example, traffic infractions in California are not punishable by imprisonment; violations require the payment of fines only; and persons charged with an infraction are not entitled to a trial by jury or the services of a public defender.[8]

TRAFFIC LAWS AND INTERPRETATIONS

During our research of traffic laws we found that those states whose laws are closely patterned after the guidelines of the Uniform Vehicle Code are relatively uniform in nature. Since a high degree of similarity of traffic laws exists between states, significant Uniform Vehicle Code sections will be covered in terms of application and court interpretation. It is hoped that the scope of this approach will be broad enough to have widespread application. Because of obvious limitations, we suggest that respective state vehicle codes be used as a primary reference for local and state laws and as a supplement to this chapter.

The clarity of traffic laws is enhanced if one understands the commonly used terms. Major categories to be covered are (1) components of the traffic environment, (2) components of the highway system, and (3) traffic environmental controls.

Components of the Traffic Environment

Components of the traffic environment are of various types. As used in the following context, they are those elements of the traffic environment that are subject to traffic regulations. These elements are identifiable with the term *traffic,* and traffic is defined by section 1-177 of the Uniform Vehicle Code as:

> Pedestrian, ridden or herded animals, vehicles, streetcars and other conveyances either singly or together while using any highway for purpose of travel.

---

7. Pennsylvania, *Vehicle Code,* sec. 1202 (1958).
8. California, *Penal Code,* sec. 19c (1974-1975).

Within the traffic environment some traffic components are encountered more frequently than others. The ones most commonly encountered are vehicles, pedestrians, bicycles, and ridden animals. While using the highway for purposes of travel, each is subject to traffic regulations.

Traffic regulations are designed to control traffic in order to provide a safe and economical traffic environment. Most traffic laws deal with the operation of vehicles upon the highways. The term *vehicle* is too broad, so a more succinct definition is needed. The Uniform Vehicle Code, section 1-184, states that a vehicle is:

> Every device in, upon or by which any person or property is or may be transported or drawn upon a highway, excepting devices moved by human power or used exclusively upon stationary rails or tracks.

The classification of a vehicle is modified by the term *motor;* thus, *motor vehicle* becomes an identifiable term. Also, many traffic laws define violations in terms of motor vehicle operation. The Uniform Vehicle Code, section 1-134, defines motor vehicle as:

> . . . every device which is self-propelled and every vehicle which is propelled by electric power obtained from overhead trolley wires, but not operated upon rails.

An essential part of the operation of a vehicle is the *driver.* A driver is "every person who drives or is in actual physical control of a vehicle."[9] To drive a vehicle means to control its speed or direction while in motion. Thus, steering a car being pushed by another is "driving" it, since the person steering the car is controlling *its* direction.[10] In contrast, steering a towed car is not "driving" since the person steering cannot control the direction of the car.

The operation of a vehicle, which is an integral part of the driving of a vehicle, requires actual physical handling of the controls. One is operating a vehicle when starting the motor of a vehicle; steering a vehicle with the engine shut off while coasting down a sloping highway; or pushing and steering a disabled vehicle down a highway.[11] Being in physical control of a vehicle not only includes "driving" and "operating"; it is more inclusive than either, as was found in the Arizona case of *State* v. *Webb,* 78 Ariz. 8, 274 P. 2d 338 (1954). In this case it was established that "one found asleep in his car with head and arms resting on the steering wheel, the motor running and lights on, is in 'actual physical' control of the vehicle."

---

9. *Uniform Vehicle Code,* sec. 1-114 (1968).
10. *Hester* v. *State,* 196 Tenn. 680, 270 S.W. 2d 321, 47 ALR 2d 568-570 (1954).
11. Fisher, *Vehicle Traffic Law,* p. 276.

Another component of the traffic environment is the pedestrian. A pedestrian is "any person afoot," as defined by section 1-143 of the Uniform Vehicle Code. The actions of pedestrians are regulated, and their responsibilities according to section 11-501, Uniform Vehicle Code, are:

(a)   A pedestrian shall obey the instruction of any traffic device specifically applicable to him, unless otherwise directed by a police officer.

(b)   He is subject to traffic and pedestrian control signals.

The activities of "ridden or herded animals" within the traffic environment are provided for and limited by section 11-104, Uniform Vehicle Code. It states:

Every person riding an animal or driving any animal-drawn vehicle upon a roadway shall be granted all the rights and shall be subject to all duties applicable to the driver of a vehicle . . . , except provisions . . . which by their very nature can have no application.

In modern-day traffic, the number of bicyclists is ever increasing. Of the various devices called bicycles, only those meeting the definition of *bicycle,* as defined by statutes, are subject to traffic regulation. Section 1-105, Uniform Vehicle Code, defines bicycle as "every device propelled by human power upon which any person may ride, having two tandem wheels either of which is more than 14 inches in diameter." According to section 11-1202, Uniform Vehicle Code, "every person riding a bicycle upon a roadway shall be granted all the rights and shall be subject to all the duties applicable to the driver of a vehicle . . . except as to those provisions . . . which by their very nature can have no application."

This list of traffic environment components could be expanded to include variations of those mentioned. For example, motor vehicles include motor trucks, motorcycles, school buses, and specially constructed vehicles. There are limitations imposed on each. The scope of this chapter is limited to broad categories with the intent of conveying some basic concepts and how they relate to the whole scheme of traffic control and investigation.

Components of the Highway System

As stated earlier, traffic laws are designed to control the operations of vehicles upon the highways in order to provide a safe and economical traffic environment. We will now look at some of the components of the highway system, where traffic activities are engaged. For clarity and understanding, again there is a need to define some terms. Inherent within some of the terms are the limits of the traffic environment. With the exception of a few traffic laws which cover off-highway operation of vehicles, the scope of most traffic laws is confined to the operation of vehicles upon the highways.

Alley.   An alley, as a component of the highway system, imposes the same obligation on users as any other street or highway. That is, the usual rules of the road apply. By definition an alley is "a street or highway intended to provide access to the rear or side of lots or buildings in urban districts and not intended for the purpose of through vehicular traffic."[12] Some jurisdictions, by statutes, limit the width of alleys to twenty-five feet or less, exclude alleys intersecting other highways from forming "unmarked crosswalks," and extend alleys to unincorporated areas (communities outside of cities).[13]

Variations in the definition of alley have elicited a variety of court interpretations. In the case of *Irwin* v. *City of Manhattan Beach,* 51 Cal. Rptr. 881 (1966), it was held that ". . . alley does not include 'street' as the lesser does not include the greater. Further an alley differs from a street in quality as well as quantity, in that 'it is a right of way . . . to serve a limited neighborhood for local convenience and not for general passage or travel as in the case of streets,' 64 C.J.S. Municipal Corporation, sec. 1653, p. 24."

The Uniform Vehicle Code, section 1-102, limits alleys to urban districts. As held in North Carolina in the case of *Faw* v. *Town of North Wilkesboro,* 253 N.C. 406, 117 S.E. 2d 14 (1960), "'alley' relates exclusively to a way in a town or city." This case implies that by definition limitations can be set as to where alleys can exist. Namely, they do not exist outside of towns or cities in North Carolina.

Crosswalk.   Since highway users are required to yield the right-of-way to pedestrians using a "crosswalk," it is important to clarify what highway conditions impose such duties. There are two basic conditions regarding the existence of crosswalks. They are "unmarked crosswalks" and "marked crosswalks." The case of *Well* v. *Alderman,* 117 Ga. App. 724, 162 S.E. 2d 18-23 (1968), brought this out when it was ruled that "only two kinds of crosswalks are recognized in the law — a marked or painted one which may or may not be at an intersection, and an unmarked one which may be only at an intersection."

An unmarked crosswalk can be defined as "that part of a roadway at an intersection included within the connection of lateral lines of the sidewalks on opposite sides of the highway measured from the curbs or, in the absence of curbs, from the edges of the traversable roadway."[14] All

---

12.   *Uniform Vehicle Code,* sec. 1-102 (1976).
13.   California, *Vehicle Code,* sec. 110 (1978).
14.   *Uniform Vehicle Code,* sec. 1-111(a) (1976).

states do not include the phrase ". . . connection of lateral lines of the sidewalk on opposite sides of the highway. . . ." However, those states using this phrase by definition imply that an unmarked crosswalk can exist only if a street's sidewalk is intersected and continues beyond such intersection. Therefore, unmarked crosswalks do not exist at "T" intersections at those locations where the sidewalks do not continue beyond the intersection (see fig. 8-1).

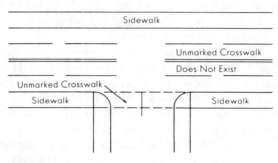

FIGURE 8-1

"T" Intersection

The Supreme Court of Georgia in *Griffin* v. *Odum,* 108 Ga. App. 572, 133 S.E. 2d 910-912 (1963), has held that "there is no 'unmarked crosswalk' where there is no sidewalk on the opposite side of the street with which 'lateral lines' may connect." This case was responding to the Georgia Vehicle Code section defining crosswalk in accordance with the Uniform Vehicle Code section on crosswalk.

At least one state's statute excludes ". . . prolongation of such lines from an alley across a street" from the definition of an unmarked crosswalk. Thus, as previously mentioned regarding alleys, unmarked crosswalks in that state do not exist where alleys intersect with other streets or highways.[15]

The other crosswalk condition, the "marked crosswalk," is straightforward and clear. Its Uniform Vehicle Code definition — "any portion of a roadway at an intersection or elsewhere distinctly indicated for pedestrian crossing by lines or other markings on the surface" — is self-explanatory.[16]

Highway.   The Uniform Vehicle Code's section on rules of the road refers exclusively to the operation of vehicles upon highways. State statutes, likewise providing for the commission or omission of acts upon highways,

---

15.   California, *Vehicle Code,* sec. 275 (1978).
16.   *Uniform Vehicle Code,* sec. 1-111(b) (1976).

necessarily become one of its essential elements. The Uniform Vehicle Code, section 1-122, defines highway as "the entire width between the boundary lines of every way publicly maintained when and part thereof is open to the use of the public for the purposes of vehicular travel" (see fig. 8-2). This definition also defines *street*. *Street* and *highway* are synonymous and interchangeable terms. Those locations outside of these parameters, as a general rule, do not apply to the operation of vehicles. Streets and highways are not just for the use of vehicles. As stated in *Armstrong* v. *Sengo,* 17 Cal. 2d 300 (1949), "streets and highways are maintained for the use of pedestrians as well as for vehicles."

Included within the boundaries of highways are shoulder or sidewalk areas of the road.[17] The shoulder is not required to be paved to be part of the highway. As held in a Virginia case, *Crouse* v. *Pugh,* 188 Va. 156, 49 S.E. 2d 421, 4 ALR 2d 1242-1249 (1948), "the dirt shoulder of a highway is included therein, since it is built not only for the support of the paved surface but also for the protection and safety of highway users. It provides a place where users may drive off the hard surface when necessary, hence is a place 'open to the use of the public for vehicular travel.'"

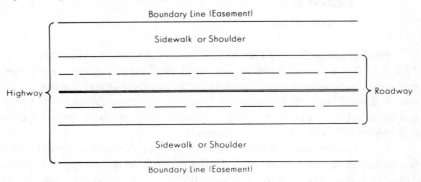

FIGURE 8-2

Highway

Intersection.   Traffic laws prescribing the movement of vehicles at, near, or in an intersection exist in many jurisdictions. Whether such traffic regulations are applicable in a particular situation is frequently determined by what constitutes an intersection within the meaning of the law. The Uniform Vehicle Code, section 1-126, definition of intersection is:

(a)   The area embraced within the prolongation or connection of the lateral curb line, or, if none, then the lateral boundary lines of the

---

17.   *Mecchi* v. *Lyon Van and Storage,* 38 Cal. 2d 474 (1940).

roadways of two highways which join one another at, or approximately at, right angles, or the area within which vehicles traveling upon different highways joining at any other angle may come in conflict (see figs. 8-3 and 8-4).

(b)   Where a highway includes two roadways 30 feet or more apart, then every crossing of each roadway of such divided highway by an intersecting highway shall be regarded as a separate intersection. In the event such intersecting highway also includes two roadways 30 feet or more apart, then every crossing of the two roadways of such highway shall be regarded as separate intersections (see figs. 8-5 and 8-6).

(c)   The junction of an alley with a street or highway shall not constitute an intersection (see fig. 8-7).

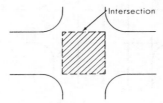

FIGURE 8-3

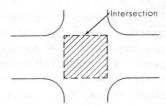

FIGURE 8-4

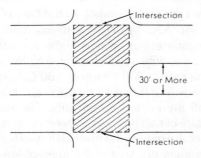

FIGURE 8-5

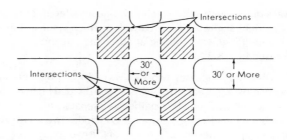

FIGURE 8-6

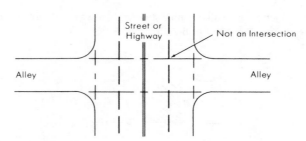

FIGURE 8-7

In *Connors* v. *Dobbs,* 77 Ohio App. 247, 32 Ohio Ops. 552, 66 N.E. 2d 546 (1942), it was said that "where two improved streets or highways intersect, the term 'intersection' means the improved area embraced within the lateral boundary lines of the two streets or highways, as improved, extended to their point of juncture with the lateral boundary lines of the intersecting street and highway, as improved." We find that this court's reasoning is consistent with the Uniform Vehicle Code definition as far as it goes.

In a number of cases an intersection has been construed under the applicable traffic regulation as the area in which vehicles traveling on the respective street may come into conflict. In the case of *Shedlock* v. *Marshall,* 186 Md. 218, 46 A2d 349 (1946), it was held that "an accident occurred within the intersection of two highways intersecting at acute angles when the cars traveling upon respective highways came into conflict." However, in the case of *Bell* v. *Huson,* 180 Cal. App. 2d 820, 4 Cal. Rptr. 716 (1960), it was found that "a collision did not occur within the intersection when all the evidence indicating the point of impact was outside of the boundary of two highways intersection at approximately 55 degrees and outside of the path of the normal flow of traffic which must be considered in determining the area of the intersection."

Strict interpretation of the Uniform Vehicle Code definition of intersection seems to suggest that no intersection exists where intersecting streets or highways do not cross. This thought is derived from the emphasis placed on the prolongations of lateral boundary lines. However, in the case of *Commonwealth* v. *Cassidy*, 209 Mass. 24, 95 N.E. 214 (1911), it was brought out that "intersecting way shall mean any way which joins another at an angle, whether or not it crosses the other." Therefore, "a so-called 'T'-intersection at which one street meets with another at an angle without crossing the other is generally held to constitute an 'intersection' within the means of the application of traffic regulations."[18] It should be noted that the same principles apply to the so-called "Y" intersections.

Roadway.   Some statutory provisions make references to the term *roadway*. The term ordinarily applies to the main travelled portion of the highway. More commonly, roadway is defined as "that portion of a highway improved, designed or ordinarily used for vehicular travel, exclusive of the berm or shoulder" (see fig. 8-2). The terms *highway* and *roadway* as used in statutes are not synonymous. Regulation of traffic is generally in reference to the movement of vehicles on the roadway of a highway.[19]

During hours when designated parking lanes incorporated with the highway system are occupied, some have concluded that the roadway was exclusive of the parking lanes. However, in the case of *Shachunazarcan* v. *Widmer*, 159 Cal. App. 2d 180 (1958), it was held that "a city street is a 'roadway' from curb to curb, since it is open to travel in all of its parts." Generally, under the components of the highway system, we have established the environment within which traffic activities can be regulated. Now we will proceed to traffic environmental controls.

Traffic Environmental Controls

There are a host of traffic regulations covering most conceivable traffic situations in need of controls. A driver, in order to contribute to the safety of the traffic environment, must have some expectation as to what he is being held responsible for while using the highway system. To deal with this issue and as a limiting factor, Uniform Vehicle Code sections selected for discussion were chosen largely because of judgmental factors. That is, these sections require the exercise of reasonable judgment. In many cases people are unable to exercise judgment primarily because they do not understand the traffic regulations.

---

18.   *United States Fidelity and Guaranty Co.* v. *Duet*, La. App. 1, 177 S.O. 2d 302 (1965).
19.   *Bates* v. *Legette*, 239 S.C. 25, 121 S.E. 2d 289, 292 (1961).

Traffic Control Devices. Traffic control devices such as traffic signs, signals, and markings are designed to regulate, guide, and warn traffic. Their purpose is to minimize conflicts between highway users vying for the same space through the assignment of right-of-way. The Uniform Vehicle Code provides that:

> The driver of any vehicle shall obey the instructions of any official traffic control device applicable thereto placed in accordance with the provisions of this act, unless otherwise directed by a police officer, subject to the exception granted the driver of an authorized emergency vehicle in this act.[20]

One type of device provided is the traffic control signal legend, which consists of sequential red, green, and yellow lights. Typically, red means stop, green means proceed, and yellow warns of an impending red light. The greatest burden placed on a driver is the obedience to a red traffic signal. In terms of regulation it is provided that:

> Vehicular traffic facing a steady red signal alone shall stop at a clearly marked stop line, but if none, before entering the crosswalk on the near side of the intersection, or if none, then before entering the intersection and shall remain standing until an indication to proceed is shown.[21]

When someone fails to stop for a red traffic signal, he often raises the question of whether the signal was functioning properly at the time he proceeded through the intersection. A New York case dealing with this question, in response to an officer's testimony that the signal was functioning properly when he returned to check it, said "It is reasonable inference that a traffic device which was properly functioning a matter of minutes after a violation was also properly functioning at the time of the violation."[22]

Provisions of the Uniform Vehicle Code do not prohibit traffic from entering the intersection when the yellow or caution light is exhibited. The only requirement is that traffic not enter or be crossing the intersection when the red or "stop" signal is exhibited.[23] It must be shown the light changed to red prior to entry into the intersection in order to prove that a violation took place.

Following too closely. Many drivers are familiar with the practice of following too closely behind a vehicle proceeding ahead. Sometimes this

---

20. *Uniform Vehicle Code*, sec. 11-201 (1976).
21. *Uniform Vehicle Code*, sec. 11-202(c) (1976).
22. *People* v. *Elsessor,* 52 Misc. 2d 588, 276 N.Y.S. 2d 232-241 (1967).
23. *Atlanta Stone Work, Inc.* v. *Hollon,* 112 Ga. App. 862, 146 S.E. 2d 358, 361, 363 (1965).

is done deliberately and sometimes it is done inadvertently. In any event, it is an extremely dangerous practice that frequently results in personal injuries, death, or property damage.[24]

Statutes sometimes prescribe the distance to be maintained by a motor vehicle from the one ahead — some in general language, such as a "reasonable and prudent" distance, and others in a specified number of feet. In a Maryland case it was held that "the driver of a motor vehicle should not follow another vehicle more closely than was reasonable and prudent having due regard for the speed of such vehicles and traffic upon and the condition of the highway."[25] Typical of statutes requiring specific distances to be maintained is one noted in an Arizona case. It provided that, outside of a business or residence district, the driver of a motor truck should not follow another such truck within 100 feet but might overtake and pass another motor truck.[26]

In formulating a general rule respecting the distance to be maintained between motor vehicles, some courts have stated that the following motorist must remain behind a sufficient distance so as to be able to avoid a collision.[27] In other cases it has been held that this rule was applicable only so long as the driver ahead observed the rules of the road and that the following driver was not required to anticipate unusual contingencies.[28] In any event, the distance maintained according to the standard of reasonable care should be sufficient to avoid danger in the case of a sudden stop or decreased speed by the vehicle ahead under circumstances which are reasonably anticipated by the following driver.[29] Further, it is reasonable for a driver to assume that the car ahead will not stop instantaneously, but at the same time he can not assume that the car ahead will always slow down and travel a short distance before coming to a complete stop.[30]

The Uniform Vehicle Code relative to following too closely provides that "the driver of a motor vehicle shall not follow another vehicle more closely than is reasonable and prudent, having due regard for the speed of such vehicles and the traffic upon and the condition of the highway."[31] The similarity between this section and the language used in the Maryland case is obvious. Since the distance to be maintained is relative, it must be recognized that, in applying the statutory standard, the trier of fact must weigh a great many considerations, including speed, amount of traffic, road conditions, and opportunities for clear vision.[32]

---

24. 85 ALR 2d 613.
25. *Brehm v. Lorenz,* 206 Md. 500, 112 A. 2d 475 (1955).
26. *Southwestern Freight Lines v. Floyd,* 58 Ariz. 249, 119 P. 2d 120 (1944).
27. *Jackson v. Camp and Brown Produce Co.,* 92 Ga. App. 359, 88 S.E. 2d 540 (1955).
28. *Billington v. Schaal,* 42 Wash. 2d 878, 259 P. 2d 634 (1953).
29. *State v. Bush,* O.L.A. 161, 182 N.E. 2d 43-48 (Ohio 1962).
30. *Hibner v. Lindauer,* 18 Wis. 2d 451, 118 N.W. 2d 873-877 (1963).
31. *Uniform Vehicle Code,* sec. 11-310 (1976).
32. *Phillips v. Haring,* 262 Wis. 174, 180, 54 N.W. 2d 200-203 (1952).

Right-of-way. Right-of-way rules are designed to standardize duties and obligations of highway users with respect to the establishment of priority rights between persons at a particular location in a particular situation. They furnish standards by which users may readily determine who has the right to proceed when both are about to use the same highway space. The primary purpose of the regulations is to minimize uncertainty and confusion at intersections and elsewhere and to make movement of traffic both practical and safe.[33] The Uniform Vehicle Code defines right-of-way as:

> The right of one vehicle or pedestrian to proceed in a lawful manner in preference to another vehicle or pedestrian approaching under such circumstances of direction, speed and proximity as to give rise to danger of collision unless one grants preference.[34]

Simply stated, several courts, including California and New York, have said "right of way" merely means a preference to one of two vehicles asserting the right of passage at the same place and at approximately the same time."[35] By definition it is implied that the question of right-of-way arises between two users of the highway only when there is danger of collision between them if both proceed on their respective ways without delay.[36]

An important qualification of right-of-way is that before anyone is entitled to it, the driver himself must be proceeding in a lawful manner. One cannot acquire the right-of-way by violating the law. It was held in a Maine court that right-of-way presupposes approach of vehicles at lawful speed; otherwise, no right-of-way is acquired.[37] In California it has been held that before a vehicle driver is entitled to right-of-way, he must be operating a vehicle within the law and not in violation thereof.[38]

The Uniform Vehicle Code covers various conditions in which right-of-way rules apply. Those selected for discussion are (1) section 11-401, vehicle approaching or entering an intersection; (2) section 11-402, vehicle turning left; (3) section 11-403, vehicle entering a stop or yield intersection; and (4) section 11-502, pedestrians' right-of-way in crosswalks.

Section 11-401   Vehicle Approaching or Entering Intersection

(a)   When two vehicles approach or enter an intersection from different highways at approximately the same time, the driver of the vehicle on the left shall yield the right of way to the vehicle on the right.

33.   *Martin* v. *Stevens,* 121 Utah 484, 243 P. 2d 747-750 (1952).
34.   *Uniform Vehicle Code,* sec. 1-156 (1976).
35.   *Cowan* v. *Market St. Ry.,* 8 Cal. App. 2d 642, 47 P. 2d 752-754 (1935).
36.   *State* v. *McLachan,* 36 Cal. App. 2d Supp. 754 (1939).
37.   *Ricker* v. *Morin Brick Co.,* 22 A. 2d 536-540 (Maine 1966).
38.   *Carley* v. *Zeigler,* 156 Cal. App. 2d 643 (1958).

(b)   The right of way rule declared in paragraph (a) is modified at through highways and otherwise as stated in this chapter.

Paragraph (b) implies that paragraph (a) is designed to regulate traffic at uncontrolled intersections, and on this basis we will proceed. Refer to the section on intersections for clarification as to what a street or highway intersection is within the traffic rule.

When two vehicles approach an uncontrolled intersection at approximately the same time, the vehicle on the left must yield the right-of-way to the vehicle on the right. The two vehicles must not only enter the intersection at the same time but also must by necessity have approached the intersection at approximately the same time.[39] The words "at approximately the same time" do not mean at precisely the same instant. In order for the vehicle on the left to secure the right-of-way, it must enter the intersection at a sufficient interval of time ahead of a vehicle approaching from the right so that it may be said that vehicle did not enter at approximately the same time. Such an interval must be of appreciable duration.[40]

If a driver is so far in advance of a vehicle on his right and has reasonable belief that he can clear an intersection without danger of a collision, the driver on the left may proceed into the intersection. He must not do so where the margin of safety is so narrow that a reasonably prudent person would not test an obvious danger.[41]

Section 11-402   Vehicle Turning Left

The driver of a vehicle intending to turn left within an intersection or into an alley, private road or driveway shall yield the right of way to any vehicle approaching from the opposite direction which is within the intersection or so close thereto as to constitute an immediate hazard.

Responsibility is placed upon the driver of a car desiring to make a left turn to ascertain before attempting to do so that such a maneuver can be made safely and without danger or undue delay to overtaking or oncoming traffic. He must refrain from making a left turn unless the way is clear.[42]

Generally, "immediate hazard" are words which are easily understood and require no special definitions. Their meaning is similar to "imminent peril," "timely warning," and "reasonable warning." As far as the application of law is concerned, "immediate hazard" has no precise set of measurements and must be judged on the basis of common sense in light of existing circumstances.[43]

---

39.   *Smith* v. *Murphy*, 48 Tenn. App. 299, 346 S.W. 2d 276-278 (1960).
40.   *Brower* v. *Stolz*, 121 N.W. 2d 624-627 (N.D. 1963).
41.   *Pugh* v. *Ludwig*, 409 Pa. 577, 186 A. 2d 911 (1963).
42.   *Desormeaux* v. *Continental Ins. Co.*, 153 So. 2d 128-138 (La. App. 1963).
43.   *Lafferty* v. *Wattle*, 349 S.W. 2d 519-529 (Mo. App. 1961).

Some drivers are of the opinion that if they are first in the intersection (controlled intersections) they have the right-of-way. It has been found to the contrary that where vehicles proceeding in opposite directions are stopped momentarily for a traffic control signal, the driver intending to turn left has no right to make a quick left turn across the path of the other, and being first in the intersection does not give him the right-of-way. A driver must give a plainly visible signal of his intention to turn and must ascertain if the turn can be made safely.[44]

Section 11-403 (b)   Vehicle Entering Stop or Yield Intersection

Except when directed to proceed by a police officer or traffic-control signal, every driver of a vehicle approaching a stop intersection indicated by a stop sign shall stop at a clearly marked stop line, but if none, before entering the crosswalk on the near side of the intersection, or, if none, then at the point nearest the intersecting roadway where the driver has a view of approaching traffic on the intersecting roadway before entering the intersection. After having stopped, the driver shall yield the right of way to any vehicle which has entered the intersection from another highway or which is approaching so closely on said highway as to constitute an immediate hazard during the time when such driver is moving across or within the intersection.

The failure to yield right-of-way at a street controlled by a stop sign and failure to stop at a stop sign are separate offenses. One may be guilty of failing to come to a complete stop even though he yielded to oncoming traffic. Conversely, even though a driver came to a complete stop at a street controlled by a stop sign, he may be guilty of failing to yield the right-of-way to traffic approaching so closely as to constitute an immediate hazard.[45]

If a reasonably prudent person does not believe he can pass through an intersection with safety, and a vehicle is approaching so closely as to threaten safety, mere stopping is not sufficient. He must remain stopped and shall not proceed until such movement can be made with safety.[46] If a vehicle approaching on a highway is close enough, considering the rate of speed, so that it would be reasonable to assume that a collision would occur if another vehicle stopped at the entrance of the intersection moved into its path, the stopped vehicle should remain stopped until it is safe to enter the intersection.[47]

The duty imposed upon a driver at a yield sign is less than the absolute duty to stop at a stop sign. The duty to stop at a stop sign is absolute,

---

44. *Wiggins* v. *Ponder*, 259 N.C. 277, 130 S.E. 2d 402-404 (1963).
45. *Parsekian* v. *Cresse*, 75 N.J. Super, 405, 183 A. 2d 426-429 (1962).
46. *Herman* v. *Wohler*, 419 P. 2d 45-47 (Ore. 1966).
47. *Magun* v. *Bemis*, 17 Wis. 2d 192, 116 N.W. 2d 129-133 (1962).

followed by a duty of lookout, including a calculation of interference with the right-of-way of other vehicles. The duty to stop at a yield sign arises after the required efficient lookout, including calculations.[48]

Section 11-502   Pedestrians' Right of Way in Crosswalks

(a)   When traffic-control signals are not in place or not in operation the driver of a vehicle shall yield the right of way, slowing down or stopping if need be to so yield, to a pedestrian crossing the roadway within a crosswalk when the pedestrian is upon the half of the roadway upon which the vehicle is traveling, or when the pedestrian is approaching so closely from the opposite half of the roadway as to be in danger.

(b)   No pedestrian shall suddenly leave a curb or other place of safety and walk or run into the path of a vehicle which is so close that it is impossible for the driver to yield.

A driver has the greater burden of careful lookout and extreme caution at locations provided for the passage of pedestrians, for it is the driver who has the power (because of the dangerous instrument which he controls) to reduce the status of a pedestrian to that of a statistic in a split second. The pedestrian poses no such threat. Because of this burden of response, a driver is entitled to adequate notice of the existence of a street condition that imposes upon him this special duty. A marked crosswalk normally would be clearly identifiable on the street by distinct and adequate markings.[49] Refer to the section on crosswalk for details of the two street conditions of crosswalks.

It may not be commonly known that stop signs do not apply to pedestrians. Stop signs are posted at intersections to control vehicular traffic only.[50] This does not mean that it is open season on drivers at intersections controlled by stop signs. Pedestrians are prohibited from suddenly stepping from the curb into the path of a vehicle that is so close that it is difficult for a driver to yield. A pedestrian is not entitled to the right-of-way even though he is crossing within a crosswalk at an intersection. Regulation patterned after the Uniform Vehicle Code, section 11-502(b), applies when a pedestrian unexpectedly leaves a place of safety at a time when a vehicle is so close it is virtually impossible to stop, but it does not apply when pedestrians are well into the intersection.[51]

Speed.   Two major schools of thought have developed relative to speed restrictions. One group insists speed restrictions should be flexible, de-

---

48.   *Sailing* v. *Wallestad,* 32 Wis. 2d 435, 145 N.W. 2d 725-728 (1966).
49.   *White* v. *McAllister,* 443 S.W. 2d 541-542 (1969).
50.   *Folck* v. *Anthony,* 228 Md. 73, 178 A. 2d 413 (1962).
51.   *Spann* v. *Ballesty,* 81 Cal. Rptr. 229 (1969).

pending upon conditions and circumstances, leaving a wide area of determination for the driver's prudence and judgment. From this school of thought the "basic speed law" concept evolved.[52]

The other school of thought insists the "basic speed law" with greater restrictions leaves too much to drivers' judgment, many of whom cannot be relied upon to make proper decisions. Also, it contends such laws are virtually unenforceable because a question arises in every case, not merely as to the rate of speed but almost exclusively as to the conditions and what was reasonable under the circumstances. Variances in physical and mental abilities of drivers along with limited enforceability of the basic speed law make it essential to provide firm "absolute" limitations that drivers may violate at their peril. From this school of thought the "maximum speed law" concept evolved.[53]

Some states have a combination of the two speed laws: (1) a basic speed law with prima facie limits and (2) an overall (absolute) maximum speed beyond which it is unlawful to proceed under any circumstances. They usually provide for reasonable and prudent speed, with prima facie limits in designated speed zones, and absolute maximum on the open highways. Consistent with uniformity, the Uniform Vehicle Code provides for both restrictions.

Section 11-801   Basic Rule

No person shall drive a vehicle at a speed greater than is reasonable and prudent under the conditions and having regard to the actual and potential hazards then existing. Consistent with the foregoing, every person shall drive at a safe and appropriate speed when approaching and crossing an intersection or railroad grade crossing, when approaching and going around a curve, when approaching a hill crest, when traveling upon any narrow or winding roadway, and when special hazards exist with respect to pedestrians or other traffic or by reason of weather or highway conditions.

Section 11-801.1   Maximum Limits

Except when a special hazard exists that requires lower speed for compliance with section 11-801, the limits hereinafter specified or established as hereinafter authorized shall be maximum lawful speed, and no person shall drive a vehicle at a speed in excess of such maximum limits.

Practically all of the states embody the essentials of section 11-801 in their motor vehicle codes. It is the rule of safety stated in the form of a criminal

---

52.   Fisher, *Vehicle Traffic Law,* p. 223.
53.   Ibid., p. 224.

law and applies regardless of the presence or absence of stated speed limits, either absolute or prima facie.

What is meant by prima facie speed? *Prima facie* limits merely implement the basic speed law and serve as an aid in its enforcement. A prima facie case is complete when it is shown that the accused was exceeding the stated speed limit; that is, the law furnishes a presumption that the accused speed was greater than was reasonable and proper under the conditions. The degree of excess of speed over the stated speed limit is an important factor to be considered by the trier in determining whether, under all the circumstances, a motor vehicle has been operated at a speed greater than was reasonable.[54]

During prosecution all the circumstances enumerated must be taken into consideration, but it is not required that all of them be other than reasonable at the time of the alleged violation. It is for the trier to determine under all of the circumstances, some of which may be favorable to the accused, whether or not the speed was greater than was reasonable at the time.[55]

Absolute maximum speed limits are arrived at through the use of sound engineering practices. They in fact represent reasonable and prudent limits, and the speeds in excess thereof are fairly certain to be dangerous. Generally, maximum speed limits are based upon engineering and traffic surveys on existing highway segments or upon the basis of approaching design standards, and they project traffic volumes in the case of newly constructed highway segments.[56] Maximum limits set a level at which the movement of vehicular traffic would be orderly, reasonable, and safe. Occasionally, other factors influence the establishment of maximum limits, such as the imposition of the 55 mph maximum speed limit for the purpose of energy conservation. Speeds in excess of this maximum limit are not necessarily unsafe as measured by reasonable standards of traffic safety.

Turning from Direct Course.   Multilane highways have greatly promoted safe travel, but at the same time their use has created some problems not associated with the two lanes of traffic proceeding in opposite directions. One problem is the movement of vehicles across right or outside lanes of a multilane highway to leave the road. Statutes in many jurisdictions require that right turns be made from the right lane of travel, or as closely thereto as practicable.[57] The Uniform Vehicle Code, section 11-601, covers these movements similarly. A driver who makes a right turn "wide" so as to

54. *State v. Simon*, 2 Conn. Cir. 642, 204 A. 2d 320-321 (1964).
55. Ibid.
56. California, *Vehicle Code*, sec. 22356 (1978).
57. 7 ALR 3d 282.

permit a car to maneuver between him and the right curb or edge is in violation of such statutes.[58] This positioning criterion applies not only at intersections but also includes turning into private roads, driveways, or elsewhere.[59] When making a left turn, a driver must exercise reasonable care under existing conditions to ascertain whether such movement can be made with safety. It does not mean that he has to refrain from making a left turn unless the circumstances are absolutely free from danger. Infallibility is not required.[60] However, the responsibility is placed upon the driver wanting to make a left turn to ascertain before attempting to do so that such movement can be made safely and without undue delay to overtaking or oncoming traffic. He must refrain from turning left unless the way is clear.[61]

Before turning from a direct course upon a highway, the driver is responsible for seeing that such movement can be made in safety. Whenever the operation of any other vehicle may be affected by such movement, he must give a signal plainly visible to the drivers of such other vehicles of his intention to make the turn. The responsibility for ascertaining that a left turn across a highway can be made safely is placed upon the driver attempting the movement. This rule applies to vehicles changing from one lane to another on multilane highways.[62]

SUMMARY

Traffic laws have but one legitimate purpose — to establish standard rules of procedure to be followed by drivers in the operation of their vehicles so as to promote the safe and orderly flow of traffic. Early development of traffic laws brought about speed restrictions because automobile speed capacity increased faster than people's ability to cope with it. As automobiles increased in number and began to span greater distances, the impact of conflicting traffic regulations became great. Lack of standardization contributed to the confusion of drivers crossing geographical boundaries. The legitimate purpose of traffic laws during this period was not being fulfilled.

The need for uniform traffic laws nationally became evident. A National Committee on Uniform Traffic Laws and Ordinances was formed, and it was responsible for the publication of the Uniform Vehicle Code and Model Traffic Ordinance in 1926 and 1928, respectively. The acceptance of these publications as guidelines has been almost universal.

58. *Luna* v. *Tecson*, 227 Cal. App. 2d 655, 39 Cal. Rptr. 24-28 (1964).
59. *Crouch* v. *Nicholson*, 116 Ga. App. 12, 156 S.E. 2d 384-387 (1967).
60. *Clarke* v. *Holman*, 274 N.C. 425, 163 S.E. 2d 783-786 (1968).
61. *Roy* v. *Edmonson*, 221 So. 2d 583-585 (La. App. 1969).
62. *Barker* v. *Thompson-Hayward Chemical Co.*, 152 So. 2d 649-651 (La. App. 1963).

The evolution of traffic laws went through the processes of conforming to criminal law principles. They were defined as crimes and noncrimes of various classifications: felonies, misdemeanors, petty offenses, infractions, and summary offenses, or some combination thereof depending on the locale.

The application of traffic laws has not been without its difficulties. Over a period of time, law application has been reviewed by the courts and general rules and interpretations have been established. In this chapter we examined selected Uniform Vehicle Code sections in terms of the types of highway traffic interaction within the traffic environment under defined constraints.

When we study court decisions of the period following the advent of the motor, we see a gradual awakening of the judiciary to the preventive nature of traffic laws. This is of great significance, since it is in the courts that the law enforcement efforts culminate. Recognizing that the true purpose of traffic laws is to prevent collisions has been of inestimable value in promoting traffic safety through enforcement of laws enacted for that purpose.

DISCUSSION QUESTIONS

1.   Identify and discuss the major problems confronted by the developers of early traffic laws.

2.   Discuss the pros and cons of adopting uniform traffic laws for local traffic regulation.

3.   Discuss the rationale for designating certain traffic laws as summary offenses or infractions.

4.   Discuss why it is important to define elements of the traffic environment.

5.   Discuss why it is important to define components of the highway system.

6.   Discuss why it is sometimes difficult to apply statutory requirements of traffic laws.

chapter **9**

Accident Investigation

Today, as in the past and as will be in the future, accident investigation will be a constant challenge to law enforcement agencies throughout the United States. Within our modern, contemporary industrial society the automobile has become an integrated, economic necessity. Without it our economy would collapse because neither people nor materials would be capable of movement sufficient to sustain our present way of life.

When physical objects are put into motion, there must be some inherent controls placed upon these objects or there surely will be conflict. The degree of conflict depends upon the space available for movement, the controls placed, and the number and the size of the objects in motion. The objects we refer to are motor vehicles, and the controls are a combination of drivers and the statutory vehicle laws (that govern our behavior) which affect the very operation of these objects. While chemists can effect compounds of materials that combine without occupying additional space, drivers of motor vehicles cannot so blend their conveyances without causing damage, injury, or death. Efforts are continually being made to enlarge the space available to motor vehicle and pedestrian traffic. As more streets are widened and freeways, expressways, toll roads, turnpikes, and the interstate highway system completed, so is there an increase in motor vehicle traffic. Space is not only an intangible passage of openness, but it is also something that may be occupied by various objects of different size and shape. Therefore, every citizen should know that a combination of number and size of motor vehicles will likewise increase space. Thus, conflict is inevitable.

EDUCATION, ENGINEERING, AND ENFORCEMENT

Traffic crashes continue to cause damage and injury so extensive that all citizens are affected either directly or indirectly. Based on past experience, it is a foregone conclusion that traffic collisions cannot be eliminated, but they can be effectively reduced to an acceptable minimum. The problem is attacked by using the techniques of *education, engineering,* and *enforcement.* Through education public interest is stimulated so that all persons not only understand the extent of the problem, but they also become aware of the skills and attitudes necessary to reduce collisions. Properly engineered highways and vehicles reduce both the cause and effects of traffic collisions. The enforcement of governmental regulations aimed toward the reduction of traffic conflict, accidents, and their resulting damage and injury both guide and direct highway users in order to solve our society's transportation problem. Forceful implementation of each of these three measures will produce a three-pronged attack against the traffic problem within every community of our country. If effectively done, it will produce a more orderly system of mobility in our society. The real importance of accident investigation is to determine the who, what, when, where, why, and how these problems were created and how they may be resolved so they do not occur as often. It is also of great importance to the police in relationship to other police activities, and likewise, it is important as a community service. Without a proficient and professional accident investigation program, the entire traffic supervision program will fail or be seriously weakened.

While fatal and critical injury accidents are usually investigated by law enforcement officers dispatched to the scene by police radio, less serious property-damage accidents may not require the same detailed investigation. A growing number of police agencies are saving time and labor by sampling less serious accidents rather than attempting to investigate all of these property-damage-only or minor personal injury accidents.[1]

Information essential for effective planning of the "three E's" is obtained mainly through accident investigation. Accident investigation reports provide one of the few sources of unbiased information available and thus a great public service. Accident investigation is therefore the cornerstone of the foundation of any system or program of traffic supervision. Without accurate information upon which to base plans, this function cannot be progressive or effective.

If planning to prevent accidents is to be valid and productive, it must be based upon consideration of accident causes. To achieve this, there

---

1.   Paul B. Weston, *The Police Traffic Control Function* (Springfield, Ill.: Charles C Thomas, 1969), p. 164.

must be careful investigation, together with complete and accurate reporting, to determine cause. The question then arises, Which accidents should be investigated and reported? Fatal accidents alone, fatal and injury only — or to develop the complete picture, should all collisions be investigated?

The number of damage or injury accidents that occur for each fatality is unknown. Their incidence in cities, with slower speeds, is greater in proportion to the fatal accidents occurring in rural areas, where higher speeds are attained. If planning were based on fatal accidents alone, only about 20 to 25 percent of the total reported accidents would be considered. This is but a small percentage of the total. If planning is expanded to include injury accidents, this base is expanded to about 55 percent of the collisions. However, 40 percent of the known crashes would still not be considered; thus, planning would still be based on only a little over half of the total accidents.

The investigation and reporting of all known accidents is suggested for two reasons — adequate planning and good public relations. No matter how minor an accident may appear to one not directly affected, it is an important matter to those people actually involved. They look to the police for help. Although the police are primarily concerned with the criminal aspects of the investigation, parties concerned expect (and are entitled to) an impartial evaluation of the circumstances so that the rights of all may be protected. The investigator should not attempt to establish civil liability or fix the blame, but he should impartially record the facts so that in the future civil action an unbiased, intelligent, and complete factual record will be available.

However, the time necessarily consumed by investigation of all accidents known to a department may not be available. There is validity in the argument that prosecuting the violator who has caused an accident happens too late to make a difference. The officer's presence on visible patrol, which deters other potential accident-causing violators, is time better spent than in the investigation of minor property damage collisions — especially those in which no violation is immediately discernible. Instead of basing investigations upon the severity of accidents, the professional approach would be to consider the incidents in terms of possible violations — an enforcement viewpoint. Thus, a one-car fatality in which the victim was alone in his car might take a minimum of investigation (in spite of its grave consequences), as contrasted to a property-damage accident involving violations by both drivers. As an enforcement officer, the investigator must not lose sight of his objective. Obviously, the same amount of time cannot be devoted to all minor accidents because there are too many of them. Evaluation of the occurrence in terms of possible violation appears to be a firm basis to use as a guide to investigative effort.

The accident investigator should keep in mind throughout his investigation that the ultimate test of the quality of his work will be the convincing force it carries in the courtroom. Prosecution after the accident is one of the most equitable types of enforcement. Much time is spent in apprehending and citing drivers whose violations might cause an accident. If these drivers are prosecuted, it follows that in all fairness prosecution should be instituted against those whose violations have caused accidents. By pointing out the relationship between collisions and violations, the public may be brought to realize the need for strict enforcement of all traffic laws as a preventive measure. The entire enforcement program will be bolstered by the public as they begin to realize that if traffic violations were not combated by enforcement, a terrific increase in highway casualties would surely result. The philosophy of "haven't they suffered enough already" is no valid reason for failing to prosecute. The fleeing felon who is seriously wounded during an escape attempt undoubtedly suffers from his wound. Society, however, spares no effort to keep him alive in order that he may stand trial for his offense. Why should personal suffering, no matter how great, limit prosecution of the traffic violator?

This type of prosecution is readily understood by the general public. People who witness or are involved in an accident where there is a violation expect the police to do something about it. They are perplexed if nothing is done. Prosecution of violators is an objective lesson to the general public, acts as a strong deterrent, and lessens opportunities for further deaths, injuries, and economic losses. It presents the officer to the public as someone who is doing something tangible for them. It engenders a feeling of protection, which in turn creates a desirable relationship. To the violator it points out that all traffic laws must be obeyed.

In contrast to the crime rates, which steadily increase, the accident rate not only can be but also has been lowered. With increased travel, America's mileage death rate (known as M.D.R. — deaths per 100 million miles traveled) has risen over the past several years. On our nation's highways in 1977, 47,876 persons were killed as a direct result of traffic crashes. The mileage death rate for that year was 3.24 persons killed for every 100 million miles that were traveled. In 1978 deaths rose to an estimated 50,145, for an M.D.R. of 3.27. This was the first time since 1973 (when the estimated deaths rose to a staggering 54,052) that the death toll rose above 50,000.[2] While it is true that the number of fatalities attributed to motor vehicle collisions has risen, it can be seen that the attack against the problem has been successful. The statistics prove that the chance of being killed in an accident has been significantly reduced.

---

2.   U.S. Department of Transportation, *Traffic Statistics for 1978* (Washington, D.C.: National Highway Traffic Safety Administration, 1979), p. 6.

Accident investigation is not only important but also is interesting. The investigator deals with human problems, frailties, and suffering. In turn, he renders a service to humanity. His immediate action may directly save one life and indirectly many lives. Each investigation presents a new challenge, calling for the utmost in skill, knowledge, and ability.

Because of lack of motive, accident investigation is different from other types of police investigations. If the occurrence was planned, it would no longer be an accident. Accidents happen unexpectedly, without design, or by chance. The element of surprise is a part of any traffic accident.

Successful accident investigation requires considerable basic back-, ground knowledge. To know what questions to ask and what to look for, the investigator must have some fundamental ideas about accidents and their causes. To avoid wasting time and making mistakes, especially during the urgent activities at the scene of an accident, the investigator needs to plan what he is going to do and to continually revise the plan as he proceeds.[3]

TRAFFIC COLLISIONS

During recent years, scientists have turned to the word *crash* in preference to the term *accident* in reference to traffic collisions. Their belief is that traffic collisions are *caused occurrences* rather than incidents involving chance alone. In almost every traffic crash there has been human failure — someone has made a mistake by neglecting to obey either traffic laws or the laws of defensive driving. For police investigative purposes, however, *crash* and *accident* may be used interchangeably since the officer's objective is to determine collision cause. Accident investigation offers a challenge to the investigator and gives him an unlimited opportunity to use his initiative, skill, and experience to uncover the factors that caused the crash.

Accident investigators are given the opportunity to perform a public service. Not only are the results of investigations used in research, but officers also render immediate assistance to those involved in the collision. They become the protectors of the suffering. The public views favorably actions to expedite traffic and assist victims of accidents. Such positive actions are necessary in order to elicit public support of enforcement organizations.

Many major arrests will follow accident investigations. These include arrests for misdemeanor and felony drunk driving, manslaughter, hit and run, reckless driving, auto theft, and other crimes. Obviously, a great amount of care must be used in case preparation. Essential evidence must

3. J. Stannard Baker, *Traffic Accident Investigator's Manual for Police* (Evanston, Ill.: The Traffic Institute, Northwestern University, 1966), p. 7.

be recognized, identified, and properly preserved. The investigator must be careful to make a thorough investigation, prepare his case meticulously, and present it well in court. The officer whose work is inadequate will fall short of accomplishing his duty to the people whose rights he is sworn to defend, protect, and uphold.

In civil cases, too, courts have come to rely upon the investigating officer for unbiased and informed testimony. The traffic accident investigator has acquired an enviable reputation in this connection, and judges and attorneys give great weight to the officer's testimony. The investigator should always be conscious of this, and he must realize that a poor investigation or presentation of evidence will destroy the trust that has taken years to build.

In order for the officer to be able to relate the events of the crash, through results of a thorough investigation, to the court and/or other government and civilian agencies, he should have a working knowledge of some of the causes of these same accidents.

First, we must put into some perspective how the puzzle is to be assembled. The operation of an automobile is like a puzzle, where all the pieces must fit properly into place so that we may reach our destination. We consider the route we are to take, the operation of the motor vehicle we are to drive, and at the same time the alternatives available should we need to take evasive action when a hazard appears. One must, of course, be able to recognize a hazard. This calls for a certain amount of driving strategy, or evasive action of an operational nature. There are four steps in one's driving that may be a part of the crash potential: (1) *recognize* the situation that may require some type of action; (2) *anticipate* the potential of an emergency situation; (3) *decide* what action is to be taken and also what *alternatives* are available; and (4) there must be *performance* of what has been decided or the alternative chosen.[4]

At this point the investigator may be able to assemble the pieces of the collision puzzle, which will give the essential *how* of the crash but will not include the *why* of the accident. Here the officer is faced with the real need to understand the term *investigate* in order to trace certain needed facts. To investigate is "to search minutely for the truth, also to inquire and examine with care and accuracy, or careful inquiry to find out what is unknown." This covers *what* the officer is supposed to do and *how* he is to set about the task of unraveling the problem at hand. Unfortunately, one cannot arrive at the accident scene and easily determine the guilty party. It requires time to make an investigation, so an officer has no reason for not making it a good one. There is a difference between "attending" and "investigating" an accident. Many reasons given for the "investigating" of an accident by an

---

4.   Ibid., pp. 27-28.

officer are merely the reasons for his attending, such as the preserving of peace and protection of life and property. Any officer "attending" an accident will direct traffic, care for the injured, and so on but make no effort to investigate.

The predominant cause of an accident is not always a violation. The officer should not narrow his work to a possible prosecution only but always check for *secondary causes* that might have been contributing factors. What did the violation stem from — situation or circumstance? Ascertaining causes requires deliberate, painstaking effort and a lot of weighing, which we sometimes call "expert opinion." The officer must use his expert opinion and intelligence. He may distinguish between provable opinion and provable fact, but the officer must be sure to include any opinions he has formed.

Because accident investigation is important, the successful accident investigator must possess certain qualities and abilities. This will assure that the task is accomplished satisfactorily from the standpoint of the individual, the public, and the department that the investigator represents.

CHARACTERISTICS OF AN ACCIDENT INVESTIGATOR

The first characteristic of an accident investigator is *enthusiasm*. The individual must be interested in his work, zealous, and anxious to do the best possible job. Each new investigation must be accepted as a challenge. Lacking enthusiasm, the operation becomes routine, something to be accomplished with a minimum of time and effort. The completed investigation will fall short of the quality that is necessary. It will be a recording, not an investigation.

Determination is essential for the successful investigator. He must possess tenacity of purpose to do a competent job — get the job done and done well — or the investigation will lack the completeness that marks a good report.

The investigator must possess *sincerity*. He must truly believe in his work and its importance as a public service. His feelings must direct his actions toward a definite goal. Believing fully that what he is doing is worth doing well, he will be content with nothing less than sincere effort to achieve the best in each investigation.

A sense of *responsibility* is important — a desire to be an asset to the organization he represents. He must recognize the need to make a thorough investigation, do a proper job of enforcement, write a complete and concise report, and represent his department well at the accident scene. He should realize that investigation goes far beyond mere recording of readily available information on an official form.

The *ability to communicate* is essential. As an investigator, he will be expected to know more about the accident than a layperson. This information must be written so that any reader will have as much knowledge of the circumstances as the investigator. The investigator's report must contain all of his knowledge of the accident. *If, after reading the report, the reader cannot ask a relevant question regarding the accident, the investigator has in some measure failed.* Either the investigation or the report has been in some way inadequate.

Proper representation of his department at the scene entails the ability to *represent authority* without a display of excessive command. The officer need not remind people who he is — they will recognize him the moment they see the uniform. The investigator is being observed all the time. Some welcome him, some believe in him, but others would like to criticize him. The actions of the officer reflect not only upon himself but also upon his department and the whole police profession.

The investigator must possess *investigative ability.* He must be able to interview, observe efficiently and completely, reach sound conclusions, and make his investigation meaningful and valuable. Some fatal accident investigations may be very difficult, as in those cases without survivors. With no witnesses, the accident must be reconstructed from physical evidence alone. There have been attempts to make it appear that victims of murder met death as the result of a traffic crash. Casual examination of the scene would have led to a false conclusion, allowing the murderer to escape. In many cases, however, proper application of investigative techniques has uncovered evidence that the incidents were not what they appeared to be and the responsible parties have been brought to justice. The ability to analyze situations — measure statements against physical evidence and probability — so that his opinions will approach reality is essential for the investigator.

Dealing as he does with people who are not in a normal situation, the investigator must possess the qualities of *leadership.* It is necessary that he quickly bring order to the chaos existing at accident scenes. He must have the ability to control emotionally and physically upset people. He must use skill and tact in answering or asking questions. An attitude of disinterest or levity is out of place at the scene of any accident. No matter how commonplace or routine the particular incident may appear to the investigator, he must always bear in mind that to the participants there is nothing routine about it. To them it is an unusual, frightening, and sorrowful experience. The investigator must approach his task with empathy. As a further instance of leadership, the investigator must be able to recognize how much authority he can delegate to volunteers as well as properly evaluate their actions to determine if they will actually assist rather than hinder him in the investigation.

Initiative is essential. Many times the investigator will not have a supervisor to direct him, so he must be able to think logically and clearly under conditions of duress and pressure. He must persevere to conduct a thorough and complete investigation with a minimum of guidance and direction.

A basic knowledge of *photography* will be of value. The investigator must plan his picture for its evidential rather than its news value. He should know where a photograph will help in his investigation and where one will not help.

A *sense of duty* to protect the rights of the participants is essential to the investigator. He must strive to get the facts. He must realize the need for conducting an impartial investigation without preconceived opinions that may color or slant it. It will help if he considers participants as things, materials, and formulas rather than people. He should approach the investigation in terms of what each vehicle did in relation to other physical conditions. With this viewpoint, he is less apt to be swayed by prejudices as to age, sex, race, color, occupation, or personality. Any of these may subconsciously affect the unbiased consideration of all the elements which he must collect and evaluate. His report of the investigation must reflect the true accident picture.

Knowledge of these as well as other police techniques and qualities will help. The successful investigator will always be alert for new knowledge, ideas, and techniques. When he uncovers a new way of doing things, he will pass on the information. Progress in any field is a group effort, built upon the contributions of many individuals. The accident investigator today profits from the experience of past investigators, and he in turn can contribute by making available to others the results of his experience and knowledge.

PROCEDURAL STEPS IN ACCIDENT INVESTIGATION

Of course, one of the most important steps to developing a good accident investigator is the method in which he is trained. This may include one of several ways: training through a certified course at a local college or university; training taught to the individual at the basic or advance police academy, or by a police or traffic investigator during an in-service training session; and finally, training through actual field experience on a one-to-one basis.

However it is done, training must be done thoroughly and with great care to determine that all the important aspects have been covered. This should then be followed by field observation by the training officer or supervisor to validate the knowledge and skills learned by the officer. When this has been done to the satisfaction of his department, then the officer is ready to handle many of the routine types of accidents. The role of the individual from that of a basic police or traffic officer to that of an investigator is not an easy or fast transition. It will take many years of hard work, investigating many accidents to obtain what we call "professional expertise." What should the investigator be familiar with in order to properly work an accident situation?

Every action of the investigator, from the original accident call to the completion of the report, falls within one of the three reasons for investigating accidents. Steps in normal accident investigation will be grouped under these three broad headings in the order in which they most logically fall.

To assure uniformity of understanding, certain terms must be narrowly defined. The following basic definitions are in common use in the accident investigation field.

There are three basic types of accident investigation:

1. The "normal" accident investigation, which includes the investigation of those accidents where the principals are present, vehicles are approximately as they came to rest, physical evidence is unaltered, and witnesses were possibly present.

2. The "late reported" or late investigated accident, in which knowledge of the accident is gained and the investigation, if any, is made after some lapse of time.

3. The hit-and-run accident, in which the operator knowingly causes damage or injury and/or death and leaves the scene without identifying himself.

A Fixed System of Operation

Some type of fixed procedure is extremely valuable in accident investigation, although it should not be a limitation of the investigator's actions. *It should be flexible.* Steps should be taken as conditions warrant rather than by rote. By realizing the need for a fixed procedure, the investigator will use it as a sort of mental checklist. It will make the task easier for the officer — assist in determining the cause and gathering data, tend to make sure that nothing is overlooked in the investigation, give a definite starting point, and help to prevent duplication of effort. A planned procedure impresses the public with the efficiency of the investigator's department and builds favorable public opinion. Officers will find that accident investigation will consume a great part of their time. The better they know the correct procedure, the more reliable their reports will be and the more pleasant their job will be. When one is familiar with a task, it is easier to perform.

Responsibility to Protect Life and Property

In a normal accident investigation, there are various steps which may be conveniently grouped under the broad heading of protection of life and property. Not all of these steps will be required in all accident investigations, nor will they always be done in any particular order. The important thing for the investigator to remember is that each investigation should be evaluated in the light of each of these steps, assigning top priority to that which in each instance is most important. The best procedure is a planned procedure that can be adapted to each event.

Before any investigation can commence, the investigator must be at the scene. Therefore, his *safe* arrival is essential. There are many reasons why the investigation should be made as soon as possible after the occurrence of the accident. It follows, then, that prompt arrival at the scene is also important. The first thing the investigator has to do is get to the scene safely, yet quickly.

Since the accident has already occurred, the investigator can do nothing to prevent it; he should consider this fact and protect his life and others' by driving at a safe speed. Taking unnecessary chances may lead to the investigator being involved in an accident himself. This not only slows down the investigation of the accident he was assigned to cover, but also provides an additional accident that must be investigated. Bad public relations can be caused by the officer becoming involved in an accident while en route to the original accident scene.

The investigator arrives at the scene to protect the scene and other traffic, to preserve evidence that might be lost, and, in some cases, to save life by applying first aid. Another accident may occur because the highway is obstructed. Traffic congestion is usually present, and the investigator must attempt to restore normal vehicular movements. By prompt arrival, he will prevent driver irritation and poor public relations. To those involved in an accident, time is fleeting. Each minute they wait seems much longer than it really is. Also important is the fact that witnesses, who might be of great value, often become impatient and leave the scene once their curiosity is satisfied, and the investigator will not benefit from information they might give.

A safe but quick arrival is a challenge to the investigator. One way is to *plan the approach over the quickest route* (not necessarily the shortest). The investigator must know the area — the shortcuts, detours, construction zones, and areas of congestion. A few seconds spent thinking out the best route may save minutes of hazardous high-speed driving. The officer should start at once upon receipt of the call. A short delay in getting started will have to be made up on the road, and a long delay means that time is lost which can never be regained.

Upon arrival at the scene, the investigator should *park safely and conveniently.* Consideration should be given to the safety of the officer, the patrol car, and other traffic. If he parks opposite the accident, he will have to cross the traffic stream each time he needs to return to the patrol vehicle. Parking on the same side of the highway will be safer and more convenient. By proper parking, the warning lights on the patrol car may be used to help protect the scene. The investigator should consider the safety and availability of the equipment in the vehicle as he will need to use the radio, flares, first aid equipment, and the like. Also, unguarded equipment may offer an incentive to potential looters. By safe parking, the investigator will help to establish a safe parking and passing pattern, and his task will be much easier if he has various items close at hand and where they can be kept under observation.

The investigator should *protect the accident scene* to prevent the occurrence of further accidents and to preserve the evidence that he will need. This may require placing flares at night or under conditions of poor visibility. Thought should be given to the proper location of flares to give approaching drivers a chance to slow down before running into the obstruction and to channel traffic into a safe path around the accident. It may be necessary to direct traffic around the scene. In many cases, bystanders will volunteer to assist. If their aid is enlisted, they should be told what to do; otherwise, their undirected efforts may hamper rather than help the investigation. Attempts should be made to keep onlookers in a safe location. This at times poses an extremely difficult problem to the investigator.

Where gasoline or oil is spilled on the highway, it may be necessary to request fire equipment to wash it from the pavement or highway crews may be needed to sand the area to eliminate the hazard. Where a fire hazard exists, such as from gasoline, liquid petroleum gas, or similar fluids, the investigator should use care in placing flares, warn onlookers of the danger of smoking, and, if necessary, clear the crowd from the area.

Where there is injury, *first aid* will be necessary. In certain instances, this may be the most important thing and should be given without delay. Where injury is minor, protection of the scene may warrant top priority. Placing flares and directing traffic while a person bleeds to death would undoubtedly be the wrong order of operations, as would bandaging slight injuries before protecting the scene when a high-speed road was blocked in an area of low visibility. The investigator must consider each situation on its own merits. The most important thing should come first, regardless of its position on the checklist of procedures. An ambulance should be ordered, if required. This is one of the first considerations when there is serious injury. Where there is a fatality, the coroner must be notified. Any doubt as to whether the victim is dead or alive should be resolved in his favor. He should be treated as alive unless, by the very nature of the injuries, there can be no doubt that he is dead.

The investigator must *care for the property* of those injured. A tow car may be needed, and it should be ordered as soon as it can be conveniently done. If possible, the driver's preference as to towing service should be ascertained and the tow car of his choice ordered. When the driver is unable to care for his own vehicle and the investigator orders it stored for safe keeping, a report of stored vehicle must be filled out and the contents of the car listed and inventoried, securing the signature of the tow truck driver on the inventory form as a receipt for the vehicle and its contents.

Evidence Collection and Finding the Cause

The remaining steps of the investigation come under the headings of gathering evidence for prosecution and determining the cause of the accident. These two objectives are common to accident investigations and cannot be separated. Evidence as to the cause will lead to the cause. From evidence and statements of witnesses and participants, the investigator must determine the cause of the accident. He must bear in mind that there probably will be more than one cause in any but the most simple type of accident; where more than one vehicle is involved, there may be one or more violations on the part of each driver.

There are three factors in any accident: (1) the highway, (2) the vehicle or vehicles, and (3) the people involved. All three should be checked for evidence. Although it is impossible to get all the facts about everything, the investigator should strive to get all the pertinent facts. If a violation is indicated, an effort should be made to secure sufficient evidence to prove the elements of that violation.

Usually the officer will begin to form an opinion of what happened early in the investigation and will look for evidence to confirm it. At this point he should take care not to overlook evidence that does not agree with the investigator's theory. Evidence that tends to disprove his first impression may be very important. Things are not always what they seem. The officer must never attempt to distort facts to fit his theory; the opinion must be adjusted to fit the facts. He must never be reluctant to accept negative or conflicting evidence, no matter how convinced he is that the accident happened in a different way.

Every fact, each statement, and every shred of evidence must be analyzed and evaluated in order to get a true picture of what happened. To start with, the investigator is faced with a result. Step by step he must work backwards from that result to find the causes. He must proceed from the "what" of a situation to determine, insofar as possible, the "how" and the "why."

A logical first step is to *locate and question the drivers and witnesses.* This is done by making a quick preliminary check to see that all drivers are present, then attempting to locate witnesses. The investigator should get the operator's license of each driver, determine which vehicle each was driving, then look for persons who might have seen the accident. Many persons may remain at the accident until the police arrive, then leave before the officer has had an opportunity to question them. An early search for these people may provide the investigator with information which he would not otherwise obtain.

The person who begins this search with the query "Were there any witnesses to this accident?" will probably not be very successful in finding any. The word *witness* has an unpleasant connotation in the minds of many people. They have been conditioned by motion pictures and other types of entertainment to visualize a witness in court being badgered by the opposing attorneys to the point of acute discomfort, and they want no part of it. The indirect approach is inherently much more productive. The officer should find out from the drivers, if possible, who was the first one they saw or talked to after the accident, then approach these persons and ask them what they saw. They might say that the accident had already happened when they stopped, but they may be able to furnish information as to who was there when they arrived. Thus, a witness may be discovered indirectly. Many times, while giving first aid or performing some of the other duties incidental to the investigation, the officer may overhear someone telling how the accident occurred. This person may or may not be a witness. He may have talked to someone who did see it, and in this way, too, a witness may be located. A check and recording of the license numbers of the vehicles parked closest to the scene may be valuable. Drivers of these vehicles are most apt to be the first arrivals. Even if witnesses cannot be found at the scene, contacting these drivers at a later date may develop the fact that one or more of them may have witnessed the accident. However, witnesses should be located as soon as possible. Not only are they prone to leave when the excitement is over, but also their statements may be valuable in offering leads to develop during the actual interrogation of the drivers. They may also suggest what physical evidence the investigator should look for.

In all contacts with witnesses or potential witnesses, the investigator must act with tact, diplomacy, and understanding. It must be remembered that he is asking for something, and that these people have no obligation to tell him anything. Their assistance may be very valuable, if freely given, but if coerced into making a statement, their feeling of resentment toward the interrogator will probably destroy the value of any statement he may extract.

Drivers must be thoroughly checked as to their *physical condition*. Intoxication is a state that often changes rapidly. Tests for intoxication should be conducted without unnecessary delay. The condition of the driver at the time of the accident, not the condition an hour or two after the accident occurred, is important.

Early in the investigation the investigator should *determine if it is a hit-and-run*, for the procedures in this type of investigation are different from normal accident investigation. Time is of the essence, and the sooner the hit-and-run procedures can be put into effect, the more likely will be the chance of apprehension.

The second factor to be considered is the vehicle. Much evidence may be developed by thoroughly examining and testing the vehicles involved. It should be determined if all the visible damage was the result of the current accident. The investigator should note the exact location and extent of damage. Evidence of crumpled fenders and broken glass that does not tie in may be the result of a previous incident. Fresh damage, not connected, may lead to the solution of an earlier hit-and-run.

The driver's statement may give the investigator a clue as to what to look for. Perhaps the driver's statement is not correct, and damage which he does not explain may lead to the true account of the accident. A check of the mechanical devices — brakes, lights, windshield wipers, turn indicators, and mirrors — should be made to see if they are adequate. In some cases, operator's licenses are restricted to the operation of vehicles equipped with certain safety devices. The officer should check to determine if safety devices are employed if required. The officer should note the condition of each tire on the vehicle and check the front end, unless the damage makes the test impossible. Brakes may fail or be faulty or inadequate. Loss of control may suggest a worn steering assembly. A fresh break in the steering mechanism will probably be a result of the accident rather than a cause. Other points to check are lack of safety devices on commercial vehicles, inadequate lighting equipment, defective windshield, and vision obscurements.

Tire failure is often claimed as the cause of an accident, but many times it is a result rather than the cause. The investigator should know whether or not vehicle failure contributed. In the event of prosecution, the driver may claim vehicle failure as a defense. If the investigator has not checked, he will be unable to refute this type of argument. However, if a thorough check has been made, he will have the answers to any questions that may arise.

The third factor involves the *surrounding physical conditions*. Any conditions that might have contributed to the accident should be carefully observed by the officer: holes in the roadway surface; loose material on the pavement; the weather; visibility from the driver's path of view, including obstructions to vision such as hedges, trees, poles, or signboards; traffic control devices; and warning signs. *All observations should be made from the driver's line of sight.* The operator of a truck ten feet above the highway has a far different field of view than the driver of a low-slung sports car. Skid marks, gouge marks, tire marks, and vehicle position should all be checked and the information recorded in notes at the scene, for both the accident report and possible use when testifying.

Necessary photographs should be taken. They may be a great aid to the prosecution as they present physical circumstances of a case in a manner that is easily understood. Most people are visually oriented. A photograph of large or perishable evidence is accepted in place of the original. Include such items as skid marks, footprints, or a body to show the location and type of injury. But before the shutter is snapped, the investigator should ask, "What will this tend to prove?" If the answer is "nothing," the photo should not be taken.

The photographer must be qualified. He must know what he is doing and why, for the more important the picture, the stronger will be the attempt to discredit or disprove it. A commercial photographer is usually not satisfactory for several reasons. In addition to being expensive, he may not know what is required, is often reluctant to appear in court, and may not keep proper data to insure that the photograph will be admitted as evidence. If a commercial photographer is used, the officer should direct the photographer to take the type of picture the officer needs and record exposure and other related data. It should be remembered that these photographs are not for publicity but are evidence, as is the sketch of the scene. Valuable as they may be, the investigator should not depend on photographs only. They may be an important part of the case, but photographs alone do not constitute a complete investigation.

Pictures of the following subjects are often needed as evidence or to complete the records of a case: general scene from driver's viewpoint; point of impact; traffic control devices; skid marks showing length and direction; condition of roadway at location, showing defects, position of cars, victims, and parts of vehicles after impact, indicating distances from point of collision; view obstructions or the lack of them; blood, flesh, hair, fabrics, scrape marks, and the like, which are frequently useful in hit-and-run cases; tire prints; footprints; defects in vehicles involved, such as missing headlight, stickers obstructing driver's vision, or trucks lacking turn indicators; the roadside, showing the kind of district; sagging springs of an overloaded vehicle; and the license number of the vehicle for identification.

Photographs, however, do not show measurements or dimensions. The photo may be incorrectly exposed, blurred, or otherwise worthless. The accident sketch, therefore, is important as the record of the investigator's intricate, personal examination of the scene.

Sketching the Accident Scene

In every investigated accident, the investigating officer is usually required to submit a sketch of the crash along with his report. A sketch is similar to a photograph. It represents a graphic picture of the investigating officer's impression of the crash scene. Upon arrival at traffic crashes, he observes numerous bits of activity taking place along with the resting places of the involved vehicles. All of this information is, of course, not necessary to record, but the pertinent facts directly relating to the accident are. The officer must rely on his ability to make not only a thorough investigation but to skillfully preserve and record the facts. Thus, a well-prepared diagram will be extremely helpful to all the parties involved in the crash. Should the case go to court, the officer will have better recall of the accident through his sketch.

The rough sketch should be drawn freehand at the scene. The officer should always keep in proper perspective the vehicles involved, roadway width and traffic lanes, skid marks, gouge marks, and other supportive evidence. He should use a sturdy clipboard, some type of a straightedge (ruler), a pencil, and a good eraser. Using a blank piece of paper and a clipboard, he starts the sketch by indicating the direction of north. North is indicated by an arrow in the upper right-hand corner of the sketch and placing a capital N directly below the stem of the arrow, drawing a circle around the entire symbol (see fig. 9-1).

Some basic scale, such as one inch equals ten feet, should be used. Of course, the officer can use other types of equations to reproduce compiled distances, but he should remember to keep them the same throughout the sketch. The scale should be large enough to make it clear, yet small enough to show the whole area. Everything that might have a bearing on the accident should be included: length and position of skids; distance traveled after collision; width of streets, shoulder and roadways; distance and height of view obstructions; location of traffic control devices; distance from the pavement to any fixed object that was struck; victims or parts of vehicles; and debris. Distances should be measured rather than estimated or stepped off.

The investigator should not neglect to locate and record the evidence that may be hidden beneath the vehicles. When making the sketch, the

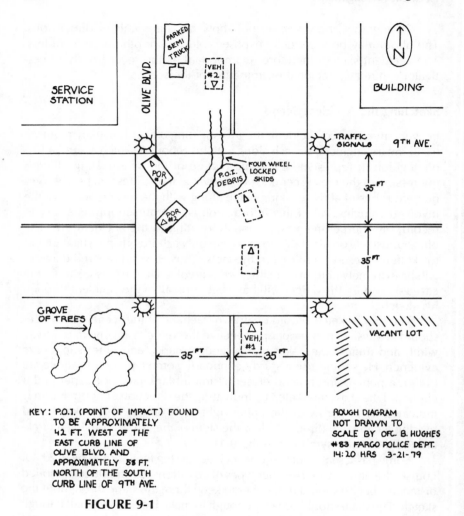

KEY : P.O.1. (POINT OF IMPACT) FOUND
      TO BE APPROXIMATELY
      42 FT. WEST OF THE
      EAST CURB LINE OF
      OLIVE BLVD. AND
      APPROXIMATELY 58 FT.
      NORTH OF THE SOUTH
      CURB LINE OF 9TH AVE.

ROUGH DIAGRAM
NOT DRAWN TO
SCALE BY OFC. B. HUGHES
#83 FARGO POLICE DEPT.
14:20 HRS 3-21-79

FIGURE 9-1

officer should treat vehicles as transparent, viewed from the top, and record evidence in its proper location.

Completing the Accident Report

If the investigation of the crash is to be a truly professional job, the officer should remember two important objectives. First, the report must reflect an accurate summary of all relevant and material evidence obtained at the scene. The knowledge he obtains through his interviews of the involved parties and witnesses must be accurately reflected in the report. No matter how thorough the investigation, an officer who fails to supply the needed information on the accident report will find that he will spend countless additional hours trying to repair the incomplete report. Second, the report must be in such form that it is self-explanatory. Anyone who reads the report should be able to understand exactly what it says and know exactly what the officer meant to say. A report that does not speak for itself requires additional investigation; additional investigation requires time, money, and labor that may very well be needed in other police areas.

Most traffic accident reports are submitted on a printed departmental form (see figs. 9-2, 9-3, 9-4 and 9-5). Such forms provide spaces for both a narrative review or summary of the officer's completed investigation and a place for a finished diagram. Although some departments require such finished accident reports to be completed in the field, other departments may allow their officers to complete their reports at the end of their tour of duty. There are even some departments that have their officers telephone in their reports over a dictating device, and the reports are later transcribed by a secretarial pool. In these cases the officer, at the completion of his shift, simply turns in the finished accident diagram to accompany the completed report.

There has been a trend to simplify the mechanics of accident diagraming. One method uses very simple symbols, as shown in figure 9-6. Using these standard symbols for a collision diagram can speed up the accident report writing process and is also more easily read. Figure 9-6 is the same rough diagram as seen in figure 9-1, but this time the standard symbols have been used to pictorially describe the crash scene.

Each police, sheriff, state police, or highway patrol department has a prescribed format to be used in the narrative portion of the accident report. A standard format might consist of four parts. The FACTS would include (1) the method of receiving the call; (2) the description of the crash scene: the type of area — residential, business, open area, etc.; number of traffic lanes; type of roadway surface; any traffic controls; (3) vehicle location, damage, and defects and how those defects were detected for each vehicle involved in the crash; (4) all physical evidence, such as skid marks, gouge marks, debris, vehicle parts, and any fixed property damage; (5) name, age, date of birth, sex, address, vehicle number (as listed on your report), and location in the vehicle at the time of the crash (e.g., right rear, right front seat, etc.) of passengers who were not injured or are not included as witnesses; and (6) what, if any, photographs were taken at the crash scene. The last item includes official police photographs and any photographs taken by the press or other interested persons. The officer should include the names, addresses, and phone numbers of these people and record the number of all photographs taken.

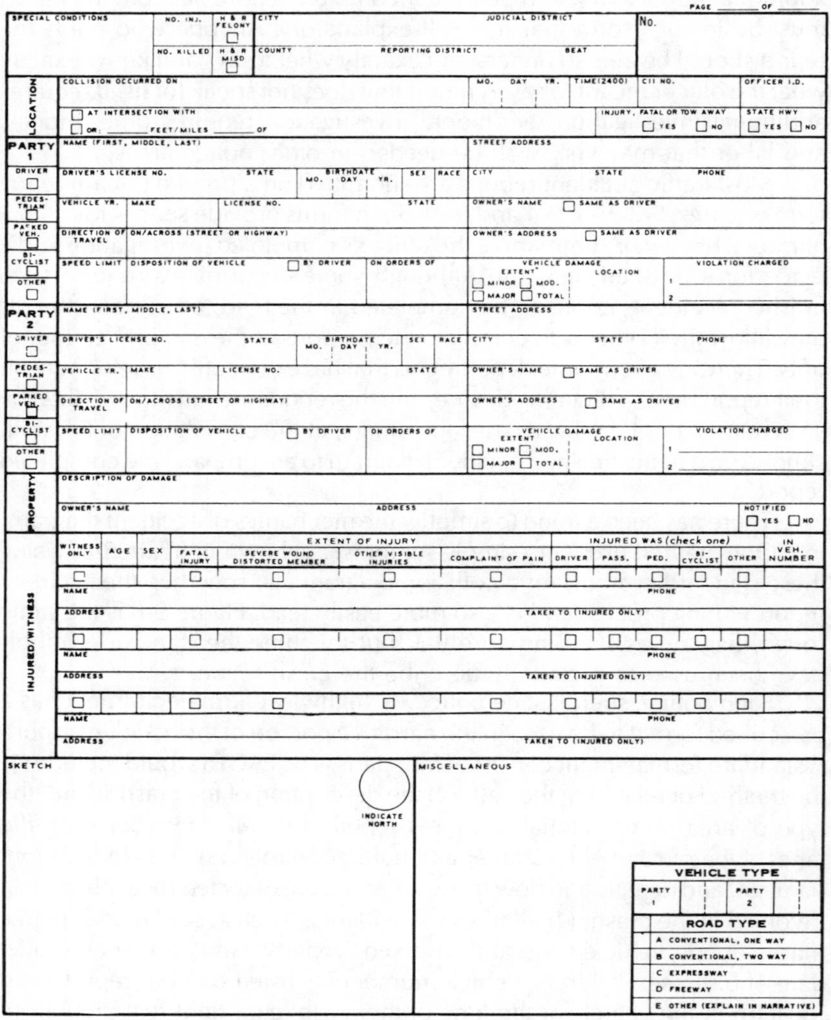

FIGURE 9-2

PAGE _____

COLLISION NARRATIVE

PRIMARY COLLISION FACTOR	RIGHT OF WAY CONTROL	1	2	3	4	TYPE OF VEHICLE	1	2	3	4	MOVEMENT PRECEDING COLLISION
A VC SECTION VIOLATION ____	A CONTROLS FUNCTIONING					A PASSENGER CAR (INCLUDES STATION WAGON)					A STOPPED
B OTHER IMPROPER DRIVING*	B CONTROLS NOT FUNCTIONING					B PASSENGER CAR W/TRAILER					B PROCEEDING STRAIGHT
C OTHER THAN DRIVER*	C CONTROLS OBSCURED					C MOTORCYCLE/SCOOTER					C RAN OFF ROAD
D UNKNOWN*	D NO CONTROLS PRESENT					D PICKUP OR PANEL TRUCK					D MAKING RIGHT TURN
WEATHER	TYPE OF COLLISION					E PICKUP OR PANEL TRUCK W/TRAILER					E MAKING LEFT TURN
A CLEAR	A HEAD-ON					F TRUCK OR TRUCK TRACTOR					F MAKING U TURN
B CLOUDY	B SIDESWIPE					G TRUCK OR TRUCK TRACTOR W/TRAILER(S)					G BACKING
C RAINING	C REAR END					H SCHOOL BUS					H SLOWING - STOPPING
D SNOWING	D BROADSIDE					I OTHER BUS					I PASSING OTHER VEHICLE
E FOG	E HIT OBJECT					J EMERGENCY VEHICLE					J CHANGING LANES
F OTHER ____	F OVERTURNED					K HIGHWAY CONSTRUCTION EQUIPMENT					K PARKING MANEUVER
LIGHTING	G AUTO/PEDESTRIAN					L BICYCLE					L ENTERING TRAFFIC FROM SHOULDER, MEDIAN, PARKING STRIP OR PRIVATE DRIVE
A DAYLIGHT	H OTHER					M OTHER ____					
B DUSK - DAWN	MOTOR VEHICLE INVOLVED WITH										M OTHER UNSAFE TURNING
C DARK - STREET LIGHTS	A NON-COLLISION					OTHER ASSOCIATED FACTOR (MARK ONE TO THREE ITEMS)	1	2	3	4	N CROSSED INTO OPPOSING LANE
D DARK - NO STREET LIGHTS	B PEDESTRIAN					A VC SECTION VIOLATION ____					O PARKED
E DARK - STREET LIGHTS NOT FUNCTIONING	C OTHER MOTOR VEHICLE					B VC SECTION VIOLATION ____					P MERGING
ROADWAY SURFACE	D MOTOR VEHICLE ON OTHER ROADWAY					C VC SECTION VIOLATION ____					Q TRAVELING WRONG WAY*
A DRY	E PARKED MOTOR VEHICLE					D VC SECTION VIOLATION ____					R OTHER ____
B WET	F TRAIN					E VISION OBSCUREMENTS					SOBRIETY - DRUG - PHYSICAL (MARK ONE TO THREE ITEMS)	1	2	3	4
C SNOWY - ICY	G BICYCLE					F INATTENTION					A HAD NOT BEEN DRINKING
D SLIPPERY (MUDDY, OILY, ETC.)	H ANIMAL					G STOP & GO TRAFFIC					B HBD - UNDER INFLUENCE
ROADWAY CONDITIONS (MARK ONE TO THREE ITEMS)	I FIXED OBJECT					H ENTERING/LEAVING RAMP					C HBD - NOT UNDER INFLUENCE
A HOLES, DEEP RUTS	J OTHER OBJECT ____					I PREVIOUS COLLISION					D HBD - IMPAIRMENT UNKNOWN*
B LOOSE MATERIAL ON ROADWAY	K OTHER ____					J UNFAMILIAR WITH ROAD					E UNDER DRUG INFLUENCE
C OBSTRUCTION ON ROADWAY	PEDESTRIAN'S ACTION					K DEFECTIVE VEHICLE EQUIPMENT ____					F OTHER PHYSICAL IMPAIRMENT*
D CONSTRUCTION-REPAIR ZONE	A NO PEDESTRIAN INVOLVED					L UNINVOLVED VEHICLE					G IMPAIRMENT NOT KNOWN
E REDUCED ROADWAY WIDTH	B CROSSING IN CROSSWALK AT INTERSECTION					M OTHER*					H NOT APPLICABLE
F FLOODED	C CROSSING IN CROSSWALK - NOT AT INTERSECTION					N NONE APPARENT					
G OTHER ____	D CROSSING - NOT IN CROSSWALK										
H NO UNUSUAL CONDITIONS	E IN ROAD - INCLUDES SHOULDER										
	F NOT IN ROAD										
	G APPROACHING/LEAVING SCHOOL BUS										

INVESTIGATED BY	I.D. NUMBER	INVESTIGATED BY	I.D. NUMBER	REVIEWED BY

*EXPLAIN IN NARRATIVE

FIGURE 9-3

ORIGINAL NO.				

PAGE _____

CHECK ONE	SUPPLEMENTAL	DATE OF ORIGINAL INCIDENT	TIME (2400)	CII NUMBER	OFFICER I.D.
		MO. DAY YR.			
	SUPPLEMENTS FORM 555	LOCATION/SUBJECT			CITATION NO.
	TRAFFIC COLLISION REPORT				
	OTHER:				BEAT
	FORM 555 NARRATIVE	CITY		COUNTY	REPORTING DISTRICT
	CONTINUATION ONLY				

PREPARED BY	I.D. NUMBER	PREPARED	REVIEWED - APPROVED BY	I.D. NUMBER	DATE
NAME/RANK		MO. DAY YR.	NAME/RANK		MO. DAY YR.

FIGURE 9-4

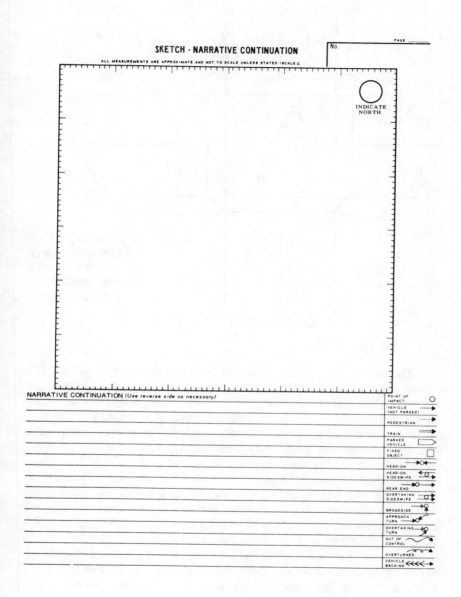

FIGURE 9-5

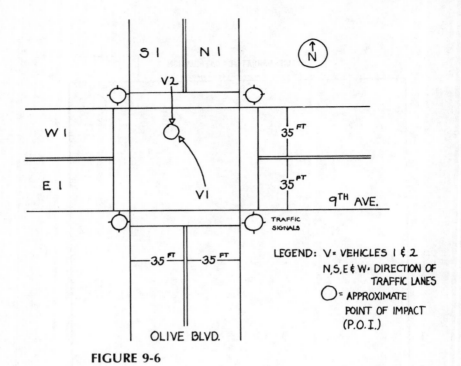

FIGURE 9-6

The next portion of the narrative report should include STATEMENTS. These are statements made by the involved drivers, pedestrians, and witnesses. If the officer's department requires that all statements be written in the first person — that is, exactly what that person said — then they should be enclosed in quotation marks. Other departments may require that the statements be made in third person; that is, the statements simply reflect what it was that the driver or witness said to the officer. The officer should always arrange the text of these statements in a logical and meaningful order. He may record statements after he asks a series of questions and listens to the answers. If he takes statements at locations other than the crash scene, he should include the date and location of the interview, the time, and the name of the investigating officer.

After the officer has included all the statements taken either at the scene or at other locations, he is ready to add the OPINIONS AND CONCLUSIONS. The purpose of this section is to explain, from the facts of the investigation, just how the crash occurred. The officer should give his opinion of *what* took place, show *how* it occurred, and explain *why* it happened the way it did. He should establish the proof for a vehicle code violation.

The remaining unit to the report is the RECOMMENDATIONS. In this section, the officer suggests any investigative follow-up that may be necessary to the case that was not done at the time of the original investigation (see figure 9-7).

SUPPLEMENTAL/NARRATIVE (Check one)	DATE OF ORIGINAL INCIDENT 3/21/79 MO. DAY YR.	TIME (2400) 1300hrs	NCIC NUMBER	OFFICER I.D. 83	NUMBER 79-3609	PAGE 3
☐ NARRATIVE CONTINUATION TRAFFIC COLLISION REPORT (CHP 555 OR 555-01)	LOCATION/SUBJECT				CITATION NUMBER	
☐ SUPPLEMENTAL TRAFFIC COLLISION REPORT (CHP 555 OR 555-01)					BEAT	
☐ OTHER:	CITY/COUNTY				REPORTING DISTRICT	

```
  FACTS:      Included here would be the time you received the call and when
              you arrived at the scene.

              SCENE:   Describe the crash scene as you found it upon your
                       arrival.  Type of location (business, residential,
                       commercial, open area,etc.) Directions the streets
                       run, type of roadway surface, number of traffic lanes.
          VEHICLES:    Location where the vehicles were found, description
                       of the vehicles, and the location of any and  all
                       damage.  List any mechanical defects to any of the
                       involved vehicles.
          PHYSICAL EVIDENCE:  Skidmarks, debris and photographs taken.
          INJURIES:  This includes injuries to drivers and passangers.

  STATEMENTS:   Include statements of the involved drivers,and witnesses.

  OPINIONS AND CONCLUSIONS:  The investigation officer describes his
                       findings as a result of his complete investigation.
                       This includes the results of any field sobriety tests,
                       brake or skid tests, etc.
          POINT OF IMPACT:  From your investigation, the physical
                       evidence, statements of drivers and witnesses you are
                       able to identify the approximate location where the
                       vehicles crashed.
            CAUSE:     Include the determining cause of the crash. The
                       KEY event that resulted in the impact.

  RECOMMENDATIONS:     Any follow-up investigation necessary should be
                       described here.  The disposition of your invest-
                       igation, such as submission of the report to the
                       prosecuting attorney's office.
```

PREPARED BY NAME/RANK Officer B. Hughes	I.D. NUMBER 83	PREPARED MO. DAY YR. 3 21 79	REVIEWED APPROVED BY NAME/RANK E. Flannigan Sgt.	I.D. NUMBER 17	APPROVED MO. DAY YR. 3 21 79

FIGURE 9-7

An accident investigator should be aware of the following list of cautions:

1. Do not discuss the accident with anyone outside of your department or outside the line of duty.

2. Do not take sides. The investigator is an impartial fact finder.

3. Do not tell any participant that he is either blameless or at fault. These are matters for adversary proceeding.

4. Do not tell anyone you will be a witness for or against him. You will be a witness for no individual. Testimony must be honest and impartial.

5. Do not mention garage charges, repair bills, or civil liability, as these are not part of the investigation.

6. Do not enter into any discussion of a probable or possible fine. This is a court function.

7. Do not be hasty in making decisions as to cause. Consider every possible cause, gather all the evidence, then analyze to exclude factors not involved.

With the information gathered, the investigator should now determine the cause or causes of the accident. He should be very careful in this phase, as it is one of the most important parts of the investigation. It should be approached in terms of the violation, and facts should be gathered to prove the essential elements of the action. It is quite probable that there may be one or more violations on the part of each driver.

What the investigator faces upon arrival at the scene is the result of a combination of circumstances. He must start from this result and work backwards as the investigation progresses, until at its conclusion he knows the cause or causes of the accident.

The Probable Result

A traffic collision (crash) is classified as one of three types: (1) running off the road; (2) noncollision on the road; and (3) collision on the road.

Running off the road is when the driver of a motor vehicle loses control of his car and one or more wheels run off the main traveled portion of the highway or the car strikes a curb. Should the driver strike an object after leaving the roadway, this would be considered a second event. The second classification, noncollision on the road, covers cases where a motor vehicle strikes a large pothole in the highway, causing the driver to lose control and overturn on the roadway, or where a car traveling on a roadway catches fire and burns without striking anything or running off the road. The third classification covers a collision on the road with a pedestrian, railroad train, bicycle, animal, fixed object, or other object (such as a large crate that may have fallen off a truck).

These classifications, termed *events*, characterize the manner in which a motor vehicle traffic accident occurred. When we identify a specific event by the exact time, place, and type of accident (one of the three previously described classifications), it is called the *key event*. The key event actually fixes the accident with respect to the factors of time (the actual time of the crash), place (the exact location of the crash), and type (running off the road, noncollision on the road, or collision on the road).

When an investigator seeks that event which characterizes just what occurred to each traffic unit (motor vehicle or pedestrian), he is attempting to determine the *available path* of each respective unit, or what is commonly referred to as the *crucial event*. There are five kinds of crucial events:

1. Leaving the available path (not the same as running off the road).

2. Turning over in the path without collision.

3. Other noncollision in the path.

4. Collision with a nontraffic object in or adjacent to the path.

5. Collision with another traffic unit in the path (not a parked vehicle).[5]

When the investigator determines that there may have been more than one event by which the accident may be classified, then he must assign the classification of the accident to the event that occurred first. This is referred to as the *rule of first harmful event* and is the same as the key event.

The *direct cause* of a crash would be characterized as the *dynamic situation* that led to the point of no escape for the driver, hence the ultimate collision. In other words, the direct cause would be the particular vehicle code violation that actually caused the accident. Examples might be excessive and unsafe speed for prevailing roadway conditions, failure to stop for a red traffic signal or a stop sign, or driving across the double solid center lines.

Mediate causes are those circumstances beyond the driver's immediate control that surround him as he heads in a collision course. These may include unknown faulty brakes, an opposing sleepy or drunken driver, a driver following too closely to the rear, a slippery roadway, foggy condi-

---

5. Ibid., p. 13.

tions, or an upset or angry driver. These conditions, in turn, may be preceded by what is referred to as *remote conditions* or *causes,* such as driving habits, a roadway design that is outdated for present demand and usage, failing to heed an earlier highway warning sign, or failing to have a leaky brake cylinder repaired.

Finally, the investigator must determine if and when the involved drivers and/or pedestrians might have actually realized they were about to become involved in an accident. At what point *could* the involved parties have seen one another, and would there have been sufficient time, distance, and opportunity to take some type of evasive action? This is known as the *point of possible perception.* The investigator must then determine at what point they actually saw each other and thus attempted to take evasive action, which is called the *point of actual perception.* This could be determined by locating the skid marks (light or faint) left by one of the vehicles. It is at that moment that the driver and/or pedestrian arrives at the point of no escape. No matter what he does (skidding, turning his vehicle from a direct course, and so on), it is too late to correct his mistake. The crash is now imminent and soon occurs. The result is *engagement at its maximum* (when the greatest amount of damage occurs) and the final stages of *disengagement* (separation of the colliding units). The final stage is when the traffic units have stopped moving and come to rest. The accident has now *stabilized* and the vehicles are at the *point of rest.* The first actual point of contact (initial impact) is called the *point of impact* (POI). The POI is extremely important to the investigator, because it is from this point that he determines the violating traffic unit that caused the accident. Chapter Ten discusses some of the basic vehicle code violations and the proof needed in establishing the direct causes of accidents. This will aid the investigator in compiling the necessary evidence to establish his case.

In an uncomplicated accident, a vehicle runs off the road and overturns, injuring the driver. In this case, there is an injury accident. The key event would be skidding on a curve, which might have resulted from a combination of mediate causes, including a slippery highway surface, excessive speed, smooth tires, improper brake application, and an inadequate signing of the hazard. These in turn may have many *early causes;* rain, poor driver attitude, insufficient funds for adequate highway signing, construction and policing, lack of driver education as to proper care of equipment, and many more acts, neglects, or conditions that lead up to mediate causes. The area of improvement in all three phases of traffic supervision falls within the area of mediate causes. Many of the early causes may also need improvement, but others are so remote as to be of little immediate concern to the investigator, although they may play a part in the total picture of traffic supervision.

Catastrophic Crashes

Presently, there is great concern with catastrophic crashes. The federal government recently provided federally funded grants to the California Highway Patrol to set up two Multidisciplinary Accident Investigation Teams (MAIT). Funds were approved by the California Office of Traffic Safety for the purchase of two specially constructed vans equipped with cameras, photographic material, tape recorders, skid testing apparatus, psychrometers to test humidity, and anemometers with compasses to check wind speed and direction. With each van there is a team of specially trained investigators consisting of three members of the California Highway Patrol (CHP) and one member of the California Department of Transportation (Caltrans). The specific members of the team are (1) a sergeant with special training in accident reconstruction; (2) a state traffic officer who is an expert on speed and skidding; (3) a nonuniform member of the CHP who is a motor carrier operations specialist; and (4) a Caltrans highway engineer. The team has access to other specialists such as medical experts and metallurgical engineers.

These highly specialized teams investigate accidents involving spillage or leakage of hazardous materials, accidents where a possible manufacturing defect was the cause, accidents in which four or more fatalities occurred, and accidents with two or more fatalities in which one or more trucks or other commercial vehicles were involved. The MAIT will respond to any of these catastrophic crashes to perform detailed accident reconstruction and augment the investigations of local commands.

Other states will be following the progress of the MAIT project. Some states already have a type of accident reconstruction team that is available on an "as needed" basis, but there is a very definite need to expand these highly specialized units throughout the country. Today we are seeing an alarming growth of catastrophic crashes involving commercial vehicles. The causes of the crashes can only be fully determined if a thorough investigation can be conducted at the crash scene and all the events and other causative factors are both analyzed and equally weighed in the reconstruction of the accident. Professional accident investigation can only be enhanced by expert scientific study.

SUMMARY

We have noted many reasons for the necessity of a sound accident investigation program. However, we must recognize also that unless we prepare our police officers in the proper techniques of traffic accident investigation, no program, however elaborate, will succeed.

To do an effective job of traffic supervision, a complete analysis of the causes of accidents should be carefully undertaken. While in recent years the mileage death rate has shown a decrease proportionate to the number of motor vehicles and miles traveled, most states have been unable to reduce their overall accident problem. This could be due to a number of factors, but especially to an inattention to the three "E's" — education, engineering, and enforcement.

The accident investigator needs certain qualities to do an effective and efficient job. However, there is no substitute for carrying out fully all of the procedural steps necessary in a complete field investigation. First, it is necessary to recognize the three basic types of accident investigation: normal, late reported, and the hit-and-run. Although there should be a fixed system of operation in accident investigation, it must always remain flexible to accommodate any unusual problem that may arise.

It must be emphasized that in any motor vehicle accident there are three factors that, when all linked together, form the chain reaction leading to traffic mishaps. These three factors are the highway, the vehicle, and the people. Sufficient physical evidence must be gathered to identify each of these factors with some contributing cause that brought about property damage, injury, or death.

It is finally up to the investigating officer to zero in on the key event, analyze and/or reconstruct the accident, look at possible alternatives, make a decision based on the facts, and then submit a comprehensive factual report to his agency describing the resulting traffic accident.

DISCUSSION QUESTIONS

1. Describe in full the terms key event, direct, and mediate causes. Apply them to the principles of traffic accident investigation and analyze.

2. Discuss why it is so important to understand the various characteristics of accident causation. Identify some of the more prevalent types of accident causes.

TRUE — FALSE

1. Accident investigation is the cornerstone of the foundation of any program of traffic supervision.

2. During recent years, scientists have turned to the word *crash* in preference to the term *accident* in reference to traffic collisions.

3. Good traffic collision reporting is really of little value in the overall traffic program.

4. The *direct cause* of the accident is the unconventional behavior of a traffic unit which leads directly to the key event.

5. Measurements of fatal accidents require only approximate distances and, therefore, the pacing off of distances is acceptable.

6. An investigator's duty upon arrival is to protect the scene from further accidents before any other task is performed.

chapter

Special Accident Investigation Problems

THE HIT-AND-RUN ACCIDENT

With the hit-and-run accident, the officer is faced with a situation where he is really conducting two investigations. There is the investigation to determine the cause of the accident and the one to determine the identity of the driver who has left the scene. This is one type of accident where it is readily apparent that a violation has already occurred, that being evasion of responsibility. The officer, however, must not lose sight of the fact that leaving the scene is not a cause of the accident. The investigation, insofar as determining cause, must be complete and thorough in addition to locating the missing driver.

Hit-and-run may be a felony, as in cases resulting in injury or death, or a misdemeanor, wherein only property damage is involved. In either case, the accident should be investigated just as any other accident, except that the hit-and-run procedure should be followed.

The elements of felony hit-and-run, as established by the Vehicle Code, are (1) a driven vehicle involved in an accident resulting in injury or death; (2) failure to stop immediately (not instantly) at the scene and furnish identification by giving name and address of driver, name and address of the vehicle's registered owner, and upon request and if available, to show operator's license; and (3) failure to furnish aid, if requested or required.

To prove a case of felony hit-and-run, therefore, it is necessary to prove each of the foregoing elements. It must be shown that a driven vehicle was involved in an accident in which someone was injured or killed and that the driver had knowledge of the accident. Knowledge of the injury or death is not necessary. It must be proved that the driver *either* failed to stop *or* identify himself, *or* offer aid if it was necessary or requested. The driver may stop or return to the scene, but unless he identifies himself, the elements of the crime still exist. The investigator may prove knowledge, identity, and the offense by means of witnesses or entirely by circumstantial evidence. The owner of the vehicle, as a passenger, may be as guilty as the driver if he makes no attempt to stop at the scene and comply with the hit-and-run statute. The owner, under these circumstances, may be convicted of hit-and-run driving. Actual collision or contact between the vehicles involved is not necessary. "Involved in" is given the broader construction so that physical contact is not required. However, the driver involved must have committed the violation that caused the accident if there is no physical contact.

Time is important in hit-and-run investigations. The longer it takes to locate the driver, the more time he will have to repair the damage, destroy evidence, and establish an alibi. Therefore, the investigator faced with a hit-and-run investigation should get information on the air for the benefit of radio-equipped units as quickly as possible so that a wide search for the violator may be instituted at once.

Procedure at the scene of a hit-and-run investigation should be keyed to this need. A check should be made first for injuries, then to be sure that the drivers of all vehicles involved are present. As soon as the investigator determines that it is a hit-and-run, he should secure a description of the responsible vehicle, the driver and occupants, direction of travel, area of possible damage, and probably paint transfers and broadcast the preliminary information as soon as possible so that a minimum amount of time is lost in launching the search.

Having arranged for this immediate lookout to be broadcasted, the investigator should question the witnesses fully. He should get their complete story and determine the amount of damage and injury. If there was a collision, how did the witness know? If a license number was obtained, how was it obtained and by whom? It is essential to maintain a chain of continuity of all evidence so the case will not break down in court.

The investigator should determine whether or not the suspect stopped at any time. If he did, did he converse with anybody? Any conversation should be recorded in the exact words, if possible, as an aid in questioning the suspect. Was any identification offered? Did the victim ask for any? The witness should be questioned as to whether he would be able to identify the driver. The best possible description of the driver as well as of the passengers should be obtained. An accurate description of the vehicle should be requested, including the damage, make, model, year, color, and anything unusual or outstanding about the car. This should be as complete as the witness or witnesses can make it and supplemented by physical evidence that the investigator discovers. Any new developments should be furnished to the radio dispatcher so that other units may be advised.

It should be determined whether or not the witness actually saw the accident. A person who did not see the accident itself might have seen the damaged vehicle leave the scene. Persons working in nearby areas or motorists arriving from the direction of the suspect's flight might come under this category. A thorough canvass of the area should be made for witnesses.

No detail should be overlooked. If there was an injury, was it apparent? Did the suspect make any attempt to assist the victim? Was the victim conscious? How long from the time of the accident was it before the investigator arrived? Were there other violations on the part of the suspect such as excessive speed or driving while intoxicated? This is a twofold investigation, and no particle of evidence should be overlooked.

The scene should be literally combed for physical evidence. Extremely small parts broken from the suspect's car may be matched with the vehicle to make a positive identification. Paint transfers or chips may be discovered. Clothing should be preserved to be analyzed, using great care not to handle clothing unnecessarily or roughly as paint is invisible to the naked eye in many cases and might be lost. The clothing of persons killed should be obtained from the coroner. In auto-pedestrian cases clothing should be analyzed whenever possible. Chain of possession should be maintained, and clothing should be handled as little as possible and properly marked for identification. Photographs of the accident scene, victim, and vehicle should be taken, and other evidence photos obtained as indicated by the circumstances.

The investigator should be alert for the return of the responsible driver to the scene of the accident. Mingling with the crowd, even going so far as to follow the officer closely, the driver may attempt to ascertain the progress of the investigation. The inquisitive person who displays an unusual interest might well be the wanted driver trying to discover how close the investigation is coming to him, possibly going so far as to destroy evidence.

Follow-up activity will include checking garages, wrecking establishments, service stations, and repair shops and putting them on the alert for the wanted vehicle. Many other channels of group activity will be followed by other members of the department as well as the investigator.

If no suspect is apprehended, the investigator should revisit the scene periodically at the same time of day, day of the week, and date of the month. Through this pattern he may discover route salespeople, delivery drivers, or others who have a regular routine and may have been witnesses to the accident.

Once the vehicle is located and identification established, the driver will have to be found and connected to the crime. When he is located, the approach should be positive. The suspect may spontaneously make a statement that will identify him as the driver involved. However, officers must remember to properly admonish the suspect.

Hit-and-run investigation and apprehension is one of the most difficult and interesting jobs of the investigator. There is no apparent motive. The driver may have acted spontaneously through fear or nervousness to avoid apprehension because of being intoxicated, unlicensed, with "the other woman/man," uninsured, or wanted for another crime.

After apprehension is made, it is vitally important that the broadcast be cancelled and all alerted establishments notified. A word of thanks for their cooperation would not be amiss. They might prove useful in a later case.

Good hit-and-run investigation and reporting involve digging a little deeper to obtain more facts. It is the small, easily overlooked detail which, if found and checked, could start the chain of events leading to apprehension of the violator. Success in this field is a group effort, calling for much cooperation with other agencies as well as within the department. Cases are solved by common sense, hard work, and a small amount of technical knowledge.

ESTABLISHING TRAFFIC ACCIDENT VIOLATIONS

One of the primary purposes of a traffic accident investigation is to obtain evidence of violations that have occurred and record the information in such a manner that a complaint can be issued against the violator. The following Uniform Vehicle Code sections are shown in modified form to assist officers in recognizing the necessary elements. A complaint cannot be obtained if one or more of the elements is missing or cannot be proven. It is not necessary, however, that any one person witness *all* of the elements. A conviction can be sustained, for instance, where several witnesses contribute only portions of the elements individually, but together can supply all of the elements. To illustrate, this procedure is often used in drunk driving cases, with police officers testifying to intoxication only and other parties or witnesses testifying to driving only.

When interviewing parties and witnesses at the scene of a traffic accident involving any traffic violation, *the investigating officer must question each party or witness concerning each element of any suspected traffic violation.* How each element of the intended prosecution can be proven should be covered in the opinions and conclusions section of the particular state's accident investigation form. *No element should remain unresolved.* Every person interviewed should make one of the following statements:

1. That the element *was* present.

2. That the element was *not* present.

3. That he does not know whether it was present or not.

The "investigation" portion of the following material does not include the basic information needed for every accident investigation, such as direction of each vehicle, speed of vehicle, location when danger was first noticed, location of witnesses, or other general information, unless it is specifically needed as an element to obtain a conviction of a particular vehicle code section.

HIT-AND-RUN FELONY

The driver of any vehicle involved in an accident resulting in injury to any person other than himself or death to any person shall:

1. Stop immediately at the scene.
2. Comply with his state's vehicle code requirement dealing with persons injured as a result of a traffic accident, i.e.,
   a. give name and address,
   b. give registration number of the car,
   c. give name of the car's owner,
   d. exhibit his operator's license, if available, to the person struck or any police officer, if requested.
3. Render reasonable aid to the person struck.

NOTE: Failure to comply with *any* of these elements would constitute a violation of this section.

Investigation

In addition to the above elements (although not an element by statute), it is difficult to obtain a conviction without proof of guilty knowledge of the accident. Therefore, an investigator should gather evidence to show that:

A. The suspect knew or should have known of the accident because of extensive damage, loud noise, or other unusual circumstances.
B. Did the suspect stop? If so, where? Did he leave and then return? Why did he leave? How long was he gone?
C. If he stopped, did he give:
   1. Correct name?
   2. Correct address?
   3. Registration number of his vehicle?

   4. Name of the registered owner?
   5. Help to the victim?
   6. Did he exhibit his operator's license? (Was it requested?)
D. What did the suspect do that would indicate that he knew that he had
    been involved in an accident? Did he:
    1. Slow down and look back?
    2. Stop and look back? Walk back, look, then leave?
    3. Leave, then drive past again without stopping?
    4. Swerve, or take evasive action?

FELONY DRUNK DRIVING

To sustain a conviction of this section, the following four basic elements
must be present; that is, an investigation must cover each in order to be
complete.
   Any person who:

1. while under the influence of intoxicating liquor or under the com-
    bined influence of intoxicating liquor and any drug,
2. drives a vehicle,
3. and does any act forbidden by law, or neglects any duty imposed by
    law,
4. which act or neglect proximately causes bodily injury to any person
    other than himself

is guilty of a felony.

NOTE: Driving a *motor* vehicle is not a requirement. The act or neglect
       must "immediately precede and produce" the injury. All reports
       should show a strong relationship between the proximate cause
       and the injury.

Investigation

A. Suspect
    1. What have you been drinking? How much? Where? When?
    2. Where were you going when the accident happened? (Establish
        driving)
    3. How did the accident happen? (Establish violation)
    4. What injuries were sustained? By whom?
B. Other parties and witnesses
    1. Has he (suspect) been drinking? Why do you think so? What is
        your opinion of his degree of intoxication? Has it affected his
        ability to drive?

2. Was he driving the car? Did you see him in the driver's seat shortly after the accident?
3. Did he commit any traffic violations? Were they the cause of any injuries?
4. Who was injured besides the driver?

MISDEMEANOR DRUNK DRIVING

It is unlawful for any person who is:

1. under the influence of intoxicating liquor,
2. or, under the combined influence of intoxicating liquor or *any* drug,
3. to drive a vehicle on a highway.

This charge is valid when:

1. The arresting officer witnesses the arrestee commit the elements of driving on a highway while under the influence of intoxicating liquor or combined influences, or
2. A witness can establish the element of driving on a highway, and the arrestee is intoxicated at the time of arrest.
3. The element of driving can be established by circumstantial evidence.
4. A peace officer arrests said driver without warrant out of an accident.

NOTE: There are numerous degrees of intoxication from "barely under the influence" to "falling down drunk." The word *intoxicated,* rather than the phrase "under the influence of intoxicating liquor," *should* be used in reporting officers' opinions.

Investigation

A. Suspect
    1. What have you had to drink? How much? When? Where? If you have not had anything to drink, why can't you do the balance tests?
    2. Where were you driving? How did the accident happen?

DRIVING AND NARCOTIC DRUGS

It is a felony to drive a vehicle under the influence of narcotics. It is unlawful for any person who is:

1. addicted to the use, or
2. under the influence of narcotic drugs,
3. to drive a vehicle upon a highway.

NOTE: The suspect should be taken to a specialist or doctor to obtain expert opinion of the cause for objective symptoms. No accident or injury is necessary to investigate. The charge is not valid if the driving is on private property, but the Health and Safety Code is still applicable.

Investigation

A. Suspect
  1. Why are you unable to perform balancing test? What medicine are you taking? What is your doctor's name? How long since your last "fix"? Check for needle marks, "hype kit," and so on.
  2. Where were you driving the car? From where?
B. Parties and witnesses
  1. Are his actions normal? Does he appear to be under the influence of anything? If so, did you notice the odor of alcohol? (To disprove drunkenness)
  2. Did you see him driving? Where? Was he in the driver's seat?

DRIVING AND NONNARCOTIC DRUGS

Driving a vehicle under the influence of nonnarcotic drugs may be either a felony or a misdemeanor depending on the individual state laws. Any person who:

1. while knowingly under the influence of any drug other than a narcotic,
2. to a degree which renders him incapable of safely driving a vehicle,
3. drives a vehicle,
4. does an act forbidden by law or neglects any duty required by law,
5. which proximately causes injury to another person,

is guilty of this offense.

NOTE: It is not necessary for the substance to be a narcotic, not required for the vehicle to be a *motor* vehicle, and not necessary for the act to be on a highway. The act or neglect must "immediately precede and produce" the injury, and the injury must be to someone other than the driver. Death is not included in this section (use manslaughter charge). Clearly establish the traffic violation; the charge may later be reduced.

Investigation

A. Suspect
  1. Are you under a doctor's care? Doctor's name? If so, what drugs are you taking? Where are they? How many? How long?

    2.   How did you feel just before the accident? Have you felt that way before? (Safe driving in question)

    3.   Where were you driving?

    4.   How did the accident happen?

    5.   Who was injured? What were the injuries?

B.   Parties and witnesses

    1.   Does he appear normal? Do you think he is under the influence of anything? Why?

    2.   Is he a safe driver? Would you ride in a car with him driving?

    3.   Did you see him driving? Was he in the driver's seat?

    4.   Did he do anything illegal that caused the accident? Any traffic violations?

    5.   Was anyone besides the suspect injured?

LEFT TURN AT AN INTERSECTION

In this maneuver, a left-turning vehicle is required to yield the right-of-way to vehicles that:

1.   have approached an intersection (waiting at red signal), public or private property, or an alley, or

2.   are approaching and are close enough to constitute a hazard at any time during the turning movement.

NOTE: Right-of-way violations occur when there is "danger of conflict" because this section involves a left turn. Other Vehicle Code sections may be involved, such as wrong lane, required signal from 100 feet, driving left of double lines, and nonturner yield.

Basic Investigation

A.   Approach to intersection, public property, or an alley

    1.   Lane traveled.

    2.   Speed (mph).

B.   Signaling

    1.   Type of signal, hand or mechanical.

    2.   Distance prior to turn that signal was given.

C.   Arrival at turning point

    1.   Determine if party stopped or rolled into turn (mph).

    2.   Locate point in relation to where party started his turn.

D.   Yielding (or lack of same)

    1.   Describe number, speed, and location of cars yielded to.

    2.   Describe speed and location of approaching vehicle (party).

E.   Path of travel following turning point

1.   Note position of point of impact, skid marks, and obtain statements relative to same.

Questions

A.   Left turner
1.   What street were you on? Which direction were you going? Which lane? What speed? (Set the picture)
2.   Did you signal? How? Where were you at the time of start of signaling? (Turn signal violation)
3.   Where was the other car at the time you started to turn? How fast was it going? How fast were you going then? Did you slow or stop? Where? Where did your turn actually start? Did you stop, then restart?
4.   Were there passing cars going in the same direction as the other car? How many? How fast? Were you partially in a turn while you were waiting? How long did you wait there? Where was the other car when you first arrived in turn position?

B.   Nonturner
1.   Which direction were you traveling? How fast? Which lane?
2.   Where was the other car when you first saw it? Its speed? At the time it *first* started to turn, where were you? Your speed? If violator stopped, did he restart?
3.   How long was he stopped? Where were you at the time you first observed other car stopped? Were there any vehicles in front of you? How many? How far ahead?

RED SIGNAL VIOLATIONS

Traffic facing the red signal shall:

1.   stop at a limit line if marked,
2.   otherwise before entering the crosswalk,
3.   or if none, before entering the intersection.

This section requires drivers to stop at certain locations when a red signal is displayed. Therefore, parties and witnesses should be interviewed to find where the violator's vehicle was at the time the red light came on and whether he stopped for it.

Investigation

A.   Both parties
All parties should be asked the following questions in relation to every party involved:

1. Which direction were you traveling? How fast?
2. Where on the roadway were you when you first observed signal? Which signal was observed? What color was it?
3. What color was the signal when the party entered the intersection?
4. Did the signal change? To what color? Where were the parties then?
5. Where was the other party when first observed? What was the condition of the signal then?

B. Witness
   1. Where were you at the time of the accident?
   2. What attracted your attention to the accident?
   3. Which party entered the intersection against the red signal?
   4. Which signal did you observe? What color was it?
   5. How fast were the parties traveling?
   6. Do you know either party?

If witness' attention was attracted to accident by the sound of the impact:

1. Did you look at the signal? What was the condition of the signal? Which signal was observed?
2. How much time elapsed between the time of the accident and the time you first observed the signal?
3. Did the signal change after the accident? How long after?
4. What was the location of the offending vehicle when first observed and the condition of the signal at that time?

FOLLOWING TOO CLOSELY

The driver of a motor vehicle shall not follow another vehicle more closely than is *reasonable* and *prudent*, having due regard for the

1. speed of such vehicle,
2. traffic,
3. and condition of the roadway.

NOTE: Primary considerations must show that both vehicles were *in motion* at the time of the collision or that the front vehicle had been *stopped for not more than one second*. This is essentially a speed and distance violation, and the investigation must show a hazardous condition — following too closely for a period of time.

Investigation

A. Rear car driver
   1. What was the speed of the front car? Your speed?

2. How far behind were you? (Feet or car lengths)
3. How far did you follow at that spacing?
4. Condition of the road surface?
5. Did the other person signal?

B. Front car driver
   1. What was your speed before the accident? What was the speed of the rear car (if observed)?
   2. What attracted your attention to the vehicle behind you?
   3. How far behind was it? How far did he follow there?
   4. Condition of the road surface?
   5. Why did you slow or stop?
   6. What signal did you give?
   7. How long were you stopped before being struck?

YIELDING RIGHT-OF-WAY AFTER STOP

The driver of any vehicle shall *stop* at the entrance to a through highway and shall *yield* the right-of-way to *other vehicles* that have:

1. entered the intersection, or
2. are approaching so closely as to constitute an immediate hazard.

NOTE: A *stop* is required before this section becomes operative. If the driver fails to *stop,* use stop sign section. "Immediate hazard" is determined by establishing the distance and speed of the approaching vehicle at the time the starting vehicle is just starting into the through highway.

Investigation

A. Violator
   1. Did you stop? Where? How long were you stopped (seconds)? Did any vehicles pass you on the through highway?
   2. Where was the other car at the time you were *just stopped?* Its speed?
   3. Where was the other car at the time you were *just* starting into the intersection? Its speed? Your speed?
   4. (If skids are observed leading into the intersection, are those your skids?)

B. Other party
   1. Where was the other party when first observed?
   2. Did he *stop* before entering the intersection? How *long* was he stopped? If not, his speed?
   3. Where were you at the time he was just starting into the intersection? Your speed? His speed?

UNSAFE TURN OR MOVEMENT

No person shall:

1. turn a vehicle from a direct course.
2. or move right or left upon a roadway until it can be done safely, and
3. then only with an appropriate signal if another vehicle is affected.
4. The person must signal during the last 100 feet traveled.

NOTE: Even if a signal is given properly, a turn is still prohibited until it is safe to do so. Do not use this section for unsafe lane change on laned streets; it generally applies to lane changes within intersections.

Investigation

A. Violator
   1. Which direction were you going? Speed? What portion of the roadway were you traveling in?
   2. Did you signal? How? Window up or down?
   3. Where was the other car when you first saw it? Speed?
   4. Where was it when you started to turn?
B. Other party
   1. Which direction were you going? Speed?
   2. Where was the other car when you first saw it? Its speed?
   3. Did he signal to turn? How?
   4. Where were you when he started to turn? Your speed at the time?

UNSAFE START OR BACKING

It is unlawful to:

1. start a vehicle
   a. stopped,
   b. standing,
   c. or parked,
2. or back a vehicle
3. until such movement can be made with reasonable safety.

NOTE: This section is usually used for drivers suddenly pulling out from the curb or backing unsafely on a street. Do not use it for backing out from a private driveway. (Some state vehicle code sections apply to vehicles entering a highway from private property whether entering forwards or backwards.) Also note that signaling is not specifically required.

Investigation

A. Violator
    1. Where was the other party at the time you first started to move? Speed?
    2. Did you have sufficient time to complete your movement safely?
B. Other party
    1. Where were you when his vehicle first started to move?
    2. How fast were you going at that time? (Pedestrians — walking or running?)

UNSAFE LANE CHANGE

Whenever any roadway has been divided into two or more clearly marked lanes in one direction, the following rules apply. A vehicle shall be driven as nearly as practical:

1. entirely within a single lane,
2. and shall not be moved from such lane until the movement can be made with safety.

NOTE: That street must have at least two lanes in one direction and must be marked. Also the vehicle need *not* actually *change* lanes — merely "move from" is sufficient. (This includes "starting" to change lanes, then moving back.)

Investigation

A. Violator
    1. Which lane were you in?
    2. Did you signal prior to attempting to move from the lane?
    3. Were there any vehicles in the lanes on either side?
    4. Where was the other vehicle at the time you started to leave your lane?
    5. Did the other vehicle change direction or speed when you started to leave your lane? Why?
B. Victim
    1. Where was your vehicle when the other vehicle first started to turn? His speed? Your speed?
    2. Did he signal prior to the turn?
    3. Did you swerve or slow to avoid him? Why?

PEDESTRIANS

Every pedestrian crossing a roadway at any point other than within a marked crosswalk or within an unmarked crosswalk at an intersection shall yield the right-of-way to all vehicles upon the roadway.

NOTE: Traffic signals are not required at adjacent intersections.

Investigation

This section essentially is a speed and distance problem. Parties should be interviewed to determine:
1. That the pedestrian was in the roadway between intersections but not in a crosswalk.
2. That a hazard was present *due to the relative positions* of the vehicle and the pedestrian.
3. That the pedestrian *did not yield*, resulting in death, injury, or property damage.

Questions

A. Violator
    1. Where were you going? From where?
    2. Where was the vehicle when you stepped onto the roadway? Speed of the vehicle?
    3. Did you yield right-of-way to any vehicle?
B. Driver of vehicle
    1. Where were you when the pedestrian entered the roadway? Your speed?
    2. Was the pedestrian running or walking? Did he stop for you?
    3. Was your attention distracted? Could you have stopped prior to the traffic accident?

INVESTIGATION OF BRAKES AS UNSAFE EQUIPMENT

This information is presented to acquaint officers with the procedures necessary to initiate filings for violations of the Vehicle Code section dealing with brakes. The procedures to follow when investigating vehicles with air brake systems are also included.

Presentation

I. Procedure
    A. Thoroughly inspect the braking system and try to establish whether or not the brakes were faulty *prior* to the traffic accident. The following procedure has been prepared for use in checking braking systems for defects.
        1. Determine if the system is hydraulic or mechanical.

      a.   Whether hydraulic or mechanical, attempt to depress the foot pedal to the floorboard by fingertip.

          1.   If this can be accomplished and the system is hydraulic, determine if the pedal can be restored to normal by pumping it. If so, record the number of strokes required.

          2.   If the foot pedal can be depressed to the floorboard by fingertip and the system is mechanical, inspect the linkage for defects or improper adjustments.

  2.   When inspecting hydraulic systems, check the area in the vicinity of the master cylinder (usually on the engine side of the firewall on the later models) for evidence of brake fluid leakage.

      a.   Check for leaks in the hydraulic lines.

      b.   Check the inside portions of the wheels where evidence of leaking wheel cylinders would be present.

      c.   Check for evidence of leakage on the roadway.

          1.   Inspect that portion of the roadway over which the vehicle passed just prior to the place of impact.

  3.   Take photographs that will illustrate or substantiate any faulty or unsafe condition of the braking system.

  4.   When in doubt about the safety of the braking system, conduct a stopping-distance test, if feasible.

      a.   The test speed shall be 20 mph, and the legal stopping distance shall not exceed 25 feet.

NOTE: The preceding values apply only to passenger motor vehicles that are designed to carry not more than nine persons, including the driver. (Refer to the respective state code for the legal stopping distances for motor vehicles.)

  5.   Ascertain if the involved vehicle is equipped with an adequate emergency or parking brake.

      a.   It must be capable of locking the rear driving wheels and holding the vehicle stationary to the limit of traction of the brakes' wheels.

II.   Reporting Requirements

  A.   The success of the prosecution rests upon the ability of the investigator to establish the essential elements of the offense and to make a comprehensive report of all facts revealed by the investigation. It is mandatory to establish two elements in order to request a filing of the brake section.

      1.   Establish that the braking system of the involved vehicle was *faulty* or in an *unsafe condition*.

a.   The accident investigation form should include a complete, comprehensive statement of facts revealed by the investigation of the braking system, including the results of any tests that were conducted.

2.   Establish that the *driver* of said vehicle had *knowledge* of the unsafe condition of the braking system *prior* to the traffic accident.

a.   The driver's statement on the accident investigation form shall reflect positively or negatively his knowledge of the unsafe condition of the brakes prior to the accident.

WITNESSES' AND DRIVER'S STATEMENTS

Taking statements from drivers and witnesses is an important part of many investigations. This may simply consist of asking what happened and recording it in the investigator's own words or an informal, written statement signed by a witness. In serious cases, it may be a formally recorded statement taken by the prosecutor and stenographer. Statements written and signed by drivers in required reports are confidential; therefore, drivers' statements should not be written or signed by the prosecutor or stenographer.

Statements are of value for several reasons. They give the investigator a clue to what happened and in which direction he should start the investigation; and they tend to dissuade a person from changing his story at a later date and may, in some cases, be used to impeach a witness. Even if the person has not signed the statement, the fact that he has given it to the officer may keep him from changing his story. The statement may also be used to refresh the memory of a witness.

The investigator will take statements to assist him in determining facts. By statements, he may place the driver behind the wheel, determine probable point of impact if there were no skid marks, tie skid marks to a particular vehicle, and establish other circumstances of the accident.

One of the first considerations in taking statements is to talk to the person in private. Many people are reluctant to talk if others are listening. They may be afraid of what the driver or his friends might do if the statement is unfavorable. Spectators may interrupt by interjecting their own ideas, and arguments may start as the result of disagreements between participants.

If possible, the investigator should have the witness or driver tell the story from his general location at the time of the accident. This will serve as a check on his reliability and establish whether or not he could see what he claims. He should be allowed to tell his story without interruption, except as necessary to keep him from rambling too far from the subject. The investigator must be sure he understands what the person means. For example, "I was passing several cars" could indicate the speaker was either meeting or overtaking other vehicles. Words do not always mean the same thing to the speaker and listener.

Questions should be objective, positive, and specific — not "Where do you live?" but "What is your address, please?" This will save time and make statements concise and pertinent. Statements should be verified with facts and discrepancies pointed out. No attempt should be made to "coach" the witness, but by indicating points of disagreement the person may adjust his recollections.

After the person has finished his statement, if there are any points he has not covered, specific questions should be asked. When the investigator is sure the statement will be complete, he should write it out and have the witness sign it. In some cases, it may be appropriate to have a witness write his own statement to keep him occupied and from discussing the event with others. However, it is generally better for the investigator to write the statement and have the subject sign. Some people have difficulty putting their thoughts on paper, and their statements will be inadequate. By writing the statements himself, the investigator can be certain it is complete.

When writing the statement as the subject tells it, the investigator may consider deliberately including a few errors in minor details. The subject should correct these when he reads the statement and initial the correction. If he fails to notice the errors, they should be called to his attention. He should then correct and initial them. This precludes the chance of the subject saying he did not read the statement, and by having the pencil in his hand and becoming used to it he is conditioned toward signing the statement when requested.

If the witness refuses to sign, the officer must not insist upon a signature. He should use a positive approach in attempting to get the signature and, if this fails, drop the matter. The signature in itself is not essential. Having given the statement to an officer, the subject will be less likely to change his story if he knows it has been recorded.

While listening to a witness's statement, the investigator should not be in a hurry to start writing. Some people are reluctant to talk if they know the conversation is being recorded and will not give a statement. Also, the first time they make it, the statement may not be adequate and will have to be rewritten, which is time consuming.

Ordinarily, by the time the investigator is ready to take the statement, he will have a good idea as to cause and violation. He should be sure the statement covers all the necessary elements. Care should be taken to cover who was driving, direction of travel, approximate speed, and condition of pavement and weather and to tie in the skid marks, if any, with the appropriate vehicle.

A statement that does not add to the investigator's knowledge of the accident is wasted time, whereas a properly taken statement may prove of great value to the case and should be preserved. Witnesses have been known to change their stories. If a person who has given a statement in which he declares he knew nothing about the accident should turn up as a witness, the statement taken by the officer would do much to discredit the later testimony.

Questioning Drivers and Witnesses

To assist in routine investigations, the following questions should be asked in most cases. The answers to these questions should give the investigator a fairly good picture of how the accident happened.

1. *Exactly where were you when you first saw the other car?*
   The object of this question is to establish the first point and time of awareness. Therefore, the officer may have to say *heard* or even *felt* instead of *saw*. (The first point and time of awareness may be a jolt created by hitting a hole in the road or a soft shoulder.) It is better to get the driver to show the location than to tell it. It is a good idea to establish the spot so the officer can locate it later by measurements. From this spot, the officer should look for himself to visualize what the driver saw.

2. *What were you doing at the moment you first saw the other car?*
   First, let the driver tell it in his own words. If he is not clear, then ask him about two things:
   a. *His movement* — speed, direction, slowing down or speeding up.
   b. *His attention* — where had he been looking? Had he been talking, changing the radio, or doing something else?

3. *Where were you when you first realized you were in trouble?*
   This question is to establish the *point of surprise*. Again, have him show the location, if possible.

4. *What were you doing at the moment you first realized you were in trouble?*
   This question also involves establishment of movement and attention. Do not ask it if question 2 was answered satisfactorily.

5. *Exactly what did you do, if anything, to avoid the accident?*
   Here the officer tries to establish possible evasive action. If the response is slow, do not urge or coach an answer. If coached, the officer may get what the person thinks he *should* have done and not what he *actually* did. This is why "if anything" is included in the question.

6. *Then, what happened?*
    Let the driver describe the actual event in his own words.

7. *Exactly where did the collision take place?*
    This question need not be asked if the *point of impact* is readily apparent due to physical evidence.

8. *Where did you stop after the collision?*
    Again, this is not necessary if indicated by physical evidence. However, vehicles are often moved prior to the investigator's arrival and establishment of *point of rest* is often necessary to a valid investigation.

9. *What is the first thing you remember after the accident?*
    Take the time to allow an answer in his own words. Do not press for an answer. If the driver was knocked unconscious, this question is vital. The next logical question would be:

10. *What is the last thing you remember clearly before the accident?*
    Do not appear surprised at anything he says. However, if unconsciousness was a result of the accident, attempt to verify his statement by a statement from an unbiased witness.

11. *Whom did you first see after the accident?*
    This may be a good clue to an eyewitness. Witnesses have a habit of "not wanting to get involved."

12. *What did you say to him or her?*
    Here the object of the question is to get an idea of the explanation of the accident the driver gave immediately following the crash. Encourage him to say more by adding, "What else, if anything, do you remember?"

13. *What did he or she say to you?*
    This is a means of checking to see if the drivers have changed their stories by comparing this with what the other driver has already told the officer.

As in any criminal investigation, if possible, the parties involved should be separated when these questions are asked. If an officer attempts to question them together, he stands a very good chance of ending up in the center of an argument.

When asking these questions, the officer should be sincere. Although it may be another routine investigation to him, this may be the most important part to the people involved. Most people are not involved in many accidents and a $125 dent in a fender can be very important to them. If the officer handles each accident investigation as a professional, he will find that the answers he seeks will generally appear. These questions are by no means all that may throw light on what happened. They can be adapted to meet the needs of any particular incident. They do, however, answer the important questions of who, what, where, why, when, and how.

ENFORCEMENT ACTION

Having gathered the evidence that will support a prosecution, appropriate enforcement action is the next step. In most traffic accident investigations, the offense involved will be an infraction. In that case, the officer will be precluded from taking enforcement action at the scene due to the legal restraints imposed upon him. In cases where the evidence is clear cut and apparently sufficient to support a charge, the investigator should inform the violator of his intention to file a complaint. In cases where the prosecutor desires the opportunity to review the evidence before issuing a complaint, the officer should take a positive stand. If he believes there is sufficient evidence, he should tell the violator that it is his intention to ask for a complaint. This paves the way for psychological acceptance on the part of the violator of subsequent notice that a charge has been filed. If the officer attempts to evade taking a stand by advising the driver that he will make further investigation, confer with his superiors, and so on and a complaint may be filed, the door is opened in the violator's mind for a not guilty plea. He may feel that the officer is not certain in his conclusions and may be reluctant to accept his guilt to the extent he would if the officer took a positive stand. This points up the fact that an investigation must be complete, thorough, and conclusive.

Should the prosecutor wish to review the evidence before approving a complaint, the violator should be notified as soon as the complaint is filed. If the service of a warrant is his first notice of the court action, good public relations suffer. When the officer is empowered by law to take enforcement action at the scene, an arrest is in order.

It is good practice for the investigator to review the entire investigation just before leaving the scene. This serves two purposes. It gives him a double check to assure that all points have been covered and that all of the necessary information has been gathered. A physical recheck may disclose a piece of overlooked evidence, and property of the participants may be found that might otherwise be lost. If two officers are conducting the investigation, they should compare notes to be sure that each has all the necessary information. Reviewing the investigation takes a little time but may be very productive in terms of results obtained.

One possibility the investigator should not overlook is that of the "staged" accident designed to defraud insurance companies by means of nonexistent injuries supposedly sustained in a carefully engineered "traffic accident." Some individuals, including attorneys, doctors, and garage proprietors, have conspired to collect damages for fictitious injuries by carefully staging traffic accidents. This type of fraud is difficult to detect. Officers should carefully observe the demeanor of persons involved, developing good factual detail and watching for inconsistencies or fabrications. If fraud is suspected, careful questioning should be carried on to determine its motive. It may vary from the desire for easy money to outright murder.

Some of the circumstances that might suggest possibility of fraud are lack of witnesses, no plausible reason for the accident, or one person freely admitting liability while the other seems to be feigning injury. "Victims" may prefer to seek their own medical care in preference to usual facilities. While these are not conclusive evidence of fraudulent attempts, officers should not ignore the possibility that such a conspiracy might exist.

Before leaving the accident scene, the investigator must be sure that it is in safe condition: vehicles and debris must be cleared from the highway, spilled oil sanded or covered with dirt, flares extinguished, and as much evidence of the accident as possible removed. Otherwise, traffic may become involved in additional accidents due to sudden slowing or stopping as drivers observe signs of an accident.

Often it will be impossible to complete the investigation at the scene. It may be necessary to contact additional witnesses to determine the true causes. Drivers or other persons may have been injured and taken to hospitals or their homes after treatment. Sometimes the officer will do this further investigation himself, and in other cases it will be done by officers assigned to accident follow-up. Should it become necessary to interview injured persons, the officer should check with the doctor in attendance before attempting to talk to these people. In some cases their condition will be such that it would not be advisable to interview them. In other cases, they may have been given sedatives or other treatment so that their statements would not be reliable. Each instance will have to be treated on its merits by the investigator. Just as no two accidents will be alike, so no two investigations will be alike. The planned procedure must be flexible, and steps taken in the order called for by each set of circumstances encountered.

The final step of the investigation will be that of making out the accident report on a standard form. In filling out the report, the investigator will be guided by his departmental policy. He should bear in mind that to be a good report it should leave no logical questions unanswered that might be asked by any of the several agencies using it as a source of information. A good investigation will lose much of its value if the information is not transmitted by means of a thorough, accurate, complete report, including the who, what, when, where, why, and how of the accident. Similarly, without a thorough, accurate, and complete investigation, there can be no good report.

In addition to normal accident investigations and the hit-and-run investigation, a third type will be encountered — late reported accidents. Late reported accidents are those that come to the attention of the investigator after some lapse of time. Usually the vehicles involved are no longer at the scene, and much of the evidence will probably have been altered or destroyed. The degree of follow-up of these accidents will usually depend upon the severity. Fatalities will require a complete investigation. A considerable amount of investigation may be done where serious injury is involved, whereas minor property-damage accidents may only be recorded on the official forms as simply a driver's report.

SUMMARY

In this chapter, we have focused on some very critical issues: the hit-and-run violator, methods and evidence needed to establish uniform vehicle code violations, taking of drivers' and witnesses' statements, and finally the enforcement applied to accident investigation.

Space does not permit us to go into greater detail on the investigation of hit-and-run accidents. What has been discussed, however, are the essential methods for the field investigator to apply during the course of such an investigation. The investigator should understand that the hit-and-run suspect is not someone who merely left the scene by some unfortunate act which he was unable to control, but rather by impulse and by design. The field investigator must exercise every imaginative tool at his disposal in an attempt to piece the hit-and-run puzzle together. This task is not easy and sometimes may take days, weeks, or months to solve. By using some of the available physical evidence at the scene and statements of other drivers and possibly some disinterested witnesses, the investigator must work diligently in reconstructing the events that took place. Every possible detail must be examined and none should be overlooked.

There has always been a definite need for some uniform guidelines to establish traffic accident violations, and the material in this chapter should be helpful in providing some of these. It is imperative that the police officer, state trooper, county sheriff, highway patrol officer, or state police officer fully investigate each traffic crash with the same concerned diligence that he would a reported crime. The sifting of every shred of evidence to establish each element needed to prove the corpus delicti must be done in a systematic manner. By using the outlined material contained in this system, both the new and the veteran officer should be able to successfully complete each investigation with a great deal less effort. He will provide a combination of systematic, uniform, and relevant factual information needed by his department and that of the prosecuting agency.

DISCUSSION QUESTIONS

1.   Outline the various procedures used in the investigation of a hit-and-run accident. What additional steps does the agency in your state require in completing such a detailed investigation?

2.   Compare the uniform elements on establishing traffic accident violations with those of your state or its agency. How do they differ and what are the similarities, if any?

TRUE-FALSE

1.   Actual collision contact must be established in order to show that a hit-and-run accident actually occurred.

2.   It is always a good idea to revisit the scene of a hit-and-run investigation at about the same time of day and on the same day of the week possibly to locate the hit-and-run driver.

3.   As a police officer, your opinions and conclusions in your accident report should never reflect how each element can be proven.

4.   One method of interviewing a witness or driver is the question-answer technique.

5.   If an officer does a complete job of investigation, it is seldom necessary to review the entire investigation prior to leaving the scene.

chapter

Determination of Speed from Skid Marks

INTRODUCTION TO THE THEORY

In many investigations, knowing the initial speed of the accident vehicle is of great value to the investigator. Drivers may not admit accurate speeds. Often the speed estimate of witnesses will be unreliable or disbelieved due to their unfamiliarity with speed and its results. A scientific method which eliminates much of the guesswork is that of computing minimum initial speeds from the measured length of skid marks.

Excessive speed is a common accident cause. When faced with an emergency, a driver will usually apply the brakes with maximum force or swerve the vehicle sharply. The resultant skid marks provide evidence that serves as a basis for computing the minimum initial speed of the vehicle with reasonable accuracy.

Not only will this evidence be of assistance in prosecuting violators, but it may also serve to exonerate drivers who might otherwise be charged. A skid of 20 feet from 20 miles per hour does not mean that a skid of 100 feet, or five times as long, indicates five times as much speed. The actual speed in this case would be only about 45 miles per hour.

This type of evidence is particularly valuable in auto-pedestrian cases where little damage is done to the vehicle. Where extensive damage results, all that can be measured is the amount of speed the vehicle lost in sliding. Energy absorbed in the collision is above and beyond that figure.

With emergency stopping, rotation of the wheels ceases almost instantly and wheels are said to be "locked." Locking the wheels will not stop the vehicle at once. Instead, the tires will slide upon the surface until all the

231

kinetic energy of the vehicle has been transformed into heat energy, repre-
sented by the sliding of the tires. Since, by the law of conservation of
energy, energy cannot be created or destroyed, the energy of motion must
be equal to the energy of stopping.

While this energy transformation is taking place, a heavy deposit of
rubber will be left on the pavement. This can be readily identified, and the
length of the skid mark left by each wheel can be measured.

COEFFICIENT OF FRICTION

Coefficient of friction is the ratio of the force required in sliding an object
over a surface to the force (usually the weight) pressing the object against
the surface.

The force created by locking the wheels of a moving vehicle is the
same as that necessary to drag the vehicle with its wheels locked. The
coefficient of friction (also called the drag factor) is found by using the
formula $f = F/W$ (also $F = Wf$). For example, if a force of 3000 pounds were
necessary to move a 4000-pound vehicle with locked wheels, the coefficient of friction would be 75 percent:

$$f = \frac{F}{W} = \frac{3000}{4000} = 75 \text{ percent}$$

If the same vehicle were moving and the wheels were locked, a 3000-
pound force would "pull" on the vehicle until it stopped.

On dry, hard road surfaces braking forces that can be developed are
fairly uniform. The coefficient of friction will vary slightly with changes in
speed. In contrast, on wet surfaces, due to the lubricating effect of the water
and other factors, the coefficient of friction will vary with different initial
speeds. Therefore, use of the formulas for computing speed from skid
marks should generally be confined to dry pavements.

Even with a freely rolling wheel, minute particles of rubber are being
deposited on the surface of the pavement. However, these deposits are so
small that no clearly defined markings are visible. With a heavy brake
application, it is often difficult to detect any markings on the pavement if
the wheels continue to rotate. Under emergency conditions, however,
maximum braking force generally causes the wheels of the vehicle to lock.
On dry pavement the locked wheels will leave a heavy deposit of rubber,
which can be accurately assessed as to length, location, direction, and
number of wheels affected.

When a heavy braking force is exerted (even with disc brakes and/or
radial tires), the retarding force is greatest just before the wheels are locked.
This type of tire marking is termed *impending*. The wheels are just about to
cease rotating, and usually the tire marks are less visible than those made

by locked wheels. In some instances it is possible to see the design of the tire tread in the impending markings. Usually this type of mark leads directly to the locked wheel markings. A general characteristic of the locked wheel type of markings is that the path of the vehicle is straight. This is true because it is impossible to change direction by steering once the wheels are locked.

In many collisions there may be a sudden and violent change of direction due to impact with another vehicle or object. This change is usually visible, but many times results in a confusion of tire markings that are difficult to describe accurately. In some instances an abrupt change of direction is effected by the operator attempting to turn the vehicle from its path. It is possible when this occurs that clearly defined tire markings will be visible and that braking *may* or *may not* be in effect. In this case, a new force has been added to the vehicle which is described as *centrifugal force*. This new force resists the change of direction that the operator is attempting to impart by turning the wheels.

STANDARD TIRE MARK TERMINOLOGY

Investigators should be aware that it is possible to leave tire markings on the pavement that closely resemble "locked wheel" or "impending" marks *without any brake application*. Such markings are many times identified by a variety of confusing terms. These types of descriptions do not lend themselves to intelligent interpretations or evaluations in reconstructing the facts of the collision.

To improve this situation, we must develop and use a uniform terminology. To determine a vehicle's speed based upon the evidence left on the roadway, it is necessary that all deceleration factors be considered. The primary deceleration factor is the braking mechanism. Secondary factors are the surface upon which the vehicle is traveling, its grade percentage, and its condition.

First among the uniform definitions of skid mark terminology is a *tire skid mark,* defined as a mark left by a tire due to the sliding of the tire over a surface. Visible tire skid marks are made in three ways: extreme deceleration, extreme change of direction, and extreme acceleration.

Extreme Deceleration. When the braking system is sufficient to cause the wheels to cease rotating, they will lock and skid marks will be left on the surface. Even when the wheels are still turning but are *about to cease rotating,* skid marks will be visible.

Extreme Change of Direction. This action may result from effort on the part of the operator or from an impact. Resulting skid marks are usually visible to the investigator.

Extreme Acceleration.   This condition occurs when a propelling force exceeding the pavement efficiency is generated. If the driving force applied to the rear wheels is such that it will cause the wheels to "spin," skid marks will result.

The following diagrams illustrate some applications of the four basic terms that will be used throughout this discussion of the various types of tire skid marks. The first two of these terms involve straight or curved skid marks due to brake application. An *impending* skid mark (figs. 11-1 and 11-2) is left by a braked wheel *rotating* slower than the forward motion of the vehicle in a straight or curved line.

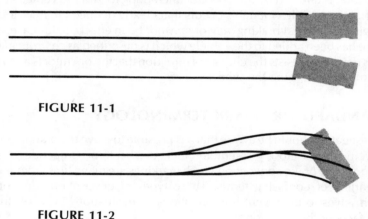

FIGURE 11-1

FIGURE 11-2

Figure 11-3 shows a *locked wheel* skid mark left by a *nonrotating* wheel of a vehicle moving in a straight or curved line in the original direction of motion.

The third term is the *slide skid* mark, which is left by a *locked,* braked, or rotating wheel of a vehicle sliding in other than a forward direction, except when caused by centrifugal force. Figure 11-4 shows a side skid due to impact with brakes applied.

The *centrifugal* skid mark, the fourth basic term, is left by a *rotating* wheel of a vehicle rounding a curve or turning at such a speed that

FIGURE 11-3

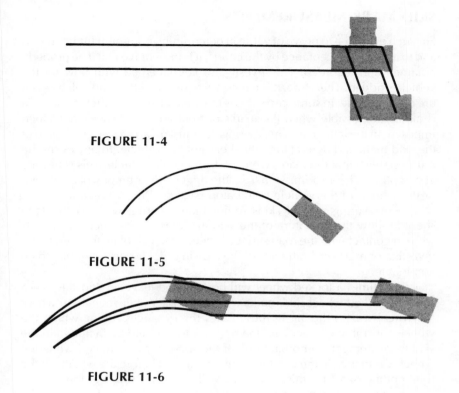

FIGURE 11-4

FIGURE 11-5

FIGURE 11-6

centrifugal force entirely or partially overcomes the frictional resistance between road and tire. Figure 11-5 shows curved light marks from a controlled rapid change of direction. Curved marks from a too rapid change of direction (fig. 11-6) end with locked wheel or side mark.

There are descriptive terms which can be used to describe skid marks *after the basic term has been used.* These may be "intermittent" to describe markings that are not continuous; "dual wheel," "single vehicle," and so on to indicate the number of wheels affected and the type of equipment; "curving," "straight line," and so on to describe direction and type. Any term that further describes the skid marks after the basic terminology has been used, and that can be employed to clarify the facts of the collision, is acceptable.

Only when the basic terminology is used by all investigators will it be possible to reach a common understanding. Thus, definite conclusions may be made concerning speed, direction of travel, and point of impact from the skid marks at the accident scene.

SKID MARK MEASUREMENTS

For such evidence to prove of value in determining minimum initial speeds and to assure its acceptance by the courts, it is imperative that it be properly obtained and recorded. The investigator is concerned with how far the vehicle skidded. Therefore, it is necessary to measure the mark left by each tire of the vehicle. In some cases this is fairly easy to do; in other instances it is almost impossible when the marks of front and rear wheels are superimposed. In the latter case, the investigator must measure the total length of the skid mark and deduct the wheel base of the vehicle. In any event, he must establish that the marks were left by a certain vehicle. This is usually accomplished by an admission from the driver, the testimony of a witness, or the wheels of the vehicle being atop each skid mark when at rest.

In measuring curved skids (other than centrifugal skids) the tape should follow the curvature of the skid mark, as the distance the wheels were in contact with the road surface is needed to calculate for speed. The investigator must see both ends of the tape in order for his testimony to be admissible.

Sometimes a locked wheel will bounce and leave a "skip skid" — a series of locked wheel skid marks with short spaces between them where the wheel was in the air. In these cases the distances during which the wheel was not in contact with the road surface should be included in the skid measurement. Although none of the speed was dissipated while the wheel was in the air, the greater energy dissipated before the wheel left the road compensates for this. The skips will be only a few feet long.

In some instances a person will apply brakes when faced with an apparent danger, leaving skid marks; then release them as the situation changes; then apply them again — or the driver may "pump" the brakes. The skid marks will have a gap between them, but the gap will generally be more than ten feet in length. Each set of marks should be measured, added, and their total used for speed computation (the gaps are *not* included, as is the case with skip skids).

Having measured the skid marks, the measurements must be properly recorded to be useful. For each wheel the length of the impending and locked wheel skids should be separately listed. It is also necessary to record the weather, the condition and the type of pavement, and the percentage of grade (noting whether it is up or down).

CALCULATING SPEED FROM SKID MARKS

When this information is secured and preserved it is simple to calculate the *minimum* initial speed of the vehicle. This can be done in several ways. What the investigator must remember is that *skid marks do not show all of the speed.* Neither the energy used in braking before the wheels began to leave visible marks nor the energy left in the vehicle at the time of the collision will appear. What can be determined is the amount of speed lost in the distance the vehicle slid. The calculation will show less speed than the actual speed of the vehicle. Any deviation from the actual speed will, therefore, be in favor of the driver.

The simplest way to estimate the minimum initial speed of a vehicle traveling on a dry, level, hard-surfaced pavement is to arbitrarily assign a coefficient of friction of 60 percent. This is a safe minimum. The percentage of grade is added to this figure if uphill, or subtracted if downhill. Skids (impending *plus* locked wheel) from all skidding wheels should be averaged and the result used to calculate the vehicle's speed.

The formula used in calculating speed from skid marks is:

$$\text{Basic Speed Skid Formula:} \quad S = \frac{V^2}{30f}$$

"S" represents the skid distance in feet, "V" (velocity) the speed in miles per hour, and the "f" the coefficient of friction. This formula may be transposed to read $V^2 = 30Sf$ or $V = \sqrt{30Sf}$, which are easier to use. What the investigator is concerned with is the speed. He simply substitutes known factors in the right-hand side of the equation, performs the multiplications, extracts the square root, and obtains the minimum speed. This can be easily done in a matter of a few seconds at the accident scene, which gives the investigator a result close enough to guide his investigation. It is a quick method of determining whether there was sufficient speed involved to warrant running test skids or further analysis.

If there is indication of excessive speed, particularly in a serious accident, test skids should be made to assure that the evidence will be as good as possible in the event of prosecution. Although it is true that the weight of the vehicle involved, the condition of tires, or the condition of brakes (provided they are sufficient to lock the wheels) is not significant, the task of convincing a jury is much simpler if test skids are made by the same vehicle that was involved in the accident. In some cases damage may prevent its use; however, if possible the vehicle involved should be used. The test should be made at the same location and in the same direction the accident vehicle was traveling. A minimum of three test skids from the same speed should be used in running test skids due to the danger involved. For all practical purposes, thirty miles per hour should be fast enough.

As an example of the use of skid marks in determining initial speeds, the following will illustrate several principles. The investigator has measured 50 feet of accident skid marks, locked wheel plus impending, on a dry, level asphaltic concrete pavement. The driver involved states he was going 20 to 25 miles per hour. The quick method of estimating initial minimum speed is

$$V = 30 \times 50 \times 0.60$$
$$= 900$$

The square root of 900 is 30. Therefore, the minimum speed is 30 miles per hour. This can be done simply and without a test skid by arbitrarily assigning a 60 percent coefficient of friction.

Desiring to arrive at a true coefficient of friction, the investigator will run three test skids from the admitted speed of 25 miles per hour. These tests give skid distances of 28, 29, and 30 feet, respectively. The longest skid from the claimed speed is 20 feet shorter than the accident skid (see fig. 11-7). This should be convincing to the driver that he was traveling faster than he admits, particularly if the investigator points out the discrepancy in the skidding distance.

FORMULAS ON SPEED AND STOPPING OF MOTOR VEHICLES

This chart of symbols and conversion factors can be used as a reference for the following discussion of how speed skid formulas are obtained.

a	= acceleration (positive or negative), ft/sec²
C	= chord, ft
CF	= centrifugal force, lbs
E	= energy, ft-lbs
f	= coefficient of friction, dimensionless
F	= force, lb
g	= accelerating force of gravity = 32.2 ft/sec²
KE	= kinetic energy, ft-lbs
m	= mass, slugs
M	= middle ordinate, distance from chord to arc, ft
p/100	= percentage of grade or superelevation
r	= radius, ft
S	= distance (space covered — skid), ft
Sa	= accident skid, ft
St	= test skid, ft
t	= time, sec
v	= final velocity
$\bar{v}$	= average velocity
vo	= original or initial velocity

$\left\{ \begin{array}{l} \text{small v designates velocity} \\ \text{in ft/sec} \end{array} \right.$

The investigator notes the necessary information, records his or her test skids, and arrives directly at the minimum speed of the accident vehicle by the following method:

Step 1
On the "Skid Distance in Feet" axis he or she plots the longest test skid, —————— in the above instance 30 feet.

Step 2
On the "Speed in M.P.H." axis of the chart he or she runs a line up at 25 miles per hour, which was the test speed.

Step 3
These lines intersect at the broken line indicating 70 percent coefficient of friction. ——————

Step 4
The investigator then, using the same steps as indicated above, plots the 50 feet of accident skid on the "Skid Distance in Feet" axis. From the point where this line intersects the 70 percent "Coefficient of Friction" line, he or she draws a line to the "Speed in M.P.H." axis and reads a minimum speed of 32 miles per hour. ——————

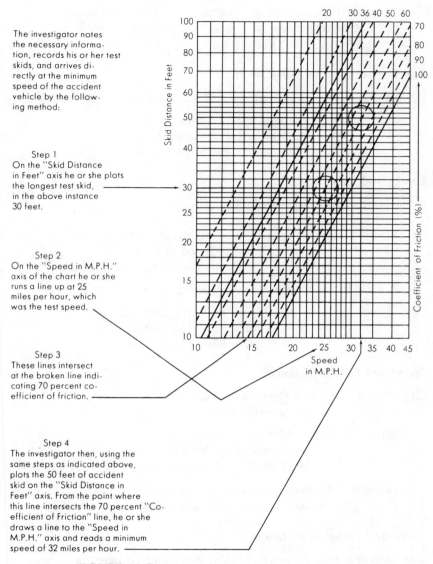

FIGURE 11-7

Calculating Speed from Skid Marks

V   = velocity, mi/hr
Vt   = test velocity, mi/hr
W   = weight

$$1.467 \ = \text{ft/sec @ 1 mi/hr} \quad (5280 \text{ ft/3600 sec})$$
$$0.6818 = \text{mi/hr @ 1 ft/sec} \quad (3600 \text{ sec/5280 ft})$$
$$\therefore v = V \ 1.467$$

Feet per Second and Miles per hour

(1)   Speed in feet per second = 1.467 times speed in miles per hour

$$60 \text{ mph} \times 1.467 = 88 \quad \text{ft/sec}$$
$$40 \text{ mph} \times 1.467 = 58.7 \text{ ft/sec}$$
$$20 \text{ mph} \times 1.467 = 29.4 \text{ ft/sec}$$

Energy and Speed

Energy varies as the square of the speed.

(2)   Kinetic Energy $= \dfrac{WV^2}{30}$ W = Weight of car in pounds
                                         V = Speed in mph
                                         Kinetic energy is in foot-pounds

A 3000-lb car has the following energies:

$$\text{At 60 mph, KE} = 360,000 \text{ ft-lbs}$$
$$40 \text{ mph, KE} = 160,000 \text{ ft-lbs}$$
$$20 \text{ mph, KE} = \ \ 40,000 \text{ ft-lbs}$$

Speed and Falling Distances

(3) $V^2 = 30 \ S$ S = Height of fall in feet
                        V = Speed in mph

$$\text{When Speed } V = 60 \text{ mph, S} = 120 \quad \text{ft}$$
$$V = 40 \text{ mph, S} = \ \ 53.3 \text{ ft}$$
$$V = 20 \text{ mph, S} = \ \ 13.3 \text{ ft}$$

Example: Running into a solid brick wall at 60 mph will do as much damage as running off a building 120 feet high.

Speed and Stopping Distances

Total stopping distance equals braking distance plus reaction distance.

(4)   Minimum original speed = Speed of car in test

$$\text{X} \ \sqrt{\dfrac{\text{Length of original skid marks}}{\text{Braking distances in test}}}$$

Example: Accident skid marks average 60.0 feet. Test skid from 30 mph gives braking distance of 40.0 feet.

$$\text{Then speed} = 30\sqrt{\frac{60}{40}} = 36.8 \text{ mph minimum}$$

Car must have been going at least this fast before the accident. It probably was going even faster.

This formula also can be written as:

$$V \text{ (original)} = V \text{ (of test)} \quad X \sqrt{\frac{s \text{ (measured)}}{s \text{ (test)}}}$$

s (measured) = average length of four skid marks following the accident

s (test) = braking distance as measured by pistol, for test run

V (test) = speed of test run in mph

V (original) = computed minimum speed of the accident vehicle (the vehicle probably was going quite a bit faster)

Speed, Friction, and Braking Distance

(5) $V = 5.5X \sqrt{fs}$ V = Speed in mph

s = braking distance in feet.

(6) $f = \dfrac{V^2}{30s}$ If wheels skid, f = coefficient of friction

If wheels do not skid,

(7) $s = \dfrac{V^2}{30f}$ $f = \dfrac{\text{Percent of braking}}{100}$

Speed on Curves

(8) $V = 15 \, r \, (e + f)$ V = maximum speed in mph

r = radius of curve in feet

e = superelevation in feet per foot

f = sideways friction coefficient

For most highway curves, e is between zero and 0.10. For comfort in rounding curves, f should not exceed 0.20. A car will skid sideways when f approaches the coefficient of friction of the pavement.

A method which saves one operation is by direct substitution in the formula $V_a = V_t \, (S_a/S_t)$, where V_a equals accident speed, V_t equals test speed, S_a equals accident skid distance, and S_t equals test skid distance. This, too, gives a result of 32 miles per hour. It can be seen by the above that the quick approximation with the assumed coefficient of friction of 60 percent gives a result close enough for practical use.

There are a variety of shortcut methods that an investigator may use in the field to determine quickly if there was a violation involving unsafe speed. The following short process determines speed and reaction, braking, and stopping distances.

SPEED: There are two suggested ways to compute feet traveled per second at different rates of speed:

1. Multiply 1.5 × rate of speed; for example, 1.5 × 60 = 90 feet per second.

2. Choose any rate of speed and add one-half the speed to it. For 60 mph, one-half the rate of speed is 30; so 30 is added to 60 to get 90 feet per second.

REACTION DISTANCE = mph × 1.1

$$55 \times 1.1 = 60.5 \text{ fps*}$$
$$65 \times 1.1 = 71.5 \text{ fps*}$$
$$70 \times 1.1 = 77.0 \text{ fps*}$$

*Distance traveled during reaction time (0.75 second is the average reaction time for a normal driver)
fps = feet per second

BRAKING DISTANCE: Multiply one-half of any rate of speed by the *first* number of the speed. The following are examples:

For 60 mph, one-half the rate of speed is 30. The first number of 60 mph is 6, so 30 × 6 = 180 ft of braking distance.

For 50 mph, 25 × 5 = 125 ft of braking distance.

For 65 mph, 32.5 × 6 = 195 ft of braking distance.

STOPPING DISTANCE = Reaction distance + Braking distance

71.5 fps	(reaction distance @ 65 mph)
+ 195.0 ft	(braking distance)
266.5 ft	(total stopping distance)

This method is only for the purpose of determining if there is a possible speed factor to consider in the investigation. To obtain an accurate determination of speed, an investigator would run tests or at least work out the formulas and include the drag factor of the highway.

In using a test skid, it is important that every effort be made to get all the impending skid; otherwise, the value of the coefficient of friction obtained will be too high. It is necessary that the speedometer be accurate so that the evidence obtained will be reliable for presentation in court.

While the investigator will be able to calculate initial speeds closely by these methods, presentation in court will probably require expert testimony, including explanation of the various physical laws and mathematical formulas involved. The expert will rely on the information given him by the investigator to reach his conclusion. This information must be accurate, understandable, and complete, for without this information skid mark evidence will be of little value. With the proper measuring and recording of skid mark evidence, accurate minimum initial speeds may be computed.

In complicated cases where not all the wheels slide, or where skid marks are on different types of surfaces, it will probably be up to the expert to determine if any use can be made of the skid mark evidence. However, it is important to record the evidence so that the expert may decide to what extent it is usable.

When a vehicle is rounding a curve, there are two opposing forces acting upon it. Centrifugal force acts to keep the vehicle moving in a straight line, while centripetal force is being applied to turn the vehicle. If the centrifugal force is greater than the frictional resistance between the tires and the pavement, the vehicle will skid. Skid marks left by a vehicle sliding on a curve can be used to tell something about how fast a vehicle was going, for centrifugal force is directly proportional to the weight of a body and the square of the velocity and is inversely proportional to the radius of the curvature of its path. The speed at which a curve can be rounded without skidding is known as the *critical speed*. When a vehicle skids on a curve without brake application it is because the critical speed was exceeded. *By calculating the critical speed of a curve the investigator will know the minimum speed at which the vehicle must have been traveling in order to slide.*

To calculate the critical speed of a curve, the investigator must know the *radius* of the curve, the bank or superelevation, and the *coefficient of friction*.

The radius of a curve is determined as follows:

1. Mark two points on the curve, using the outside edge, as the inside of curves are frequently widened to make them safer. The points used can be where the curve straightens or two points 100 feet or less apart near the accident. Use a long distance if the curve is a big one.

2. Measure the distance between these marks, but instead of rolling up the tape, release both ends of the tape carefully without moving it. Let it lie flat and straight on the ground. The distance so measured is called the *chord*. It is "C" in the formula on page 244.

3. Divide the length of the chord by two, and without moving the tape, find the middle of the chord. Mark the spot.

4. Carefully measure the shortest distance from the middle of the chord to the curve. Use a pocket tape if available. Measure to the nearest

half-inch. This distance is called the middle ordinate. It is "h" in the following formula.

Example: Measure straight across part of a circular curve with a chord of 50 feet, C. The distance from the middle of the chord (at 25 feet) to the curve is one foot. This is the middle ordinate, h. Using these figures in either of the two following formulas, we are able to determine the radius:

$$\text{Radius} = \frac{C^2}{8h} + \frac{h}{2} \text{ (in this formula the middle ordinate is in feet)}$$

$$\text{Radius} = \frac{50 \times 50}{8 \times 1} + \frac{1}{2} = \frac{2500}{8} + \frac{1}{2} = 312.5 + 0.05 = 313 \text{ feet}$$

OR

$$\text{Radius} = \frac{30^2}{2h} \times \frac{h}{24} \text{ (in this formula the middle ordinate is in inches)}$$

$$\text{Radius} = \frac{3 \times 2500}{2 \times 12} + \frac{12}{24} = 7500 + \frac{1}{2} = 312.5 + 0.05 = 313 \text{ feet}$$

It may prove easier to use a calculator, which works the formula for the investigator more quickly (fig. 11-8). By drawing a straight line across the chart, we can find the radius of the circle of which the measured curve is a part. When we use two known points (length of chord and middle ordinate), we simply connect the two on the radius calculator and read the answer on the right column (radius, feet). Using the calculator and a set of known measurements, find the radius in feet.

This same formula and calculator can also be used to find the radius of a small circle by using inches instead of feet for measurements. This might help the investigator find the size of a round headlight lens from a piece of glass found at the scene of an accident.

Coefficient of friction may be determined as previously described. Superelevation is added or subtracted just as grade percentage is in other skid mark problems. (If test skids are made, the superelevation or grade is already included in the resultant coefficient of friction.)

Superelevation or grade percentage means the steepness of the road banking or a hill. They are both measured by the number of feet the road rises for each foot of level distance along or across the road. The resulting number is less than 1.00, and, except on steep hills or banks, is less than 0.10.

When drawing a diagram of an accident scene, always draw an arrow pointing *uphill* after the grade number. Also, since uphill is plus grade, put the plus sign (+) in front of the number. *Downhill* or negative grades are written with a minus sign (−) in front of the number. Whether a grade is positive or negative depends upon the direction of travel (see fig. 11-9).

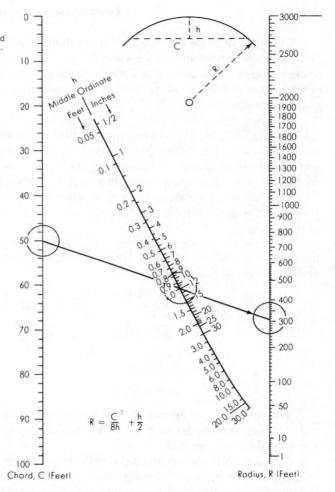

Example: Use the same measurements as in the previous example; chord 50 feet and middle ordinate 1 foot. Find the chord, 50, on the left scale, C. Find the middle ordinate, one foot, on the middle scale, h. Draw a *straight* line from the 50 on scale C through 1 on scale h to scale R. Read the radius on scale R at this point. It is 313 feet.

$$R = \frac{C^2}{8h} + \frac{h}{2}$$

Chord, C (Feet)

Radius, R (Feet)

FIGURE 11-8

Radius Calculator

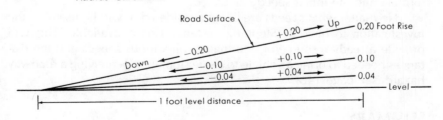

FIGURE 11-9

Superelevation of Road

245

The grade or slope of a road is the rise divided by the level distance. The bank or superelevation is the same thing *across* the road. The number representing grade is often mentioned in terms of feet of rise or fall per hundred feet of horizontal distance. It then becomes feet per hundred, grade, or percent grade.

Example: A road rises 2 feet in a level distance of 50 feet. Divide 2 by 50. The result is 0.04. (This is 4 feet per hundred, or a 4 percent grade.) This information would be indicated on a diagram by an arrow pointing *uphill* and writing +0.04 grade. This percentage of grade would be added to the coefficient of friction when computing speed from skid marks.

The formula to calculate critical speed is $V^2 = 15 \times R \times f$, or $V = \sqrt{15Rf}$, where V equals speed, R equals radius, and f is the coefficient of friction.

Example: Calculate critical speed where the chord measures 50 feet, the middle ordinate is 11 inches, the coefficient of friction is 68 percent, and the superelevation is 2 percent.

$$R = \frac{3 \times 2500}{22} + \frac{11}{24} = 341 \text{ feet}$$

$$f = 0.68 + 0.02 = 0.70$$

$$V^2 = 15 \times 341 \times 170$$

$$V = \sqrt{3580.50}$$

$$F = 59.8 \text{ mph}$$

Where brakes are applied during a centrifugal skid, the formula will not hold true, as brake application will cause skidding at lower speeds than if brakes were not applied.

The same formula used to calculate the critical speed of a curve is used to compute minimum initial speed from centrifugal skid marks. The centrifugal skid mark is the curve on which the chord and middle ordinate are measured. The radius of the curve of the centrifugal skid is entered into the formula and the initial speed calculated.

No matter what speeds are being considered, it will be useful to the investigation to have a "Stopping Distance Chart" available. This will provide a ready resource of information on various speeds and the distances needed to bring a vehicle to a safe stop upon perceiving a roadway hazard (see page 146).

SUMMARY

The investigator who uses all the tools available to him will certainly give expert credence to his investigation and to his eventual testimony in court.

Part of those tools are the various formulas used in determining speed from skids. When properly applied, the investigator becomes a valuable key in the investigation of many complicated accidents. The use of testimony in describing skid marks and speed estimates may be admissible providing the proper identifying foundation is laid. Although individual states have varying evidence codes, most of them subscribe to the prevailing rule asserting that the weight of the investigator's testimony in establishing his expertise is based on (1) the individual court's legal parameters setting forth the acceptable background for such technical testimony and (2) the jury's ability to assess that testimony in the end. The individual officer who applies these rules to his investigations is filling a critical need in the field of accident reconstruction. The expert testifying as to speeds determined from skid marks should know that it is reversible error to withhold such testimony from the court when it is properly offered in evidence. The validity of the speed estimate is dependent on a number of important factors, such as the drag factor of the particular highway in question upon which the skidding took place, the accuracy of the skilled investigator to reproduce the accident conditions as exactly as possible during test skids, and, finally, his mathematical ability to compute the drag factor and the estimate of minimum speed.[1]

To the new officer just learning accident investigation theory and faced with the challenge of developing the necessary skills in determining speed from skids, this may seem an almost endless task. Yet, with perseverance and time one may become a department's leading expert in the field of speed-skid analysis. The seasoned veteran who has worked hundreds of traffic accidents, but who has never had to testify as to the estimated speed of a vehicle prior to impact, should prepare for the possibility of having to give such expert testimony. It should be his professional concern to do so should the occasion arise. Not only is it important for the individual officer to develop the necessary vocabulary of the terms and formulas used in speed-skid analysis as well as a workable understanding of their physical application, but it is also important to continually use these scientific tools to assist in effectively bringing to justice those persons who have violated the law in the operation of their motor vehicle, especially when the speed factor resulted in a traffic accident causing loss of life and/or property.

The professional traffic accident investigator will continually strive to see that the integrity of his testimony is always above reproach and that he has constantly prepared himself to supply the factual evidence needed in assisting with the prosecution of his department's traffic accident cases.

---

1. James P. Hall, *Skid Marks: To Estimate Speed; Police Work* (Milwaukee, Wis.: Milwaukee Area Technical College, 1971).

DISCUSSION QUESTIONS

1. Discuss the theory of determining minimum speed from skids, injecting properly the various technical terms applied to speed-skid investigation and analysis.

2. Discuss the formulas for determining speed from skids by identifying the methodology by which they are derived.

TRUE-FALSE

1. The term *coefficient of friction* is synonymous with *drag factor.*

2. It is not always necessary to identify and measure all of the impending skid left by the vehicle in question in order to obtain an accurate answer as to minimal speed.

3. The term *kinetic energy* can best be described as energy a body or mass has because of its motion.

4. Centripetal and centrifugal forces are applied to a vehicle's ability to negotiate a curve.

5. A radius calculator is used in determining a roadway curve's *critical speed.*

6. *Superelevation* is a term applied to determining the slope of a grade.

Bibliography

Adams, Thomas F. *Police Patrol Tactics and Techniques*. Englewood Cliffs, N.J.: Prentice-Hall, 1971.

American Association of State Highway Officials. *Manual on Uniform Traffic Control Devices for Streets and Highways*. Evanston, Ill.: Institute of Traffic Engineers, National Conference on Street and Highway Safety, 1969.

Baker, J. Stannard. *Traffic Accident Investigator's Manual For Police*. Evanston, Ill.: Traffic Institute, Northwestern University, 1971.

Baker, J. Stannard, and Stebbins, William R., Jr. *Dictionary of Highway Traffic*. Evanston, Ill.: Traffic Institute, Northwestern University, 1964.

California Highway Patrol. *Accident Investigation*. Sacramento, 1970.

Committee on Highway Capacity of the Highway Research Board. *Highway Capacity Manual*. National Research Council, U.S. Bureau of Public Roads. Washington, D.C.: Government Printing Office, 1960.

Daily Training Bulletin of the Los Angeles Police Department. Bulletins 1–173. Springfield, Ill.: Charles C Thomas, 1963.

Department of California Highway Patrol. *Traffic Accident Investigation Manual*. Sacramento, 1966.

Department of Highway Transportation, Division of Highways, State of California. *The Highway Engineer*. Sacramento, Calif.: State Printing Office, 1966.

Donigan, Robert L., and Fisher, Edward C. *The Evidence Handbook*. Evanston, Ill.: Traffic Institute, Northwestern University, 1965.

Horgan, John J. *Criminal Investigation*. New York: McGraw-Hill, 1974.

International Association of Chiefs of Police. *Municipal Traffic Supervision Manual.* Evanston, Ill.: Traffic Institute, Northwestern University, 1971.

International City Managers Association. *Municipal Police Administration.* Chicago, Ill.: Institute for Training in Municipal Administration, 1969.

National Committee on Uniform Traffic Laws and Ordinances. *Uniform Vehicle Code and Model Traffic Ordinance.* Washington, D.C., 1972.

O'Brien, Kevin P., and Sullivan, Robert C. *Criminalistics — Theory and Practice.* Boston: Holbrook Press, 1972.

Schwartz, Louis B., and Goldstein, Stephen R. *Law Enforcement Handbook for Police.* St. Paul: West Publishing, 1970.

Soderman, Harry, and O'Connell, John H. *Modern Criminal Investigation.* New York: Funk and Wagnalls, 1962.

Stuckey, Gilbert B. *Evidence for the Law Enforcement Officer.* New York: McGraw-Hill, 1974.

Traffic Accident Investigators Manual for Police. Evanston, Ill.: Traffic Institute, Northwestern University, 1963.

U.S. Department of Health, Education, and Welfare. *Uniform Definitions of Motor Vehicle Accidents.* Washington, D.C.: Government Printing Office, 1971.

Vanderbosch, Charles G. *Criminal Investigation.* Washington, D.C.: International Association of Chiefs of Police, 1968.

Weston, Paul R., and Wells, Kenneth M. *Criminal Evidence for Police.* Englewood Cliffs, N.J.: Prentice-Hall, 1971.

———. *Elements of Criminal Investigation.* Englewood Cliffs, N.J.: Prentice-Hall, 1971.

Whisenand, Paul M., and Cline, James L. *Patrol Operations.* Englewood Cliffs, N.J.: Prentice-Hall, 1971.

DETERMINING SPEED FROM SKID MARKS

Charts and Tables for Stopping Distances of Motor Vehicles. Evanston, Ill.: Traffic Institute, Northwestern University, 1960 and 1966.

Department of California Highway Patrol. *Speed from Skidmarks.* Sacramento, 1968.

Dull, Charles E. *Modern Physics.* New York: Henry Holt, 1945.

Freeman, Ira M. *Modern Introductory Physics.* 2d ed. New York: Mc-Graw-Hill, 1957.

Rogers, Eric M. *Physics for the Inquiring Mind.* Princeton, N.J.: Princeton University Press, 1960.

Srack, C. Leonard. *Miles-Feet-Seconds.* Los Angeles, 1951.

Uses of Skidmarks in Traffic Cases. Evanston, Ill.: Traffic Institute, Northwestern University, 1969.

TRAFFIC RECORDS SYSTEMS

Probably the most comprehensive and analytical traffic records system in the world is the CARES/ACTRS system utilized by a number of communities in the San Francisco, California, Bay Area. The system was developed by Stanford Research Institute under contract to the cognizant communities. The system has been thoroughly documented, and anyone seriously contemplating the development of a traffic records system is advised to review this system. All the documents can be obtained from SRI in Menlo Park, California.

Cook, D.W., and Schlaefli, J.L. *ACTRS Citation System User's Manual.* SRI Technical Note 1011-1, May 1972.

Marcum, K.R., and Schlaefli, J.L. *ACTRS Sign System User's Manual.* SRI Technical Note 1261-1, February 1972.

Sandys, R.C., and Schlaefli, J.L. *ACTRS: Alameda County Traffic Reporting and Inventory System Procedures Manual.* SRI Project 1542, May 1972.

Schlaefli, J.L., and Bagley, M.D. *San Mateo County Computerized Accident Records System (CARES).* Final Report of SRI Project 1077, June 1972.

Schlaefli, J.L. et al. *San Mateo County Computerized Accident Records System (CARES) Systems Manuals — Volume I: File Descriptions and Maintenance Procedures.* SRI Technical Note 1077-2, June 1972.

_____. *Alameda Countywide Traffic Records System (ACTRS) User's Manual.* SRI Technical Note 8513-1, October 1971.

_____. *San Mateo County Computerized Accident Records System (CARES) User's Manual.* SRI Technical Note 1077-1, June 1972.

For a detailed description of the traffic records system implemented in the Los Angeles Police Department in the early 1970s, containing numerous flow charts and sample print-outs, see:

Optner, Stanford L. & Associates, Inc. *Traffic Information System (Phase III).* Los Angeles, 15 May 1970.

Other books treating traffic records systems include:

Eastman, George D., and Eastman, Esther M., eds. *Municipal Police Administration.* Washington, D.C.: International City Management Association, 1969. This basic treatise of police administration discusses traffic records in chapters 6 and 14.

Hewitt, William H. *Public Records Administration.* Rochester, N.Y.: The Lawyers Cooperative Publishing Company, 1968. Chapter 16 discusses in detail the legal aspects of traffic records and the essentials for documenting accidents and citations.

Whisenand, Paul M., and Tamaru, Tug T. *Automated Police Information Systems.* New York: John Wiley, 1970. A systems view of police information systems as an integral part of the overall criminal justice system. While a very theoretical treatment of police information systems, this book contains an extensive bibliography of literature about automated police information systems in existence in 1968.

Books about electronic data processing (EDP) and computers include:

Benice, Daniel D. *Introduction to Computers and Data Processing.* Englewood Cliffs, N.J.: Prentice-Hall, 1970. This introduction to EDP emphasizes the programming aspect and introduces the fundamentals of several current programming languages: System/360 Assembler, FORTRAN, COBOL, PL/1, and RPG.

Berkewitz, Nathan, and Munro, Robertson, Jr. *Automatic Data Processing and Management.* Belmont, Calif.: Dickenson, 1969. An introduction to EDP that emphasizes the implications for managers and what their responsibilities should be.

Harvard Business Review. *Computer Management Series: Reprints from Harvard Business Review.* A collection of sixteen articles appearing in HBR from 1962 through 1967. While these articles are slanted toward business uses of computers, the information can be invaluable to the officer involved in the administration of an automated traffic records system.

Martin, E. Wainwright, Jr. *Electronic Data Processing: An Introduction.* Homewood, Ill.: Richard D. Irwin, 1965. A textbook for an introductory course in EDP, the book was designed for the mature student (graduate or advanced undergraduate level). It contains the essentials for the officer who is responsible for EDP application in his or her department.

Odell, Margaret K., and Strong, Earl P. *Records Management and Filing Operations.* New York: McGraw-Hill, 1947. A thorough treatment of manual recordkeeping which serves as a guide to records department operations. It is especially useful for improving the computerized records functions that exist alongside a computerized system, or for the small police department that cannot afford a computer.

Index

253